Web Development with Java

T0255050

Tim Downey

Web Development with Java

Using Hibernate, JSPs and Servlets

 Springer

Tim Downey, BS, MS
Florida International University
Miami, FL 33199, USA

British Library Cataloguing in Publication Data
A catalogue record for this book is available from the British Library

Library of Congress Control Number: 2007925710

ISBN: 978-1-84628-862-3   e-ISBN: 978-1-84628-863-0

Printed on acid-free paper

9 8 7 6 5 4 3 2 1

Springer Science+Business Media
springer.com

To Bobbi, my sweetheart, with all my love.

Preface

I have been teaching web development for ten years. I started with Perl. I can still remember the behemoth programs that contained all the logic and HTML. I remember using a text editor to write the program. Debugging consisted of a lot of print statements. It was a fun time, full of exploration, but I do not miss them.

Five years ago, I made the move to Java and Java servlets. Life became much simpler with the use of NetBeans. It has been a critical component in developing Web applications using Java. Debugging a web application in NetBeans is just as easy as debugging any Java application.

This book is meant for students who have a solid background in programming, but who do not have any database training. Until two years ago, my students used a glorified HashMap to save data. Then a former student gave me the word: Hibernate. For anyone with a programming background in Java, using Hibernate to save data to a relational database is a simple task.

I have always been a proponent of automating the common tasks that Web applications perform. There are many packages that can simplify the job of a Web developer: Log4j, BeanUtils and Hibernate. I have created additional classes that can automate additional tasks.

Readers of this book should have a good background in Java programming. The book uses HTML, HTML Forms, Cascading Style Sheets and XML as tools. Each topic will receive an introduction, but the full scope of the area will not be explored. The focus of the book is on Java Servlets that use Java Server Pages and connect to a MySQL database using Hibernate. No SQL will be covered in the book, except for a short section in the Appendix for those who want to see what Hibernate is doing.

I am grateful to the community of web developers, who have provided all the excellent tools for creating web applications: Apache, Tomcat, Hibernate, Java Servlets, Java Server Pages, NetBeans, Log4j, Commons.

I am thankful to Bobbi, my sweetheart, for all of her love and support. Without Bobbi, this book would not have been finished. I also want to thank Kip Irvine for encouraging me to write. Without Kip, this book would never have been started.

Tim Downey
Miami, FL

Contents

1 Browser – Server Communication

This chapter explains how information is sent from a browser to a server. It begins with a description of the request from a browser and a response from a server. Each of these has a format that is determined by the *Hypertext Transfer Protocol* [HTTP].

The chapter continues with the explanation of markup languages, with a detailed description of the *Hypertext Markup Language* [HTML], which is used to send formatted content from the server to the browser. One of the most important features of HTML is its ability to easily request additional information from the server through the use of hypertext links.

HTML forms are also covered. These are used to send data from the browser back to the server. Information from the form must be formatted so that it can be sent over the web. The browser and server handle encoding and decoding the data.

Simple web pages cannot process form data that is sent to them. One way to process form data is to use a web application and a *Java Server Page* [JSP]. In a JSP, the *Expression Language* [EL] simplifies access to the form data and can be used to initialise the form elements with the form data that is sent to the page.

JSPs are processed by a program know as a servlet engine. The servlet engine receives the request and response data from the web server and processes the request from the browser. The servlet engine translates all JSPs into programs known as servlets.

Servlets and JSPs must be run from a servlet engine. Tomcat is a popular servlet engine. NetBeans is a development environment that is tailored for web development. NetBeans is packaged with Tomcat.

1.1 Hypertext Transfer Protocol

Whenever someone accesses a web page on the Internet, there is communication between two computers. On one computer there is a software program know as a browser, on the other is a software program known as a web server. The browser sends a request to the server and the server sends a response to the browser. The request contains the name of the page that is being requested and information about the browser that is making the request. The response contains the page that was requested (if it is available), information about the page and information about the server sending the page – see Figure 1.1.

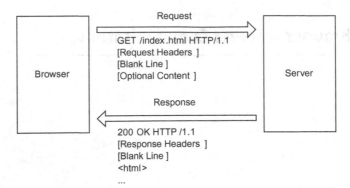

Figure 1.1 The request and response have specific formats, as specified by the HTTP protocol.

When the browser makes the request, it mentions the protocol that it is using: HTTP/1.1. When the server sends the response, it also identifies the protocol it is using: HTTP/1.1. A protocol is not a language; it is a set of rules that must be followed. For instance, one rule in HTTP is that the first line of a request will contain the type of request, the address of the page on the server and the version of the protocol that the browser is using. Another rule is that the first line of the response will contain a numeric code indicating the success of the request, a sentence describing the code and the version of the protocol that the server is using.

Protocols are used in many places, not just with computers. When the leaders of two countries meet, they must decide on a common protocol in order to communicate. Do they bow or shake hands when they meet? Do they eat with chopsticks or silverware? It is the same situation for computers, in order for the browser and server to communicate, they must decide on a common protocol.

1.1.1 Request Format

The request from the browser has the following format in HTTP:

1. The first line contains the type of request, the name of the requested page and the protocol that is being used.
2. Subsequent lines contain information about the browser and the request.
3. A blank line indicates the end of the request headers.
4. In a POST request, there can be additional information sent after the blank line.

1.1.2 Response Format

The response from the server has the following format in HTTP:

1. The first line contains the status code, a brief description of the status code and the protocol being used.
2. Subsequent lines contain information about the server and the response.

3. A blank line indicates the end of the response headers.
4. In a successful response, the content of the page will be sent after the blank line.

1.1.3 Content Type

The server must also identify the type of information that is being sent. This is known as the *content type*. There are content types for text, graphics, spreadsheets, word processors and more.

These content types are expressed as *Multipurpose Internet Mail Extensions* [MIME] types. MIME types are used by web servers and web browsers. Each will contain a file that has a table of MIME types with the associated file extension for that type.

MIME types are defined by a general type followed by a specific type. For example, there is a general type for text that has several specific types for plain text, HTML text and style sheet text. These types are represented as text/plain, text/html and text/css, respectively. When the server sends a file to the browser, it will also include the MIME type for the file in the header that is sent to the browser.

MIME types are universal. All systems have agreed to use MIME types to identify the content of a file transmitted over the web. File extensions are too limiting for this purpose. Many different word processor programs might use the extension *.doc* to identify a file. For instance, *.doc* might refer to an MS WORD document or to an MS WORDPAD document. It is impossible to tell from the extension which program actually created the program. In addition, other programs could use the *.doc* extension to identify a program: for instance, WordPerfect could also use the *.doc* extension. Using the extension to identify the content of the file would be too confusing.

The most common content type on the web is HTML text, represented as the MIME type text/html.

1.2 Markup Language

I am confident that most students have seen a markup language. I remember my days in English composition classes: my returned papers would always have cryptic squiggles written all over them (Figure 1.2).

Some of these would mean that a word was omitted (^), that two letters were transposed (a sideways "S", enclosing the transposed letters), or that a new paragraph was needed (a backwards, double-stemmed "P"). These marks were invaluable to the teacher who had to correct the paper because they conveyed a lot of

```
                    to
The old man went/\sea, he needed
a big catch, so that he would receive
a lot of money.¶The fish was waiting
in the dark sea.
```

Figure 1.2 Editors use markup to annotate text.

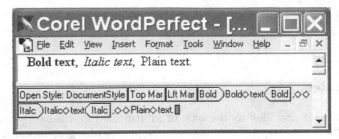

Figure 1.3 Word processors use markup to format text.

meaning in just a few pen strokes. Imagine if there were a program that would accept such a paper that is covered with markup, read the markup and generate a new version with all the corrections made.

There are other forms of markup languages. The script of a play has a markup language that describes the action that is proceeding while the dialog takes place. For instance, the following is a hypothetical script for The Three Stooges:

```
Moe: Oh, a wise guy, huh? <Pulls Larry's hair>
Larry: It wasn't me. <Hits Curly in the stomach>
Moe: What are you doing? <Tries to poke Curly in the eye>
Curly: Nyuk, nyuk, nyuk. <Places hand in front of eyes>
Moe: Ignoramus. <Bonks Curly on top of the head>
```

Word processors have an internal markup language that is used to indicate the format of the text: bold, italic, font, colour, etc. These codes are hidden from the user. *WordPerfect* has an additional view of the document that displays all of these hidden codes (Figure 1.3).

There are two parts to any markup language

1. The plain text
2. The markup, which contains additional information about the plain text

1.2.1   Hypertext Markup Language

HTML is the markup language for the web. It is what allows the browser to display colours, fonts, links and graphics. All markup is enclosed within the angle brackets < and >. Directly adjacent to the opening bracket is the name of the tag. There can be additional attributes after the name of the tag and the closing bracket.

HTML tags are intermixed with plain text. The plain text is what the viewer of a web page will see. The HTML tags are commands to the browser for displaying the text. In this example, the plain text "This text is underlined" is enclosed within the HTML tags for underlining:

```
<u>This text is underlined</u>
```

The viewer of the web page would see: <u>This text is underlined</u>.
There are two types of HTML tags: singletons and paired tags.

Table 1.1 Examples of singletons.

Tag	Explanation
` `	Insert a line break into the document.
`<input>`	Insert a form element into the document. This is a tag that has additional attributes, which will be explained below.

Singletons have a limited amount of text associated with them or they have no text at all. Singletons only have one tag. Table 1.1 gives two examples of singleton tags.

Paired tags are designed to contain many words and other tags. These tags have an opening and a closing tag. The text that they control is placed between the opening and closing tags. The closing tag is the same as the opening tag, except the tag name is preceded by a forward slash /. Table 1.2 gives four examples of paired tags.

1.2.2 Basic Tags for a Web Page

We are very sophisticated listeners. We can understand many different accents. We can understand when words are slurred together. However, if we were to write out the phonetic transcription of our statements, they would be unreadable. There is a correct way to write our language, but a sophisticated listener can detect and correct many errors in pronunciation.

For instance, most English speakers would understand me if I asked the question

Jeet yet?

In print, it is incomprehensible. A proper response might be

No, joo?

Or,

Yeah, I already ate.

As we become more proficient in a language, we are able to understand it, even when people do not enunciate clearly.

In the same way, all markup languages have a format that must be followed in order to be correct. Some language interpreters are more sophisticated than others

Table 1.2 Examples of paired tags.

Tag	Explanation
`<b>bold</b>`	The enclosed text is rendered in a thicker font.
`<u>underlined</u>`	The enclosed text is rendered with an underline.
`<i>italicised</i>`	The enclosed text is rendered in an italic font.
`<p>paragraph</p>`	The enclosed text will have at least one empty line preceding it.

and can detect and correct mistakes in the written format. For example, a paragraph tag in HTML is a paired tag and most browsers will render paragraphs correctly, even if the closing paragraph tag is missing. The reason is that paragraph tags cannot be nested one inside the other, so when a browser encounters a new <p> tag before seeing the closing </p> for the current paragraph, the browser inserts a closing </p> and then begins the new paragraph. However, if an XML interpreter were used to read the same HTML file with the missing </p> tag, the interpreter would report an error instead of continuing to parse the file. It is better to code all the tags that are defined for a well-formed HTML document, than to rely on browsers to fill in the missing details.

Standard Tags

The HTML specification defines a group of standard tags that control the structure of the HTML document. These tags will contain plain text and other tags.

```
<html>html code</html>
```

The *html* tags enclose all the other tags and text in the document.

```
<head>browser command tags</head>
```

The *head* tags enclose tags that inform the browser about how to display the entire page. These control how the page appears in the browser, but do not contain any content for the page. This paired tag belongs within the paired <html> tags.

```
<body>body tags</body>
```

The *body* tags contain all the plain text and HTML tags that are to be displayed in the browser window. This paired tag belongs within the paired <html> tags.

The <head> section does not contain normal markup tags, like bold and italic, but instead contains tags that indicate how the browser should display the page.

```
<title>title text</title>
```

The *title* tags enclose the text that will display in the title bar of the browser window.

```
<meta http-equiv="..." content="...">
```

This singleton indicates extra information for the browser. This tag can be repeated to include different information for the browser. In a standard page, there should be a meta tag with *http-equiv* of *content-type* and *content* of *text/html;charset=utf-8*. These indicate the type of text that is in the HTML page and the character set for the language that is being used.

HTML Validation

The *WWW Consortium* [W3C] publishes the HTML standard and provides tools for HTML validation that will test that a page has the correct HTML structure. In order to comply with the HTML specification, all web pages should have the following structure.

```
<!DOCTYPE HTML PUBLIC "-//W3C//DTD HTML 4.01//EN">
<html>
  <head>
    <meta http-equiv="content-type"
          content="text/html;charset=utf-8">
    <title>Simple Page</title>
  </head>
  <body>
    <p>
    This is a <i>simple</i> web page.
  </body>
</html>
```

1. The DOCTYPE defines the type of markup that is being used. It precedes the `<html>` tag because it defines which version of HTML is being used.
2. All the tags and plaintext for the page are contained within the paired `<html>` tags.
   a. Place a `<head>` section within the paired `<html>` tags.
      i. Place a paired `<title>` tag within the `<head>` section.
      ii. Place a singleton `<meta>` tag for the content type within the `<head>` section.
   b. Place a `<body>` section within the paired `<html>` tags.
3. The DOCTYPE and meta tags are required if the page is to be validated by W3C for correct HTML syntax. Go to http://www.w3.org to access the HTML validator.

There is no excuse for a web page to contain errors. With the use of the validation tool at http://www.w3.org, all HTML pages should be validated to ensure that they contain all the basic tags.

Layout versus Style

There are two different types of information that are contained in each HTML page: layout and style. The basic layout is covered in this chapter; advanced layout and style are covered in Chapter Six. Style information contains things like the colours and font for the page. The recommended way to handle style and layout is to place all the layout tags in the HTML page and to place all the style information in a separate file, called a style sheet. For the interested student, the HTML and style information from Chapter Six can be read at any time.

There are different DOCTYPE statements that can be used for HTML pages: strict and transitional. The strict one is the recommended one, since it enforces the rule that all style information be contained in a separate file. All pages for this book will use the strict DOCTYPE for HTML pages.

```
<!DOCTYPE HTML PUBLIC "-//W3C//DTD HTML 4.01//EN">
```

Word Wrap and White Space

Most of us are used to typing text in a word processor and letting the program determine where the line breaks belong. This is know as *word wrap*. The only time that we are required to hit the enter key is when we want to start a new paragraph.

Browsers will use word wrap to display text, even if the enter key is pressed. Browsers will treat a new line character, a tab character and multiple spaces as a single space. In order to insert a new line, tab or multiple spaces in an HTML page, markup must be used: if it is not plain text, then it must be placed in markup.

Browsers take word wrap one step further. Browsers will compress all consecutive white space characters into a single space character. The common white space characters are the space, the tab and the new line character. If there are five spaces at the start of a line, they will be compressed into one space.

The following listing contains a web page that has a poem.

```
<!DOCTYPE HTML PUBLIC "-//W3C//DTD HTML 4.01//EN">
<html>
  <head>
    <meta http-equiv="content-type"
          content="text/html;charset=utf-8">
    <title>A Poem</title>
  </head>
  <body>
    Roses are red
    Violets are blue
    This could be a poem
    But not a haiku

    A haiku has a fixed structure. The first line has
    five syllables, the second line has seven syllables
    and the third line has five syllables. Therefore,
    the previous poem cannot be a haiku.
  </body>
</html>
```

Even though the poem has four lines, the poem will appear as one line in the browser. This is because there is no markup to indicate that one line has ended and another line should begin. The browser will start a new line if the poem would extend beyond the right margin of the browser.

 Try It   http://bytesizebook.com/book/ch1/poem.html

Open the link in a browser and view the poem (Figure 1.4). Resize the window and notice how the browser will break the text in different places. If the window is large enough, the entire page would be displayed on one line.

Line Breaks

Two of the tags that can be used to start a new line are <br> and <p>. The <br> tag is short for *break* and starts a new line directly under the current line. It is a

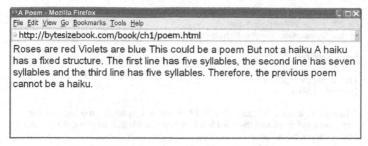

Figure 1.4 How the poem will appear in the browser.

singleton tag, so it does not have a closing tag. The <p> tag is short for *paragraph* and skips at least one line and then starts a new line. It is a paired tag, so it is closed with the </p> tag.

As was mentioned above, browsers have the ability to interpret HTML even if some tags are missing. The closing paragraph tag is such a tag. It is not possible to nest one paragraph inside another, so if the browser encounters two paragraph tags without closing tags, as in <p>One<p>Two, then it will interpret this as <p>One</p><p>Two</p>. Even the validators at *w3.org* will accept HTML that does not have closing paragraph tags.

Listing 1.1 contains the HTML page for the poem, using markup for line breaks and paragraph tags.

```
<!DOCTYPE HTML PUBLIC "-//W3C//DTD HTML 4.01//EN">
<html>
  <head>
    <meta http-equiv="content-type"
          content="text/html;charset=utf-8">
    <title>A Poem</title>
  </head>
  <body>
    <p>
      Roses are red<br>
      Violets are blue<br>
      This could be a poem<br>
      But not a haiku<br>
    <p>
      A haiku has a fixed structure. The first line has five
      syllables, the second line has seven syllables
      and the third line has five syllables. Therefore,
      the previous poem cannot be a haiku.
  </body>
</html>
```

Listing 1.1 A four-line poem displayed using HTML.

When displayed in a browser, each line of the poem will appear on a separate line. The paragraph that follows the poem will still be displayed using word wrap, since no line breaks were inserted into it.

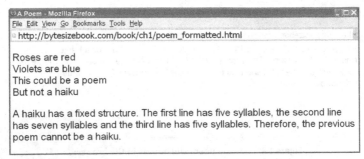

Figure 1.5 How the formatted poem will appear in the browser.

 Try It   http://bytesizebook.com/book/ch1/poem_formatted.html

Open the page in a browser to see how it looks (Figure 1.5). Resize the window and notice that the poem displays on four lines, unless the widow is very small.

Most browsers have an option for viewing the actual HTML that was sent from the server. If you view the source, you will see the same HTML code that was displayed in Listing 1.1.

1.2.3   What Is the HT in HTML?

The **HT** in **HTML** stands for *Hypertext*. Hypertext is the ability to click on a link in one page and have another page open. If you have ever clicked on a link in a web page to open another page, then you have used a hypertext link.

There are two parts to a hypertext link: the location of the new page and the link text that appears in the browser. The location of the pages is specified as a *Uniform Resource Locator* [URL], which contains four parts: protocol, server, path, name. The protocol could be http, ftp, telnet and others. The protocol is followed by a colon and two slashes (://). After the protocol is the server, followed by a slash and the path of the directory that contains the resource. The name of the resource follows the path. `protocol://server/path/name`

The URL of the hypertext link is not displayed in the browser, but it is associated with the underlined text on the web page. Another way to say this is that the URL has to be included in the markup, since it does not appear as plain text.

Anchor Tag

The tag for a hypertext link is the paired tag <a>, which is short for *anchor*.

```
<a href="hidden_URL_of_a_file">
  Visible text in browser
</a>
```

Notice that the text that is visible in the browser is not inside a tag, but that the URL of the file is. This is an example of a tag that has additional information stored in it. The additional information is called an *attribute*. The URL of the page is stored in an attribute named *href*. Attributes in HTML tags provide extra information that is not visible in the browser.

This agrees with the basic definition of HTML as having plain text and tags. The tags contain extra information about how to display the plain text. In this case, when the user clicks on the plain text, the browser will read the URL from the *href* attribute and request that page from the server.

It may not seem apparent why this tag is called an anchor tag. An anchor tag in HTML is like the anchor of a ship. The anchor for a ship connects two parts: the ship, which is visible from the surface of the water, and the bottom of the ocean. When the anchor is in use, it is not in the ship, it is in the bottom of the ocean. The anchor HTML tag connects the visible text in the browser to the physical location of a file.

Absolute and Relative References

The *href* attribute of the anchor tag contains the URL of the destination page. When using the anchor tag to reference other pages on the web, you must know the complete URL of the resource in order to create a link to it. However, depending on where the resource is located, you may be able to speed up the loading of your page by using a *relative reference*.

1. If the resource is not on the same server, then you must specify the entire URL, starting with http://. This is known as an *absolute reference*.

```
<a href="http://server.com/path/page.html">
  Some Page Somewhere on the web
</a>
```

2. If the resource is on the same server, but is not descended from the current directory, then include the full path from the document root, starting with a /.

```
<a href="/path/from/root/page.html">
  Some Page on the Current Server
</a>
```

3. If the resource is in the same directory as the HTML page that references it, then only include the file name, not the server or the directory.

```
<a href="page.html">
  Some Page
</a>
```

4. If the resource is in a subdirectory of the directory where the HTML page that references it is located, then include the name of the subdirectory and the file name.

```
<a href="subdir/of/current/dir/page.html">
  Some Page in Some Subdir
</a>
```

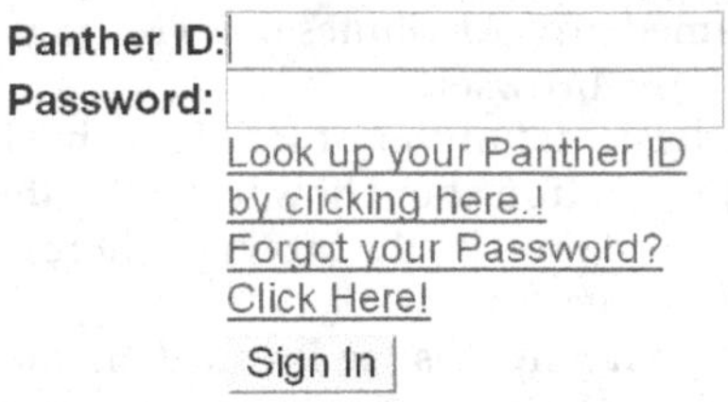

Panther ID: [   ]
Password: [   ]
<u>Look up your Panther ID</u>
<u>by clicking here.!</u>
<u>Forgot your Password?</u>
<u>Click Here!</u>
[Sign In]

Figure 1.6 An entry form from FIU.

There are three types of references.

1. Absolute
2. Relative from document root
3. Relative from current directory

There are just a few rules to determine the kind of reference.

1. If the URL begins with a protocol (like http://, ftp://, or telnet://), then it is an absolute reference to that location.
2. If the URL begins with a /, then it is a relative reference from the document root of the current server.
3. In all other cases, the URL is a relative reference from the current directory.

1.3   HTML Forms

If you have ever logged into a web site, then you have used an HTML form to supply your username and password. A form will have places where a user can enter data. These are known as *form elements* and can be for one line of text, several lines of text, drop down lists and buttons. The form in Figure 1.6, which is from Florida International University, uses several form elements for lines of text and a button for submitting the data to the server.

1.3.1   Form Elements

The form and the form elements are defined using HTML tags. The opening form tag is `<form>` and the closing tag is `</form>`. Plain text, other HTML tags and form element tags can be placed between the opening and closing form tags. There are many form elements, but only two of them will be introduced now. Table 1.3

Table 1.3 Two essential form element types.

Type	Example
text	`<input type="text" name="hobby" value="">`
	The *value* attribute is the text that appears within the element when the page is loaded.
submit	`<input type="submit" name="nextButton" value="Next">`
	The *value* attribute is the text that appears on the button in the browser.

defines the two essential form elements: *text* and *submit*. Additional form elements are covered in Chapter Six.

Each of these has the same tag name (*input*) and attributes (*type, name, value*).

1. The HTML tag name is *input*.
2. There are many different form elements that use the *input* tag. The *type* attribute identifies which form element to display.
3. There could be several form elements in a form. The *name* attribute should be a unique identifier for the element.
4. The *value* attribute stores the data that is in the element. The value that is hard coded in the element is the value that is displayed in the browser when the HTML page is loaded.
5. The *name* and *value* attributes are used to send data to the server. When the form is submitted, the data for this element will be sent as *name=value*. The value that will be sent will be the current data that is displayed in the element.

Listing 1.2 is an example of a simple web page that has a form in it.

```
<!DOCTYPE HTML PUBLIC "-//W3C//DTD HTML 4.01//EN">
<html>
  <head>
    <meta http-equiv="content-type"
          content="text/html;charset=utf-8">
    <title>First Form</title>
  </head>
  <body>
    <form>
      <p>
      This is a simple HTML page that has a form in it.
      <p>
      Hobby: <input type="text" name="hobby"
                                 value="">
        <input type="submit" name="confirmButton"
                             value="Confirm">
    </form>
  </body>
</html>
```

Listing 1.2 A web page with a form.

The form has an input element of type *text* with a name of *hobby* and an input element of type *submit* with a name of *confirmButton*. The name that appears on the button is *Confirm*. Notice that there are HTML tags, plain text and form elements between the opening and closing form tags.

Try It   http://bytesizebook.com/book/ch1/OnePage/SimpleForm.html

The page will display a text box and a submit button (Figure 1.7). Open the page in a browser, enter some data in the text box and submit the form.

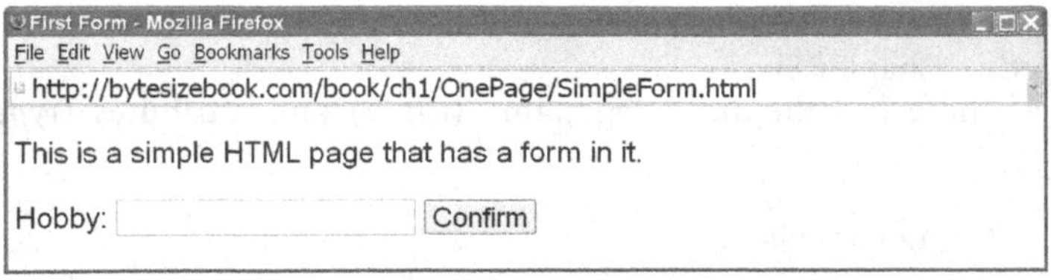

Figure 1.7 A form with a text box and a submit button.

1.3.2   Representing Data

In a two-dimensional world, it is very easy to create lists of data. For example, Table 1.4 displays a list of colour preferences in a table.

How would these be written in a one-dimensional world? In other words, how would all of this data be combined into one string of text?

In addition to the data that is in the table, the structure of the table would also need to be stored in the string. This table has four rows and two columns. There would need to be a way to indicate the end of one row and the start of the next. There would need to be a way to indicate the end of one column and the start of the next.

One technique for data formatting is to choose special characters to represent the end of a row and the end of a column. It doesn't matter which characters are used, as long as they are different. It is also helpful if the characters that are chosen are not common characters. For example, the ampersand and equal sign could be used.

1. & is used to separate rows
2. = is used to separate the two columns in a row

Using this technique, the above list could be represented as a string. The structure of the table is embedded in the string with the addition of special characters.

```
foreground=black&background=white&border=red&link=blue
```

1.3.3   Transmitting Data over the Web

When the user activates a submit button on a form, the data in the form elements are sent to the server. The default destination on the server is the URL of the current page. All the data in the form elements are placed into one string that is sent to the server. This string is known as the *query string*. The data from the form is placed into the query string as *name=value* pairs.

Table 1.4 A table of colour preferences.

foreground	black
background	white
border	red
link	blue

1. Each input element of type *text* or *submit* with a *name* attribute will have its data added to the query string as a *name = value* pair.
2. If there are many *name = value* pairs, then they are separated by an ampersand, &.
3. If a form element does not have a *name* attribute, then it is not sent to the server.
4. In the default case, the query string is sent to the server by appending it to the end of the URL. A question mark is used to separate the end of the URL from the start of the query string.

If the user entered *skiing* in the *hobby* element and clicked the *Confirm* button of the form, then the query string that is sent from the browser would look like the following string.

```
hobby=skiing&confirmButton=Confirm
```

A question mark and the query string are appended to the URL. The request sent to the browser would contain the following URL.

```
http://store.com/buy.htm?hobby=skiing&confirmButton=Confirm
```

If the user had entered the hobby as *water skiing*, then the query string would appear as the following string.

```
hobby=water+skiing&confirmButton=Confirm
```

Notice that the space between *water* and *skiing* has been replaced by a plus sign. A space would break the URL in two. This is the first example of a character that cannot be represented normally in a URL; there will be other characters that must be translated before they can be entered in a query string. Please be aware that the browser does this translation automatically and that the server will do the reverse translation automatically. This is known as HTML encoding and HTML decoding.

Try It   http://bytesizebook.com/book/ch1/OnePage/SimpleForm.html

Open the form, enter a hobby and click the *Confirm* button. The same page will redisplay, but the query string will be appended to the URL (Figure 1.8).

Many first-time observers will think that nothing is happening when the submit button on the form is clicked, except that the value that was entered into the text

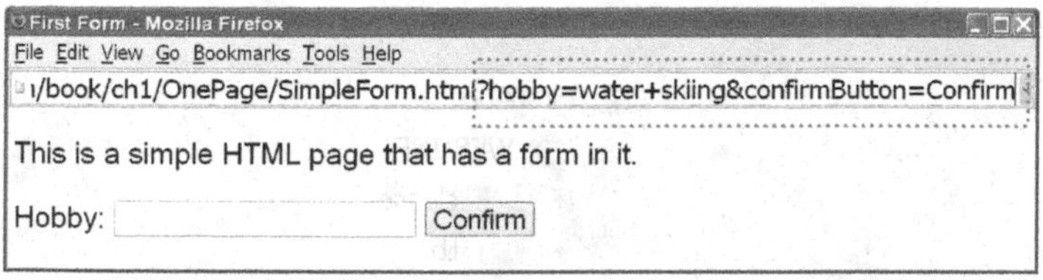

First Form - Mozilla Firefox

File Edit View Go Bookmarks Tools Help

ı/book/ch1/OnePage/SimpleForm.html?hobby=water+skiing&confirmButton=Confirm

This is a simple HTML page that has a form in it.

Hobby: [   ] [Confirm]

Figure 1.8 After entering data and clicking the button, the query string will appear in the URL.

box has disappeared. In reality, a new request for the same page was made to the server with the query string, containing the data from the form appended to the URL of the request. A complete request was made by the browser; a complete response was sent by the server.

1.4   Processing Form Data

If the data from a form is sent to a simple HTML page, then there is no way for the HTML page to retrieve the data that was sent from the browser. In order to process the data, the page should be a *JSP* or a *servlet* in a *web application*.

1.4.1   Web Application

A web application consists of a directory structure and some required files. The directory structure is the same for all web applications. One of the required files is the *web.xml* file, which is used to initialise the web application.

Directory Structure

The root directory can have any name, like *FirstApp*, but the subdirectories must have the names *WEB-INF*, *lib* and *classes* as shown in Figure 1.9.

The root directory (i.e. *FirstApp*) of the web application is the standard location for HTML files. The WEB-INF directory contains the *web.xml* file. The *lib* directory is where *jar* files will be placed to add non-standard features to the web application. The *classes* directory is where the programs and supporting files for your web application will be placed.

Only the root directory is visible from the Internet. That is why HTML files are placed in the root of the web application. Any file that is to be accessed from the web must be visible from the root of the web application.

The WEB-INF directory and its contents cannot be accessed directly from the web. A method will be covered in the next chapter for making selected files, which are descended from WEB-INF, visible from the web.

web.xml

There is one required file, named *web.xml*, that belongs in the WEB-INF directory. It contains XML that defines any special features for the web application. XML is similar to HTML, but there are no predefined tags. Each application defines its own tags. In this book, it will be assumed that the web application supports the new EL that is included in JSP 2.0. As such, the *web.xml* file for a web application

Figure 1.9 A web application has a specific directory structure.

should contain the XML in the following listing, at the least. More content will be added to the *web.xml* file as the applications become more robust.

```xml
<?xml version="1.0" encoding="UTF-8"?>
<web-app xmlns="http://java.sun.com/xml/ns/j2ee"
  xmlns:xsi="http://www.w3.org/2001/XMLSchema-instance"
  xsi:schemaLocation="http://java.sun.com/xml/ns/j2ee
    http://java.sun.com/xml/ns/j2ee/web-app_2_4.xsd"
  version="2.4">

<display-name>myApp</display-name>
<description>
  Simple Web Application with Expression Language
</description>

<session-config>
  <session-timeout>
      30
  </session-timeout>
</session-config>

<welcome-file-list>
  <welcome-file>
      index.jsp
  </welcome-file>
  <welcome-file>
      index.html
  </welcome-file>
  <welcome-file>
      index.htm
  </welcome-file>
</welcome-file-list>
</web-app>
```

Web Application Location

Web applications are run by servlet engines. Each servlet engine will have a special location for web applications. For the Tomcat servlet engine, all web applications should be located in the *webapps* directory.

NetBeans is a Java development environment that is packaged with Tomcat. It is very easy to configure NetBeans to run web applications. There will be a discussion of NetBeans in a later section in this chapter.

For other servlet engines, check the documentation to determine where web applications should be placed.

1.4.2 JSP

A *Java Server Page* [JSP] contains HTML tags and plain text, just like a regular web page. In addition, a JSP can contain Java code that is executed when the page is displayed. As long as it is contained in a web application, a JSP will be able to process the form data that is sent to it.

JSP Location

For now, the location of JSPs will be in the root directory of the web application, not in the WEB-INF directory. The WEB-INF directory is not accessible directly through a web browser. Later, you will see how it is possible to place a JSP inside the WEB-INF directory so that access to the JSP can be restricted.

Accessing Form Data

In the servlet specification 2.0, there is a new language that has been added to JSPs that simplifies access to objects that are available to a JSP. This language is known as the *Expression Language* [EL]. EL statements start with a dollar sign and are surrounded by curly braces.

```
${EL-statement}
```

The EL statement for accessing data in the query string uses the word *param* and the name of the form element that contained the data.

```
${param.name_of_element}
```

Consider the query string of hobby=water+skiing. To retrieve the value of the hobby parameter from the query string, insert ${param.hobby} anywhere inside the JSP.

```
<!DOCTYPE HTML PUBLIC "-//W3C//DTD HTML 4.01//EN">
<html>
  <head>
    <meta http-equiv="content-type"
          content="text/html;charset=utf-8">
    <title>First JSP</title>
  </head>
  <body>
    <form>
      <p>
      This is a simple HTML page that has a form in it.
      <p>
      The hobby was received as: <b>${param.hobby}</b>
      <p>
      Hobby: <input type="text" name="hobby"
                                 value="">
        <input type="submit" name="confirmButton"
                             value="Confirm">
    </form>
  </body>
</html>
```

The source code for this page looks just like the HTML page that contained the simple form in Listing 1.2, except that it includes one instance of an EL statement, ${param.hobby}, and has the extension *jsp* instead of *html*. These changes allow the value that is present in the query string to be displayed in the browser.

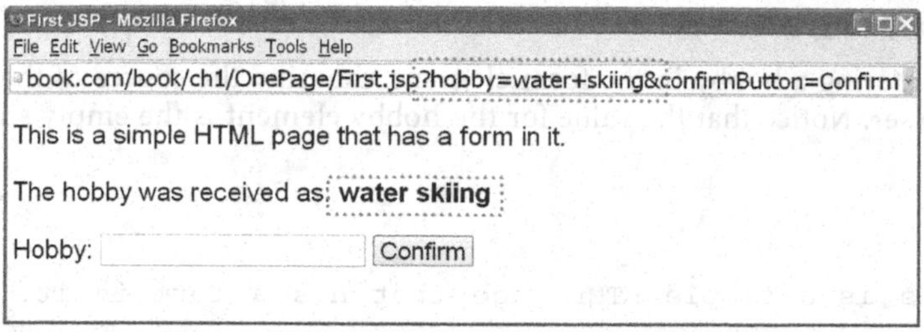

Figure 1.10 The value from the query string is displayed in the page.

This is an example of a dynamic page. It changes appearance based upon the data that is entered by the user.

Try It   http://bytesizebook.com/book/ch1/OnePage/First.jsp

Type in a hobby and click the *Confirm* button. The form data will be sent back to the current page in the query string. Figure 1.10 shows the value that is in the query string being displayed in the body of the JSP.

1.4.3   Initialising Form Elements

Using the ${param.hobby} syntax, it is possible to initialise a form element with the value that was sent to the page. The trick is to set the *value* attribute of the form element with the parameter value: value="${param.hobby}". The *value* attribute holds the data that will appear in the form element when the page is loaded.

```
<!DOCTYPE HTML PUBLIC "-//W3C//DTD HTML 4.01//EN">
<html>
  <head>
    <meta http-equiv="content-type"
          content="text/html;charset=utf-8">
    <title>Initialized JSP</title>
  </head>
  <body>
    <form>
      <p>
      This is a simple HTML page that has a form in it.
      <p>
      The hobby was received as: <b>${param.hobby}</b>
      <p>
      Hobby: <input type="text" name="hobby"
                               value="${param.hobby}">
      <input type="submit" name="confirmButton"
                           value="Confirm">
    </form>
  </body>
</html>
```

Try It   http://bytesizebook.com/book/ch1/OnePage/FormInitialized.jsp

Before entering a hobby in the form element, examine the source of the page in the browser. Notice that the value for the hobby element is the empty string.

```
. . .
<form>
  <p>
    This is a simple HTML page that has a form in it.
  <p>
    The hobby was received as: <b></b>
  <p>
    Hobby: <input type="text" name="hobby"
                             value="">
    <input type="submit" name="confirmButton"
                        value="Confirm">
</form>
. . .
```

Now enter a hobby and click the *Confirm* button (Figure 1.11).

Open the source of the page in the browser. You will see that the value that was sent from the browser to the server is now hard coded in the form element. Try a hobby that has multiple words, too.

```
. . .
<form>
  <p>
    This is a simple HTML page that has a form in it.
  <p>
    The hobby was received as: <b>water skiing</b>
  <p>
    Hobby: <input type="text" name="hobby"
                                value="water skiing">
    <input type="submit" name="confirmButton"
                        value="Confirm">
</form>
. . .
```

Remember to use the quotes around the values. If the quotes are omitted and the value has multiple words in it, then only the first will be placed in the

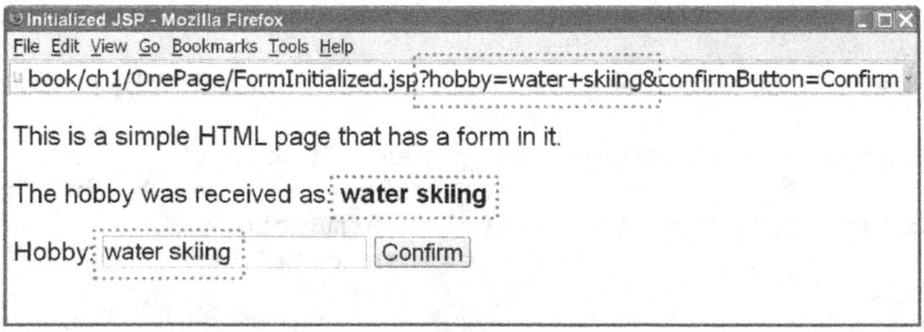

Figure 1.11 The input element is initialised with the value from the query string.

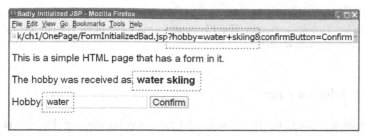

Figure 1.12 The input element is not initialised properly for values that have multiple words.

element. Never write the value as value=$ {param.hobby}; always include the quotes.

Try It   http://bytesizebook.com/book/ch1/OnePage/FormInitializedBad.jsp

In this example, the quotes have been omitted for the value. To see the problem, enter more than one word in the hobby element.

In Figure 1.12, you will see that the correct value is displayed in the plain text, but that the value in the form element is incorrect. For example, if the hobby is entered as *water skiing*, then the form element will only display *water*.

The reason becomes clear when the HTML code for the form element is viewed in the browser:

```
<input type="text" name="hobby" value=water skiing>
```

Without the quotes around the *value* attribute, the browser sees the following attributes: *type, name, value* and *skiing*. The browser doesn't know what the *skiing* attribute is, so the browser ignores it. Compare this with the correct format for the input element:

```
<input type="text" name="hobby" value="water skiing">
```

Now the browser sees the correct attributes: *type, name* and *value.*

1.5   The Truth About JSPs

JSPs look like HTML pages, but they can generate dynamic content. Whenever there is dynamic content, there is a program working in the background. HTML pages are plain text. If a JSP is not in a web application, then there would be no dynamic content and they would be treated as plain text.

JSPs are abstractions: they are translated into Java programs known as *servlets*. The program that translates them into servlets is known as the *servlet engine*. It is the task of the servlet engine to translate the JSPs into servlets and to execute them.

Servlets only contain Java code. All the plain text from the JSP has been translated into `write` statements. The EL statements have been translated into complicated Java expressions.

1.5.1   Servlet for a JSP

The following listing contains the servlet that was created by the servlet engine for the last page. The contents of the page can be seen in the `out.write` statements.

```java
package org.apache.jsp.ch2.TwoPages;
import javax.servlet.*;
import javax.servlet.http.*;
import javax.servlet.jsp.*;

public final class Edit_jsp
    extends org.apache.jasper.runtime.HttpJspBase
    implements org.apache.jasper.runtime JspSourceDependent
{

    private static java.util.Vector _jspx_dependants;

    public java.util.List getDependants() {
        return _jspx_dependants;
    }

    public void _jspService(HttpServletRequest request,
                            HttpServletResponse response)
        throws java.io.IOException, ServletException {

    JspFactory _jspxFactory = null;
    PageContext pageContext = null;
    HttpSession session = null;
    ServletContext application = null;
    ServletConfig config = null;
    JspWriter out = null;
    Object page = this;
    JspWriter _jspx_out = null;
    PageContext _jspx_page_context = null;
    try {
      _jspxFactory = JspFactory.getDefaultFactory();
      response.setContentType("text/html");
      pageContext = _jspxFactory.getPageContext(
                this, request, response,
            null, true, 8192, true);
      _jspx_page_context = pageContext;
      application = pageContext.getServletContext();
      config = pageContext.getServletConfig();
      session = pageContext.getSession();
      out = pageContext.getOut();
      _jspx_out = out;

      out.write("<!DOCTYPE HTML PUBLIC" +);
      out.write("\"-//W3C//DTD HTML 4.01//EN\">\n");
```

```
      out.write("<html>\n");
      out.write(" <head>\n");
      out.write("  <meta http-equiv=\"content-type");
      out.write("         ");


      out.write(" content=\"text/html;charset=utf-8\">\n");
      out.write("  <title>Simple Edit Page</title>\n");
      out.write(" </head>\n");
      out.write(" <body>\n");
      out.write("  <p>This is a simple HTML page that");
      out.write(" has a form in it.\n");
      out.write("  <form action=\"Confirm.jsp\">\n");
      out.write("   <p>\n");
      out.write("   If there is a value for the hobby");
      out.write(" in the query string,");
      out.write("   then it is used to initialize the");
      out.write(" hobby element.\n");
      out.write("   \n");
      out.write("   <p>\n");
      out.write("   Hobby: <input type=\"text\" name=");
      out.write("\"hobby\" value=\"");
      out.write((java.lang.String)
                org.apache.jasper.runtime PageContextImpl.
                proprietaryEvaluate("${param.hobby}",
                java.lang.String.class,
                PageContext)_jspx_page_context, null,
                false));
      out.write("\">\n");
      out.write("          ");
      out.write("<input type=\"submit\"");
      out.write(" name=\"confirmButton\"");
      out.write("            ");
      out.write(" value=\"Confirm\">\n");
      out.write("   \n");
      out.write("   </form>\n");
      out.write(" </body>\n");
      out.write("</html>\n");
      out.write("\n");
      out.write("\n");
    } catch (Throwable t) {
      if (!(t instanceof SkipPageException)){
        out = _jspx_out;
      if (out != null && out.getBufferSize() != 0)
        out.clearBuffer();
      if (_jspx_page_context != null)
        _jspx_page_context.handlePageException(t);
      }
    } finally {
      if (_jspxFactory != null)
        _jspxFactory.releasePageContext(
          _jspx_page_context);
    }
  }
}
```

It is actually a complicated matter to generate dynamic content. The EL statement in the JSP is responsible for the dynamic content. In the above servlet, the actual Java code for the EL statement of ${param.hobby} is

```
out.write((java.lang.String)
           org.apache.jasper.runtime.PageContextImpl.
           proprietaryEvaluate("${param.hobby}",
           java.lang.String.class,
           PageContext)_jspx_page_context, null,
           false));
```

The beauty of a JSP is that the servlet engine implements most of the details automatically. The developer can simply write HTML statements and EL statements to generate programs that can process dynamic data.

1.5.2   Handling a JSP

Web servers know how to deliver static content, but need separate programs to handle dynamic content. If there is a request made to the server for a JSP, then the server must send the request to another program to complete the request. In particular, if a web page has a form for entering data and sends the data to a JSP, then a special program know as a *servlet engine* will handle the request. A servlet engine is a program running on the server that knows how to execute JSPs and servlets. There are several different servlet engines: Tomcat and JRun are two popular choices.

JSP Request Process

When the user fills in data in a form and clicks a button, a request is made from the browser to the web server (Figure 1.13).

The web server recognises that the extension of the request is *.jsp*, so it calls a servlet engine to process the JSP. The web server administrator must configure the web server so that it sends all *.jsp* files to the servlet engine. There is nothing magical about the *.jsp* extension, it could be set to any extension at all (Figure 1.14).

The web server sends the request information that it received from the browser to the servlet engine. If this were a request for a static page, the server would send a response to the browser; instead, the server sends the response information to the servlet engine. The servlet engine takes this request and response information and sends a response back to the browser (Figure 1.15).

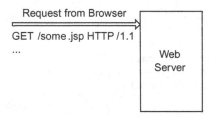

Figure 1.13 The browser makes a request to the server for a dynamic page.

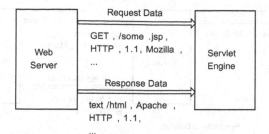

Figure 1.14 The web server sends the request for a JSP to the servlet engine.

Putting all the steps together gives the complete picture of how a request for a JSP is handled: the request is made; the server calls another program to handle the request; the other program, which is known as a servlet engine, sends the response to the browser (Figure 1.16).

Servlet Engine Response

Inside the servlet engine, there are steps that are followed to take the request information and generate a response. The servlet engine must translate the JSP into a servlet, load the servlet into memory, encapsulate the data from the browser and generate the response.

Translating the JSP The servlet engine must translate all JSPs into servlets. The servlet engine will keep a copy of the translated servlet so that the engine does not need to retranslate the JSP on every request. The servlet engine will only create the servlet when the servlet does not exist or when the source JSP has been modified.

Loading the Servlet A servlet is loaded into memory upon the first request made to it after the servlet engine has been started or restarted. The servlet .class file is stored on disk. Upon the first request to the servlet, the .class file is loaded into memory. Once a servlet has been loaded into memory, it will remain there, waiting for calls to its methods. It is not removed from memory after each request; this enables the servlet engine to process requests faster.

Request and Response Information The web server sends the request information that it received from the browser to the servlet engine. The server also sends

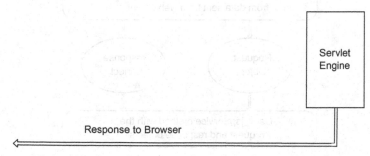

Figure 1.15 The servlet engine sends a response back to the browser.

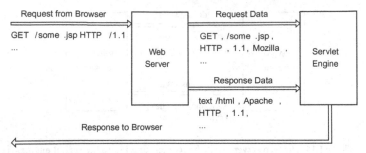

Figure 1.16 The complete request and response cycle.

the response information to the servlet engine. The servlet engine takes this information and creates two objects: one that encapsulates the request information and one that encapsulates the response information. These two objects are all that are needed to communicate with the browser; all of the information that the browser sent is in the request object; all the information that is needed to send data to the browser is in the response object.

Servlet Method to Handle Request Generating the response is done in the _jspService method of the generated servlet. The method has two parameters: the request and the response. These parameters are the objects that the servlet engine generated from the request data that was sent from the browser and from the response data that was forwarded by the web server. These objects are of the types javax.servlet.http.HttpServletRequest and javax. servlet.http.HttpServletResponse.

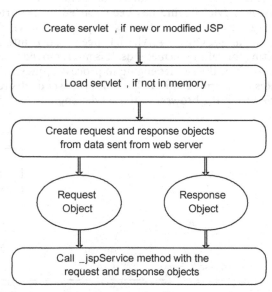

Figure 1.17 The servlet engine handling a request for a JSP.

```
public void _jspService(HttpServletRequest request,
                        HttpServletResponse response)
  throws java.io.IOException, ServletException
```

Whenever a request is made for a JSP, the servlet engine might have to create the servlet and might have to load it into memory. If the servlet is recreated, then it will have to be reloaded into memory. However, even if the servlet is not recreated, the servlet might need to be loaded into memory. Whenever the servlet engine is restarted, then all servlets are removed from memory; when the next request is made to the servlet, it will need to be reloaded into memory.

Figure 1.17 summarises the steps that are followed by the servlet engine when it receives a request for a JSP.

1.6 Tomcat and NetBeans

In order to run servlets and JSPs, it is necessary to install a servlet engine. A popular servlet engine is Tomcat, which is an Apache project.

While it is possible to download and install Tomcat, it is easier to download and install NetBeans, which is packaged with Tomcat. NetBeans is an excellent development environment for Java and it allows the developer to debug web applications just as easily as any other Java application. It is possible to use Tomcat from within NetBeans without having to know anything about Tomcat configuration. NetBeans is open source and can be downloaded for free from http://netbeans.org.

NetBeans organises applications into projects. There are several templates for creating typical projects; one of these templates is for a web application. When the NetBeans project is built, the corresponding file structure for a web application will be created.

1.6.1 Creating a Project in NetBeans

In order to work on a file in NetBeans, it is necessary to create a project.

1. From the *File* menu, select *New Project . . .*
2. Choose the **Category** of project as *Web*.
3. Choose the **Project** type as *Web Application*.
4. Enter a **Project Name** and a **Project Location**.
5. Use the default context path and use J2EE 1.4.
6. Do **NOT** set the source level to 1.4. Be sure that Java 1.5 or higher is installed on the system.
7. After clicking finish, there should be a project listed in your **Projects** tab. It will look something like Figure 1.18.

1.6.2 Web Project in NetBeans

A web project in NetBeans is a set of directories and files that allow for servlets and JSPs to be executed and debugged. By placing the HTML, JSP and servlet files in the correct folders, a web project can be executed from within NetBeans.

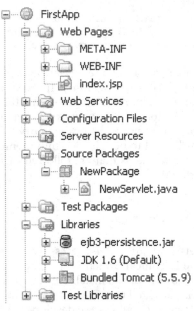

Figure 1.18 The Projects tab in NetBeans.

The web project does not have the structure of a web application; however, when a project is built, the corresponding web application structure will be created. The files from the project folders will be copied into the folders of the web application.

There are three main folders that are used for a web project: *Web Pages*, *Source Packages* and *Libraries*. The *Web Pages* folder will be discussed in this chapter, since it is the one that is visible from the web. The other two folders will be covered in detail in Chapters Two and Four.

Web Pages

The *Web Pages* folder is for HTML pages, images, CSS style sheets and some JSPs. Table 1.5 explains the directories and files that will be found in this folder when a new project is created.

 Try It   http://netbeans.org

Download and install the latest NetBeans from http://netbeans.org. In order to use the EL statements, Java 1.5 or higher must be installed on the system.

Table 1.5 Contents of the Web Pages folder.

Web Pages	This is the main folder for content that is visible from the web application. Place the JSPs from this chapter in this folder.
index.jsp	This is the default web page when this web application is loaded from Tomcat. Place hypertext links in this page to your JSPs and servlets. When the web application is run, this is the page that will appear in the web browser.
WEB-INF	This subdirectory contains the *web.xml* file. It controls the web application. More information about this file will be provided in Chapter Two.

Create a web application and copy the JSPs into the Web Pages folder. Subfolders can also be created. For now, do not place any JSPs under the WEB-INF directory.

Edit the *index.jsp* file by adding hypertext links to the JSPs.

Run the web application, follow the links to the JSPs and enjoy running a dynamic application.

1.7   Summary

The communication between the browser and server is controlled by the HTTP protocol. The two major parts of the protocol cover the request and response: the request from the browser and the response from the server must have specific formats. The server also indicates the type of the content that is being sent to the browser, so that the browser will know how to display it.

Markup languages are useful for annotating plain text. HTML is the markup language that is used on the Internet. The most common content sent on the web is HTML. Each HTML tag has a similar structure. To be well formed, an HTML page should have a set of basic tags. The most important tag in HTML is the anchor tag. The anchor tag can use relative and absolute references to other files.

HTML forms are the way that browsers accept information from a user and send it to the server. The basic input tags were covered: text and submit. When the browser sends the data to the server, the data must be formatted so that it can be passed in a URL. It is placed in the query string.

In order to process data from a user, the data must be received by a dynamic page in a web application. Of most importance in a web application is the *web.xml* file, which is used to configure the web application. A web application must have a specific directory structure. JSPs are one of the ways that dynamic content can be displayed in a web application. The expression language is used to display dynamic content from within a JSP. EL can be used to initialise form elements with data that is sent to the page.

JSPs are an abstraction: they are translated into Java programs, know as *servlets*, by the servlet engine. The servlet engine is an application that is called by the web server to handle JSPs and servlets. It is possible to write servlets directly, without creating a JSP. If a page has more Java than HTML, then it should be written as a servlet, not as a JSP. The servlet engine encapsulates the request and response information from the server into objects and passes them to the servlets.

NetBeans is an excellent development environment for web applications. Net-Beans is packaged with Tomcat and is integrated with the default browser on a system. After creating a project, a web application can be executed with the click of a button.

1.8   Chapter Review

Terms

1. Browser
2. Server

3. Request
4. Response
5. Protocol
6. URL
7. Markup Language
8. HTML
   a. Singleton Tag
   b. Paired Tag
9. Hypertext Link
   a. Relative
   b. Absolute
10. HTML Form
11. Query String
12. Web Application
13. web.xml
14. ${param.element_name}

Tags

1. HTML
2. HEAD
3. BODY
4. DOCTYPE
5. META
6. TITLE
7. BR
8. P
9. INPUT
   a. TEXT (name and value attributes)
   b. SUBMIT (name and value attributes)

Questions

1. What are the three things that belong in the first line of a request from the browser?
2. What are the three things that belong in the first line of a response from the server?
3. What types of information are contained in the request header?
4. What types of information are contained in the response header?
5. Besides the ?, = and &, list five additional characters that are encoded by the browser.
6. What is the purpose of MIME types?

7. What are the two parts of every markup language?
8. What two tags are needed in order to use the W3C validator?
9. What is word wrap?

Tasks

1. Write a complete HTML page, including TITLE, DOCTYPE and META tags. Validate the page for correct HTML syntax, at http://www.w3c.org/. Introduce some errors into your page and validate again, to see the error messages that the validator generates.
2. Write hypertext links to the following locations. Use a relative reference whenever possible.
   a. To the site `http://www.microsoft.com`
   b. To the file `page2.html` that is in the same directory as the current page.
   c. To the file `page3.html` that is in a subdirectory named `special` of the current directory.
   d. To the file `page4.html` that is in a subdirectory named `common` of the document root of the web server.
3. Write a complete HTML page that has an HTML form with a text input field and a submit button. Validate the page for correct HTML syntax, at http://www.w3c.org/.
   a. Rewrite the page so that it echoes the value for the input field if it is in the Query String.
   b. Rewrite the page so that it initialises the input element with the value for it in the Query String.
4. Write the Query String that would be created from an HTML form that has two input elements named `first` and `last`. Assume that the user has entered a value of *Fred* for `first` and *Flintstone* for `last`.
5. Create a Web Application with a complete *web.xml* file.
   a. Place the HTML page from question 1 into the web application.
   b. Place the JSP from question 3 into the web application.
   c. In the HTML page, add a hypertext link to the JSP.
   d. Access the HTML page from the web.
   e. Access the JSP from the web.

2 Controllers

Web applications are more similar than different. If you describe a web site where you buy things, you will probably say that there is a page where you enter personal information, then there is a page where you confirm that your information is correct and then the site processes your order. These pages could be named the *edit page*, the *confirm page* and the *process page*. For the next few chapters, this will be the basic structure of all the examples of web applications.

Web applications need to be able to send data from one page to the next. The form tag allows one page to send data to any other page. All data that is in named form elements can be sent to any page when a button in a form is clicked.

Pages that have visible form elements for entering data can easily send data to another page; however, not all pages have visible form elements for entering data. Typically, the confirm page will display the user's data as plain text, not in visible form elements. There is a non-visible form element that can be added to a form that will hold the user's data, so that it can be sent to the next page when a button is clicked.

Some pages in a web application need to be able to send data to more than one page. The confirm page in a typical web site is a common example. If there is an error in the data, the user will send the data back to the edit page. If the data is correct, the user will send the data to the process page. In order to handle this task efficiently, a separate page or program, known as a controller, will be used.

The main task of the controller is to determine the next page to display. Based on the button that the user clicks, the controller will forward the request to the correct JSP. A controller can be written as a JSP, but it is better to write the controller as a Java program known as a servlet.

A servlet is a Java program that is compiled to a `.class` file. The `.class` file must be in the *classes* directory of a web application in order to be executed. By default, `.class` files cannot be accessed from the web, but they can be made visible by adding tags to the *web.xml* file of the web application.

2.1 Sending Data to Another Form

When the user clicks a submit button in a form, by default, the data is sent back to the current URL. At the server, the current URL then processes the data and resends its content to the browser. It is possible to override this default behaviour so that the data entered in one page can be sent to another page (Figure 2.1).

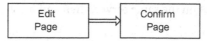

Figure 2.1 The data from the edit page can be forwarded to the confirm page.

Each form has an optional *action* attribute that specifies the URL of the page that should receive the data.

2.1.1   Action Attribute

The *action* attribute should specify the URL of a JSP or servlet that will process the data and return a new HTML page for the browser to display.

```
. . .
<form action="Confirm.jsp">
. . .
```

The *action* attribute of the form tag controls where the data is sent and the page that will be displayed. For example, Listing 2.1 shows how the edit page, could send its data to Confirm.jsp.

```
<!DOCTYPE HTML PUBLIC "-//W3C//DTD HTML 4.01//EN">
<html>
  <head>
    <meta http-equiv="content-type"
          content="text/html;charset=utf-8">
    <title>Simple Edit Page</title>
  </head>
  <body>
    <p>This is a simple HTML page that has a form in it.
    <form action="Confirm.jsp">
      <p>
        If there is a value for the hobby in the query
        string, then it is used to initialize the hobby
        element.
      <p>
        Hobby: <input type="text" name="hobby"
                                  value="${param.hobby}">
        <input type="submit" name="confirmButton"
                             value="Confirm">
    </form>
  </body>
</html>
```

Listing 2.1 A JSP that sends data to a different page.

Relative and Absolute References

Just like the *href* attribute in an anchor tag, the *action* attribute can be a relative reference to a JSP or servlet, or can be an absolute reference to a JSP or servlet on another server.

1. If the resource is not on the same server, then you must specify the entire URL, starting with `http://`.

```
<form action="http://server.com/path/Confirm.jsp">
```

2. If the JSP or servlet is on the same server, but is not descended from the current directory, then include the full path from the document root, starting with a `/`.

```
<form action="/path/Confirm.jsp">
```

3. If the JSP or servlet is in the same directory as the HTML page that references it, then only include the file name, not the server, nor the directory.

```
<form action="Confirm.jsp">
```

4. If the JSP or servlet is in a subdirectory of the directory where the HTML page that references it is located, then include the name of the subdirectory and the file name.

```
<form action="path/Confirm.jsp">
```

Retrieving the Value of a Form Element

When a button is clicked in a form, the data from the form is placed into the query string. The query string is sent to the page that is specified in the action attribute of the form. This page can retrieve the value of the form element by using EL, just as the edit page used EL to initialise the form element with the value from the query string.

The next listing shows the contents of Confirm.jsp, the JSP that processes the data and displays a new HTML page. It displays the value of the form parameter that was sent to it, using the EL statement ${param.hobby}. Once the data has been placed into the query string, it can be retrieved by any JSP.

```
<!DOCTYPE HTML PUBLIC "-//W3C//DTD HTML 4.01//EN">
<html>
  <head>
    <meta http-equiv="content-type"
          content="text/html;charset=utf-8">
    <title>Simple Confirmation Page</title>
  </head>
  <body>
    <p>The value of the hobby that was sent to
       this page is: <b>${param.hobby}</b>.
  </body>
</html>
```

 Try It   http://bytesizebook.com/book/ch2/TwoPages/Simple/Edit.jsp

Enter some data into the hobby element (Figure 2.2).

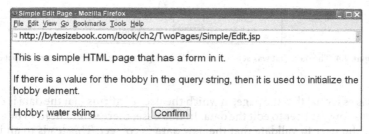

Figure 2.2 Edit.jsp with some data entered into the hobby element.

Click the confirm button and look at the URL in the browser window (Figure 2.3). The URL is for the confirm page and contains the data that was sent from the edit page: the hobby and the button. The hobby is displayed in the browser window.

Notice that

1. The URL has changed.
2. The data that was entered in the first page is sent to the second page in the query string via the URL.
3. The data that was entered in the first page has been displayed in the second page.

2.1.2 Hidden Field Technique

There are now two JSPs: `Edit.jsp` and `Confirm.jsp`. The edit page can send data to the confirm page. The next challenge is to allow the confirm page to send the data back to the edit page (Figure 2.4).

If you think about web pages that you have visited, you will realise that when a web page accepts information from the user, data can only be changed on one page: the data entry page. Furthermore, once data has been entered into the site, the user usually has the ability to confirm that the information is correct, before submitting the data to be processed.

This is the structure of the next example. The user can enter and edit data in the edit page, but cannot edit data in the confirm page; the confirm page will only display the data that was entered in the edit page and provide a button that will allow the user to return to the edit page to make corrections.

When accepting data from the user, it is important to validate that the data is correct. The simplest way to do this is to allow the user to confirm that the data is

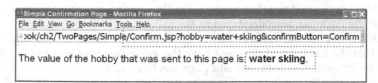

Figure 2.3 The confirm page with data that was sent from the edit page.

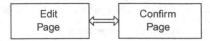

Figure 2.4 The data that was sent to the confirm page can be returned to the edit page.

valid. It is essential that the page, in which the user confirms that the data is correct, does not allow the user to edit the data. In this case, there would need to be another page for the user to validate that the new data is correct. This leads to an infinite chain of confirmation pages. It is much simpler to ask the user to confirm the data and return the user to the first page if there is an error.

First Attempt

The first attempt would be to add a form with a button to Confirm.jsp (Listing 2.2). This will allow the application to return to the edit page when the user clicks the button.

```
<!DOCTYPE HTML PUBLIC "-//W3C//DTD HTML 4.01//EN">
<html>
  <head>
    <meta http-equiv="content-type"
          content="text/html;charset=utf-8">
    <title>Simple Confirmation Page</title>
  </head>
  <body>
    <p>The value of the hobby that was sent to
       this page is: <b>${param.hobby}</b>.
    <form action="Edit.jsp">
      <p>
        If there is an error, please select <i>Edit</i>.
        <br>
        <input type="submit" name="editButton"
                             value="Edit">
    </form>
  </body>
</html>
```

Listing 2.2 A confirm page that fails to send data back to the edit page.

This approach will allow the confirm page to call the edit page, but the data from the edit page will be lost.

 Try It   http://bytesizebook.com/book/ch2/TwoPages/Error/Edit.jsp

Enter a hobby and click the confirm button (Figure 2.5). Notice that the data that was entered in the edit page has been sent to the confirm page via the query string and that the data has been displayed in the JSP.

Click the edit button on the confirm page to return to the edit page (Figure 2.6). Notice that the hobby field does not have the value that was sent to the confirm page. The original data from the edit page has been lost.

Examine the URL and you will see why it failed: there is no hobby listed in the query string. The only data in the query string is the button that was clicked in the confirm page.

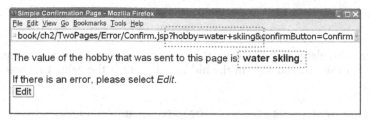

Figure 2.5 The data is sent correctly from the edit page to the confirm page.

```
.../ch2/TwoPages/Error/Edit.jsp?editButton=Edit
```

For now, the only way to send data from one page to another is to place it in the query string. Even though the value of the hobby was sent to the confirm page, the value was not put back into the query string when control was returned to the edit page. That is the reason why the value of the hobby was lost.

Second Attempt – Hidden Fields

One way to place data into the query string is to place the data in a named element within a form. This was done when the data was sent from the edit page.

```
Hobby: <input type="text" name="hobby"
                           value="${param.hobby}">
```

In the first attempt (Listing 2.2), the confirm page did not have an input element for the hobby in its form. In order to send the hobby to another page, an input element must be added for it in the form.

However, remember that the design of this application is mimicking the design of many web sites: the user should not be able to edit the data on the confirm page. If a normal text element were added to the confirm page, then the user would be able to change the data on this page. This contradicts the intended design.

The solution is to add a special form element whose value cannot be changed by the user. This is known as a *hidden* element. It is not visible in the browser, so it cannot be changed by the user. It has the same structure as a *text* element, but the *type* attribute of the form element is set to *hidden*. It will behave just like a visible element; when a button is clicked, the value from the hidden element will be added to the query string and sent to the action page.

```
Simple Edit Page - Mozilla Firefox                                    _ □ ×
File  Edit  View  Go  Bookmarks  Tools  Help
http://bytesizebook.com/book/ch2/TwoPages/Error/Edit.jsp?editButton=Edit

This is a simple HTML page that has a form in it.

If there is a value for the hobby in the query string, then it is used to initialize the
hobby element.

Hobby: [                    ] [Confirm]
```

Figure 2.6 The data is not returned from the confirm page to the edit page.

```
<input type="hidden" name="hobby"
                   value="${param.hobby}">
```

By adding this element to the form, the Confirm.jsp page will work as planned.
Notice that the value to save in the hidden element is the value that was sent to
this page.

```
<!DOCTYPE HTML PUBLIC "-//W3C//DTD HTML 4.01//EN">
<html>
  <head>
    <meta http-equiv="content-type"
          content="text/html;charset=utf-8">
    <title>Confirmation Page with Edit Option</title>
  </head>
  <body>
    <p>The value of the hobby that was sent to
       this page is: <b>${param.hobby}</b>.
    <form action="Edit.jsp">
      <p>
        If there is an error, please select <i>Edit</i>.
        <br>
        <input type="hidden" name="hobby"
                           value="${param.hobby}">
        <input type="submit" name="editButton"
                           value="Edit">
    </form>
  </body>
</html>
```

Be sure that the name of the hidden element is the same name as the original text
element in the edit page. In fact, the only difference between the visible element
in the edit page and the hidden element in the confirm page is the type attribute
of the elements (Table 2.1).

 Try It   http://bytesizebook.com/book/ch2/TwoPages/Edit.jsp

Enter a hobby and click the confirm button. Choose the edit button from the
confirm page and return to the edit page (Figure 2.7).

   This time, it works.

1. The hobby cannot be changed on the confirm page
2. The hobby can be sent back to the edit page.
3. The hobby appears in the query string that is sent to either page.
4. The name of the element is *hobby* regardless of whether it is the text element
   or the hidden element.

Table 2.1 Comparison of text and hidden elements.

Edit Page	Hobby: `<input type="text" name="hobby"` `value="${param.hobby}">`
Confirm Page	`<input type="hidden" name="hobby"` `value="${param.hobby}">`

> **Simple Edit Page - Mozilla Firefox**
>
> File Edit View Go Bookmarks Tools Help
>
> ytesizebook.com/book/ch2/TwoPages/Edit.jsp?hobby=water+skiing&editButton=Edit
>
> This is a simple HTML page that has a form in it.
>
> If there is a value for the hobby in the query string, then it is used to initialize the hobby element.
>
> Hobby: water skiing   [Confirm]

Figure 2.7 The data is returned from the confirm page to the edit page.

2.1.3   Sending Data to Either of Two Pages

The application can now pass the data back and forth between two pages and only one of the pages can change the data. This is a good start, but now there needs to be a new page that can process the user's data (Figure 2.8).

Once the user has entered data into a web site, there is usually a button that allows the user to return to the first page and edit the data. There is also a button that allows the user to confirm that the data is correct. When this button is clicked, the web site processes the user's data.

To implement this design, a new page must be added to the application. This will be the process page and will have the name Process.jsp. At this stage of development, there is nothing to do in the process page. Eventually, this is where the database will be accessed. For now, the process page will only echo the data that the user has entered (Listing 2.3).

```
<!DOCTYPE HTML PUBLIC "-//W3C//DTD HTML 4.01//EN">
<html>
  <head>
    <meta http-equiv="content-type"
          content="text/html;charset=utf-8">
    <title>Process Page</title>
  </head>
  <body>
    <p>
      Thank you for your information. Your hobby
      of <b>${param.hobby}</b> will be added to
      our records, eventually.
    </p>
  </body>
</html>
```

Listing 2.3 The process page.

Figure 2.8 The confirm page can send data to the edit page or the process page.

The first half of the intended design has been implemented in our web application. The additional requirement is that the data from the confirm page can also be sent to the process page. This presents a problem: a form can only have one action attribute, so can send data to only one page. The action attribute in a form can only specify one address. Even if there are multiple buttons in a form, they will all send the data to the same page.

Inefficient Solution: Adding Another Form

A solution to the problem of sending data to two different pages will be covered now, but a better technique will be revealed in the next section of the chapter. The current technique is being covered in order to demonstrate the limitations of only using JSPs to design a web application.

The solution to this problem, using JSPs, is not a pretty solution. The solution is to have two forms in the confirm page (Listing 2.4). Each form will have its own action attribute; each form will have its own button. One form will have an action that points to the edit page, the other form will have an action that points to the process page.

```
<!DOCTYPE HTML PUBLIC "-//W3C//DTD HTML 4.01//EN">
<html>
  <head>
    <meta http-equiv="content-type"
content="text/html;charset=utf-8">
    <title>Confirmation Page with Edit/Process Options</title>
  </head>
  <body>
      <p>The value of the hobby that was sent to
         this page is: <b>${param.hobby}</b>
      <p>
      If there is an error, please select <i>Edit</i>,
      otherwise please select <i>Process</i>.
      <form action="Edit.jsp">
        <input type="hidden" name="hobby"
                              value="${param.hobby}">
        <input type="submit" name="editButton"
                              value="Edit">
    </form>
    <form action="Process.jsp">
      <input type="hidden" name="hobby"
                            value="${param.hobby}">
      <input type="submit" name="processButton"
                            value="Process">
    </form>
  </body>
</html>
```

Listing 2.4 An inefficient solution that requires two forms.

In order to return to the edit page, the user will click the edit button, which is in the form with the action set to the edit page. In order to confirm the data and

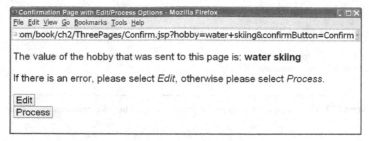

Figure 2.9 The confirm page now has two buttons.

continue to the next step, the user will click the process button, which is in the form with the action set to the process page.

Notice that the hidden data must be included in each form. Imagine if there were three possible destinations: there would be three separate forms with duplicate copies of the hidden fields. Imagine if there were ten fields of data: it would not take long for this technique to become difficult to update. This is the reason why this is an inefficient technique. As a web application becomes more robust and offers the user many different options, the technique of using a separate form for each action becomes unwieldy.

Instead of having multiple forms with one button, it would be better to have one form with multiple buttons. This could be accomplished by adding Java code to the JSP or by adding Javascript to the JSP; however, this would tend to scatter the logic for the application amongst separate pages. There is a better solution that uses a separate Java program to decide which button was clicked. Such a solution will be covered in the section on controllers.

 Try It   **http://bytesizebook.com/book/ch2/ThreePages/Edit.jsp**

Enter data in the edit page and click the confirm button (Figure 2.9). From the confirm page, it is possible to send the data back to the edit page (Figure 2.10) or forward to the process page (Figure 2.11).

This solution does have the desired effect, but it is difficult to maintain. A better solution will be discussed in the next section.

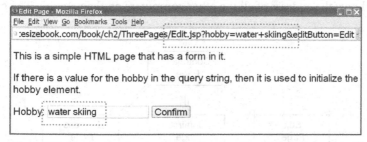

Figure 2.10 The data can be seen in the edit page. The URL contains Edit.jsp.

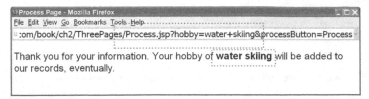

Figure 2.11 The data can be seen in the process page. The URL contains Process.jsp.

2.2 Using a Controller

A better solution to the problem of sending data to either of two pages is to use a fourth page. The idea is to use the fourth page as a control centre. In this technique, the action attribute of all the forms is set to the fourth page (Figure 2.12). The fourth page then decides which of the other pages to present. The fourth page will not contain any HTML code; it will only contain Java code. The fourth page is known as a *controller*.

In this technique, each page has only one form, but may have multiple buttons in a form. For example, the confirm page will have a single form with two buttons. The action attribute of the form will be set to the controller and each button will have a unique name. The controller will determine which page to display next, based upon the button that was clicked.

```
...
<form action="Controller.jsp">
  <p>
    <input type="hidden"  name="hobby"
                          value="${param.hobby}">
    <input type="submit"  name="editButton"
                          value="Edit">
    <input type="submit"  name="processButton"
                          value="Process">

</form>
...
```

Think of a controller as a gateway on a network. Computers on the network want to be able to communicate with each other, but each computer does not want to have to know the address of all the other computers on the network. The gateway

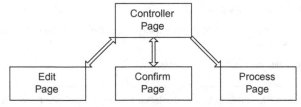

Figure 2.12 Each page only communicates with the controller.

simplifies the process of communication, since each computer only has to know the location of the gateway. The gateway knows the location of all the computers on the network. Additional computers can be added to the network and only the gateway will be affected.

2.2.1 Controller Details

The controller only contains Java code. Each JSP will send its data to the controller. The controller determines which button was clicked and then forwards control to the corresponding JSP to complete the request.

The controller simplifies the way that JSPs communicate with each other. Each JSP only knows the location of the controller. The controller knows the location of all the pages. If a new page is added, then only the controller is changed: all the other pages remain the same.

One of the functions of the controller is to determine what the next page is, based upon which button was clicked. All buttons should have a name. When the button is clicked, it will be added to the query string. By inspecting the query string, the controller can determine which button was clicked.

The query string is sent to the server as part of the request from the browser. Since the controller is a JSP, it will be handled by the servlet engine. The servlet engine creates an object that encapsulates all of the information that was sent from the browser, including the query string. This object is known as the request object and has a method in it than can retrieve the value of a parameter in the query string.

The controller also received the response object from the servlet engine. All the details for communicating with the browser are encapsulated in the response object.

Based on the button that the user clicked, the controller will send the request and response objects to the correct JSP. The JSP will use the request object to access the query string. It will use the response object to send the HTML code to the browser.

The basic tasks of the controller will be implemented with Java code. In the first example, the Java code will be embedded in a JSP. Later, the Java code will be placed in a user-created servlet.

Request and Response Objects

When the servlet engine handles a JSP, it creates an object that encapsulates all the information that was sent in the request from the browser. This object is known as the *request object* and is accessible from Java code within a JSP. The class of the object is `HttpServletRequest`.

The servlet engine also creates an object that encapsulates all the information that is needed to respond to the browser. This object is known as the *response object* and is accessible from Java code within a JSP. The class of the object is `HttpServletResponse`.

Referencing Parameters

Java code cannot use the new expression language for accessing parameters. Java code must use the traditional technique of passing parameters to a method of an object. To reference a query string parameter from Java code, pass the name of the form element to the getParameter method of the request object.

```
request.getParameter("hobby")
```

When accessing a parameter from Java code, use the Java expression request.getParameter("xxx"). When accessing a parameter from HTML, use the expression language ${param.xxx}.

Testing for the Presence of a Button

The most important test in the controller is for the presence of a named button. Even if there are multiple buttons on a page, only the one that is clicked will appear in the query string. When the getParameter method is called with a button name, then either the value of the button will be returned or null will be returned. To test if a particular button was clicked, test if the value returned is not null.

```
if (request.getParameter("processButton") != null)
```

The value of the button is irrelevant to the controller; only the name of the button is important. The value of the button is what is visible on the button in the browser window; the controller does not need to know what that value is. The controller is only concerned with which button was clicked; that can be determined by looking at the name of the button.

Control Logic

The JSP indicates the next page by the name of a button. The JSP does not know the physical location of the next page. This is analogous to a gateway on a network when a computer name is used to identify a computer instead of its IP address.
    The following list summarises how the JSP and the controller interact.

1. The action of each form in each JSP is set to the controller's URL.
2. In the JSPs, each submit button has been given a unique name.
3. By testing for the presence of a name, the controller can decide which page to call next.
4. The controller knows the URL of all the JSPs that it controls.

The controller uses a nested if block, written in Java, to decide which page to display based on which submit button was clicked.

```
...
if (request.getParameter("processButton") != null)
{
   address = "Process.jsp";
}
else if (request.getParameter("confirmButton") != null)
{
   address = "Confirm.jsp";
}
```

```
else
{
  address = "Edit.jsp";
}
...
```

Forwarding Control to Another JSP

Once the controller has determined the address of the next JSP, it must send the request and response objects to the JSP. The request and response objects contain all of the information from the browser and all of the information for sending data back to the browser. By sending the request and response objects to the JSP, the controller is sending complete ownership of the request to the JSP. It will be the responsibility of the JSP to complete the response to the browser.

Two steps are needed in order for the controller to pass control of the request to another JSP. First, a communication channel must be created for the controller to communicate with the JSP. This channel is known as a *Request Dispatcher*. The request dispatcher is created for the URL of the next JSP. Second, the controller forwards the request and response objects to this dispatcher, which passes them to the JSP.

```
RequestDispatcher dispatcher =
        request.getRequestDispatcher(address);
dispatcher.forward(request, response);
```

Forwarding control to another JSP is a two-step process, just like opening a file for writing. When writing a file, the file must be opened before it can be written. When a file is opened, the actual location of the file is specified. Once the file is opened, data can be written to the file. The request dispatcher is similar: first, open the dispatcher for the address of a JSP, then use the dispatcher to send objects to the JSP.

2.2.2 JSP Controller

Controllers can be written as JSPs or as servlets. Since the controller will not contain any HTML, it is better to write it as a servlet. However, it is easier to understand a controller if it is first written as a JSP. Therefore, the general concept of a controller will be demonstrated in a JSP, then servlets will be introduced and the controller will be rewritten as a servlet. After the first example using a JSP, all controllers will be written as servlets.

Including Java Code

JSP controllers do not contain any HTML code, they only contain Java code. A special syntax is used to include arbitrary Java code in a JSP. Place all the Java code between special opening and closing tags: <% and %>.

```
<%
//place a block of Java code here
%>
```

Controller Code

Listing 2.5 contains the complete JSP for the controller. Notice that there is only
Java code, there is no HTML.

```
<%
  String address;

  if (request.getParameter("processButton") != null)
  {
     address = "Process.jsp";
  }
  else if (request.getParameter("confirmButton") != null)
  {
     address = "Confirm.jsp";
  }
  else
  {
     address = "Edit.jsp";
  }

  RequestDispatcher dispatcher =
          request.getRequestDispatcher(address);
  dispatcher.forward(request, response);
%>
```

Listing 2.5 Listing for a JSP Controller.

Edit Page

The edit page is the same as the one from Listing 2.1, except for the action attribute
of the form.

```
...
<form action="Controller.jsp">
...
```

Confirm Page

Listing 2.6 contains the confirm page that is used with a controller.

```
<!DOCTYPE HTML PUBLIC "-//W3C//DTD HTML 4.01//EN">
<html>
  <head>
    <meta http-equiv="content-type"
          content="text/html;charset=utf-8">
    <title>
        Confirmation Page with Edit/Process Options
    </title>
  </head>
  <body>
      <p>The value of the hobby that was sent to
        this page is: <b>${param.hobby}</b>.
```

```
<p>
    If there is an error, please select <i>Edit</i>,
    otherwise please select <i>Process</i>.

<form action="Controller.jsp">
   <p>
     <input type="hidden"  name="hobby"
                           value="${param.hobby}">
     <input type="submit"  name="editButton"
                           value="Edit">
     <input type="submit"  name="processButton"
                           value="Process">

   </form>
  </body>
</html>
```

Listing 2.6 Efficient solution for sending data to one of two pages.

Notice the following about the confirm page:

1. There are two buttons in one form.
2. The action is to the controller.
3. There is one set of hidden fields.

This is a much cleaner solution than Listing 2.4 for sending data to one of two pages. It had a separate form for each button and each form had to have its own set of hidden fields.

Process Page

The process page to be used with the controller is exactly the same as Listing 2.3.

 Try It   http://bytesizebook.com/book/ch2/jspController/Controller.jsp

When the controller is accessed, the `Edit.jsp` is the first page displayed (Figure 2.13), because it was set as the default in the controller and no form button is clicked when the controller is accessed for the first time. Notice that there is no query string and that the URL points to the controller.

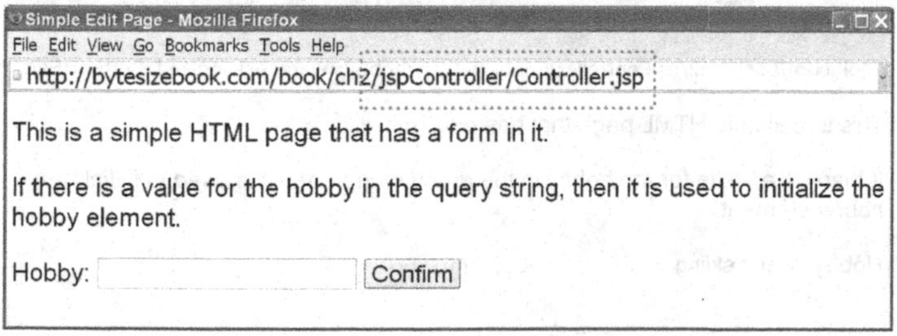

File Edit View Go Bookmarks Tools Help
http://bytesizebook.com/book/ch2/jspController/Controller.jsp

This is a simple HTML page that has a form in it.

If there is a value for the hobby in the query string, then it is used to initialize the hobby element.

Hobby: [   ] [Confirm]

Figure 2.13 The first page that the controller displays is the edit page.

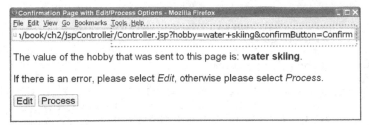

Figure 2.14 The confirm page with data sent from the edit page.

Enter a hobby and visit each page: confirm page (Figure 2.14), edit page (Figure 2.15), process page (Figure 2.16). Examine the URL and query string for each page. The URL for each page is the same.

```
.../ch2/jspController/Controller.jsp
```

The query string for each page changes. The query string will contain the name of the button that was clicked. The name of the button was chosen so that it corresponds to the actual JSP that is being displayed. For instance, when the query string contains confirmButton, the JSP being displayed is Confirm.jsp. The address of the JSP does not appear in the URL because the request was made to the controller. The fact that the controller did not complete the request, but forwarded it to another JSP is not visible to the browser.

There are four key points about the controller application.

1. The action attribute of each form has been set to Controller.jsp.
2. Each button in each form has a unique name. When a named button is clicked, its name and value will appear in the query string. If there are multiple buttons on a page, only the name and value of the button that is clicked will appear in the query string.
3. For each page, the URL contains a name and value in the query string for the button that was clicked. This name is what the controller uses to determine the next page; the value is not tested.

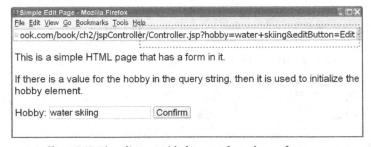

Figure 2.15 The edit page with data sent from the confirm page.

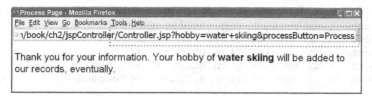

Figure 2.16 The process page with data sent from the confirm page.

4. Except for the query string, the URL always remains the same, as long as the controller is called first.

2.2.3 JSPs versus Servlets

The controller only contains Java code, there is no HTML in it. JSPs are designed to have HTML with a little bit of Java code. Whenever a JSP contains mostly Java code with very little or no HTML, then it should be written from scratch as a servlet, not as a JSP. A servlet has several advantages.

1. The servlet engine will not have to create the servlet from the JSP when it is called the first time.
2. A Java IDE can be used to develop and test the Java code. It is difficult to debug Java code that is embedded in a JSP.

Compare these with the advantages of a JSP:

1. It is easy to write HTML.
2. The servlet will be recreated whenever the JSP is modified.

The decision of using a JSP or a servlet should depend upon the mix of HTML and Java code.

1. If there is a lot of HTML with a small amount of Java, then use a JSP.
2. If there is a lot of Java with a small amount of HTML, then use a servlet.
3. If there is an equal amount of Java and HTML then redesign your application so that it uses a controller. Place most of the Java in the controller and create separate JSPs for the HTML.

2.2.4 Controller Servlet

The same application that was just written using a JSP controller will now be rewritten using a servlet. Servlets are Java programs that extend a base class for a generic servlet. Follow these steps to write a servlet from scratch.

1. Place the servlet in a package so that its location is never left to the default implementation of the servlet engine.
2. Import the following classes.

```
import java.io.IOException;
import javax.servlet.RequestDispatcher;
import javax.servlet.ServletException;
import javax.servlet.http.HttpServlet;
import javax.servlet.http.HttpServletRequest;
import javax.servlet.http.HttpServletResponse;
```

3. Make the class public and extend it from HttpServlet. This is a wrapper for the abstract class GenericServlet. It has no functionality; it only defines all the methods that are specified in GenericServlet. To create a servlet that does something, override some methods from HttpServlet.
4. Include a method with the following signature and place the controller logic in this method.

```
protected void doGet(HttpServletRequest request,
    HttpServletResponse response)
        throws ServletException, IOException
```

JSPs for Servlet Controller

The JSPs for the servlet controller are identical to the JSPs for the JSP Controller, except that the action statement in each form is set to "Controller" instead of to "Controller.jsp".

```
...
<form action="Controller">
...
```

Servlet Controller Code

Listing 2.7 contains the controller as a servlet. Notice that the contents of the doGet method in the servlet are identical to the Java code that was inserted into the JSP controller (see Listing 2.5).

```
package ch2.servletController;

import java.io.IOException;
import javax.servlet.RequestDispatcher;
import javax.servlet.ServletException;
import javax.servlet.http.HttpServlet;
import javax.servlet.http.HttpServletRequest;
import javax.servlet.http.HttpServletResponse;

public class Controller extends HttpServlet
{

  protected void doGet(HttpServletRequest request,
      HttpServletResponse response)
        throws ServletException, IOException
  {

      String address;
```

```
if (request.getParameter("processButton") != null)
{
    address = "Process.jsp";
}
else if (request.getParameter("confirmButton") != null)
{
    address = "Confirm.jsp";
}
else
{
    address = "Edit.jsp";
}

RequestDispatcher dispatcher =
    request.getRequestDispatcher(address);
dispatcher.forward(request, response);
  }
}
```

Listing 2.7 The code for the servlet controller.

Servlet Location

The source file for a servlet can be anywhere, but the `.class` file must be in a subdirectory of the *classes* directory in the web application. The servlet should be in a package.

The package must agree with the subdirectory of *classes* that the servlet is in. Do not include the *classes* directory in the package statement. The *classes* directory must already be in the CLASSPATH or Java will not search it for class files.

To determine the package, start with subdirectories of the *classes* directory. If the servlet is in the *classes/store* directory, then the package will be *store*. If the servlet is in the *classes/store/hardware* directory, then the package will have to be *store.hardware*.

For this example, the directory must be *classes/ch2/servletController* in order to agree with a package of *ch2.servletController*.

```
package ch2.servletController;
```

The package for a Java class must agree with its location in the file system.

Servlet Identity

Every servlet has a fully qualified class name that consists of two pieces of information: the package it is in and the name of its class.

```
package ch2.servletController;
...
public class Controller extends HttpServlet
```

The fully qualified class name is the combination of the package name with the name of the class. Use a period to connect the package and the name together.

```
ch2.servletController.Controller
```

The fully qualified class name uniquely identifies the servlet. It will be used to refer to the servlet without ambiguity.

Servlet Compilation

A servlet is compiled just like any other Java program: from the command line or from an *Integrated Development Environment* [IDE].

1. NetBeans is the best IDE for compiling, running and debugging servlets, because it has an instance of the Tomcat servlet engine installed with it.
2. For command line compilation,
   a. *javac* is used to compile
   b. be sure that **servlet-api.jar** and the *classes* directory of your web application are in the CLASSPATH of your environment.

2.2.5   Servlet Access

As was mentioned in Chapter One, the WEB-INF directory is not available from the web. Therefore, the *classes* subdirectory of WEB-INF is not available from the web. In that case, how can the servlet be accessed?

The answer to the question lies within the *web.xml* file. It is possible to create a shortcut in the *web.xml* file. Such a shortcut associates a `.class` file with a URL that will be accessible from the web. This shortcut is known as a *servlet mapping*.

Servlets are usually more powerful than JSPs; therefore, the servlet engine designers made it more difficult to access them from the web. By default, no servlets can be accessed without registering them in the *web.xml* file of the web application. There are two parts to registering a servlet: creating a short name and defining a servlet mapping.

Short Name for Servlet

Class files that are in packages have very long names. It is possible to create a short name for these long names. The short name is used internally by the servlet engine to refer to the servlet. Tags are added to the *web.xml* file to create a short name.

```
<servlet>
  <servlet-name>FirstController</servlet-name>
  <servlet-class>ch2.servletController.Controller</servlet-class>
</servlet>
```

This creates a short name of `FirstController` for the fully qualified name `ch2.servletController.Controller`. There is nothing special about the short name; it can be any name. Here is another example that creates a different short name for the same controller.

```
<servlet>
  <servlet-name>Overseer</servlet-name>
  <servlet-class>ch2.servletController.Controller</servlet-class>
</servlet>
```

Servlet Mapping

Associating a URL with a short name is known as creating a servlet mapping. The servlet mapping associates the short name for a servlet file with a URL that will be accessible from the web. The URL does not need to be an actual URL in the web application, it can be totally fictitious. The URL must begin with a slash. The slash corresponds to the root of the web application, not to the root of the web server.

```
<servlet-mapping>
    <servlet-name>FirstController</servlet-name>
    <url-pattern>/ch2/servletController/Controller</url-pattern>
</servlet-mapping>
```

The servlet tag and the servlet-mapping tag both have a servlet-name tag in them. The name in the *servlet-name* tag in the servlet-mapping tag must match the name in the *servlet-name* tag in the servlet tag.

The URL pattern is used to request the servlet. The request is sent to the servlet engine, which searches the *web.xml* file for a matching pattern. If a match is found, then the servlet name is used to locate the corresponding servlet definition. The definition contains the path to the actual class file. Figure 2.17 shows the order of steps for a request for a servlet.

The URL that is chosen for the servlet can simplify the servlet. In this example, the servlet has been mapped to the same directory where the JSPs it controls are located. This makes it possible for the controller to use a simple relative reference when creating the request dispatcher for the desired JSP. Even though the JSPs and servlets are in different physical locations, the servlet mapping allows the servlet engine to treat them as though they were in the same directory.

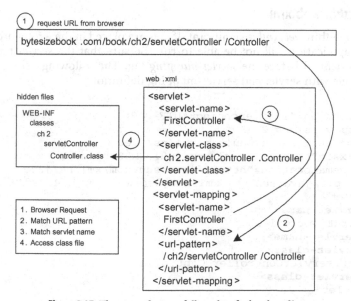

Figure 2.17 The steps that are followed to find a class file.

The URL that is chosen can be an actual directory in the web application, or it can be fictitious. A different servlet mapping for the same short name could be */Moe/Larry/Cheese*; however, in this case, the servlet would not be able to use relative references for the JSPs it controls.

```
<servlet-mapping>
   <servlet-name>FirstController</servlet-name>
   <url-pattern>/Moe/Larry/Cheese</url-pattern>
</servlet-mapping>
```

The URL pattern is always within the web application. The pattern **must** start with a /. This means that the URL starts from the root of the web application, not the root of the web server. If the name of the web application is `book`, and is running on `xyz.com`, then the URLs for the two servlet mappings just defined would be

```
http://xyz.com/book/ch2/servletController/Controller
http://xyz.com/book/Moe/Larry/Cheese
```

To determine what the complete URL is to access the controller, start with the URL to the web application root and append the name that is in the *url-pattern* tag.

When a request for a URL reaches the servlet engine, the servlet engine will look at the list of servlet mappings and find the short name for the servlet. Then the servlet engine will look up the fully qualified name of the servlet and call the servlet. For each of the above URLs, the servlet engine would call the `ch2.servletController.Controller` servlet.

Order within web.xml

The order within *web.xml* is significant. If tags are placed in the wrong order, then the web application will not be able to run. Be sure that the *servlet* tag for the servlet is defined before the *servlet-mapping* tag. The following listing shows a web.xml file with servlet and servlet-mapping definitions.

```
<?xml version="1.0" encoding="UTF-8"?>
<web-app version="2.4"
  xmlns="http://java.sun.com/xml/ns/j2ee"
  xmlns:xsi="http://www.w3.org/2001/XMLSchema-instance"
  xsi:schemaLocation="http://java.sun.com/xml/ns/j2ee
      http://java.sun.com/xml/ns/j2ee/web-app_2_4.xsd">
  <servlet>
    <servlet-name>
      FirstController
    </servlet-name>
    <servlet-class>
      ch2.servletController.Controller
    </servlet-class>
  </servlet>
```

```
<servlet-mapping>
  <servlet-name>
    FirstController
  </servlet-name>
  <url-pattern>
    /ch2/servletController/Controller
  </url-pattern>
</servlet-mapping>
<session-config>
  <session-timeout>
    30
  </session-timeout>
</session-config>
<welcome-file-list>
  <welcome-file>
    index.jsp
  </welcome-file>
  <welcome-file>
    index.html
  </welcome-file>
  <welcome-file>
    index.htm
  </welcome-file>
</welcome-file-list>
</web-app>
```

2.2.6   Servlet Directory Structure

After creating the servlet mapping, the servlet engine will look for the servlet at the URL that was specified.

For this servlet example, the JSPs are in the `/ch2/servletController` subdirectory of the root of the web application. On this site, the web application is titled *book*, so the JSPs are actually located in the directory `/book/ch2/servletController`.

The servlet is in a package named `ch2.servletController`, so it is located in the subdirectory `/ch2/servletController` in the *classes* directory of the web application. This directory is not visible from the web, so a servlet mapping is created for the servlet, which equates the servlet to a URL that is visible from the web.

The simplest way to implement the mapping is to equate it to the directory where the JSPs are located. This is what was done in this example. The URL pattern `/ch2/servletController` is relative to the root of the web application, so it is the same URL as the directory of the JSPs.

By mapping the controller to the directory where the JSPs are located, the controller can use a relative reference for the address of the next page.

```
. . .
else if (request.getParameter("confirmButton") != null)
{
    address = "Confirm.jsp";
}
. . .
```

When a *Request Dispatcher* is created, the argument contains the address of the next JSP.

```
. . .
RequestDispatcher dispatcher =
     request.getRequestDispatcher(address);
dispatcher.forward(request, response);
. . .
```

This address is similar to the *action* attribute in a form. However, the address is limited to relative references from the current directory and relative references from the root of the web application.

1. If the next JSP is in the directory where the controller is mapped, then only include the file name of the JSP.

   ```
   address = "Confirm.jsp"
   ```

2. If the next JSP is not in the directory where the controller is mapped, then the JSP must be in another directory in the web application. The address for this JSP must start with / and must include the complete path from the root of the web application to the JSP. Do not include the name of the web application in the path.

   ```
   address = "/ch2/servletController/Confirm.jsp";
   ```

Figure 2.18 is a diagram of the directory structure of the web application and the location of the JSPs and the servlet. The servlet mapping makes a logical mapping of the servlet to the same directory as the JSPs.

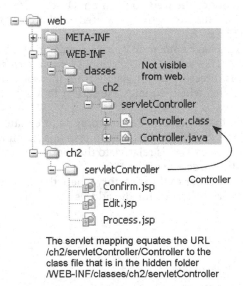

Figure 2.18 The structure of a web application.

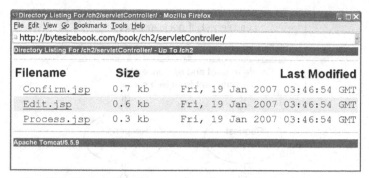

Figure 2.19 Listing of the directory where the controller servlet is mapped.

 Try It   http://bytesizebook.com/book/ch2/servletController/Controller

Access the controller by appending the url-pattern to the end of the URL for the web application.

```
bytesizebook.com/book/ch2/servletController/Controller
```

From the browser, this application behaves exactly the same as the JSP Controller example. The only difference is the URL. The URL for the controller was chosen so that the servlet appears to be in the same directory as the JSPs.

Instead of typing in the URL of the controller, type in the URL for the servletController directory. You will see a directory listing that contains all of the JSPs for this application. You will not see the controller in this directory (Figure 2.19). The servlet engine has created an internal link to the controller from this directory, but the link is not visible in the browser. The only way that you know that the link exists is by accessing the controller.

2.2.7   Servlet Engine for a Servlet

Table 2.2 summarises the key features of a servlet. The servlet engine handles a request for a servlet in almost the same way that it handles a request for a JSP (see Figure 1.17). The only differences are that the name of the method that the engine calls is different and that the servlet engine will not recompile the servlet if the *.java* file changes. The servlet engine calls the *doGet* method instead of the

Table 2.2 The key points for a servlet.

doGet	This is the method that does all the work. It is similar to the _jspService method in a servlet for a JSP.
HttpServlet	This is an abstract wrapper class. It has default implementations of all the abstract methods. In order to make a useful servlet, it is necessary to define at least one of these methods. In this first example, the class is defining the doGet method.
HttpServletRequest	This class encapsulates the information that is sent from the browser to the server.
HttpServletResponse	This class encapsulates the information that will be sent from the server back to the browser.

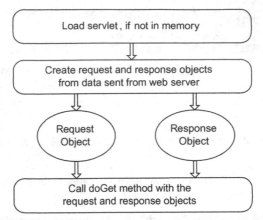

Figure 2.20 Servlet engine handling a request for a servlet.

jspService method and it is up to the developer to recompile the *.java* file whenever it changes (Figure 2.20).

The servlet engine will not automatically reload the *.class* file when it changes. It is up to the developer to reload the web application so that a servlet will be reloaded when it is requested the next time. Some servlet engines can be configured to automatically reload when a *.class* file changes, but it is not the default behaviour of the servlet engine.

2.3   Servlets in NetBeans

NetBeans is the perfect tool for developing web applications. After creating a web project, the web application can be run from within NetBeans by clicking on the *Run -> Main Project* menu. When this is done, Tomcat will be started, the servlet will be loaded into memory, a web browser will be opened and the default page for the web application will be displayed. Hypertext links can be added on this page that lead to the URLs of JSPs and servlets.

After building a web project in NetBeans, it is possible to execute servlets from it. The servlets must be placed in the *Source Packages* folder. Always place servlets in packages. When the project is built, the source packages will be copied into the *classes* folder of the web application structure.

Once a web project has been created and tested locally, it is a simple matter to upload the web application to a remote server. Every time that a web project is built, NetBeans packages all the files that are needed for a servlet engine into a *Web Archive* [WAR]. A WAR archive is a zip file containing all the files for the web application. If this is uploaded to a remote server, it can be deployed without making any modifications.

2.3.1   Source Packages

The *Source Packages* folder in a NetBeans project contains all the source files and packages for Java servlets. Place all source files in a package. All of the servlet examples in this book have been placed in packages. Place these packages in this folder. The source packages folder is added to the classpath variable, so every package that is placed in this folder can be found by Java at runtime. See the Appendix for a discussion of Java packages.

There are two ways to create the folder structure for a package. One way is to add new folders within the *Source Packages* folder. Another way is to add a new package using a NetBeans wizard. In the wizard, all of the folders for a package can be created at once. For example, if there is a servlet in a package named edu. fiu.cis, then all the necessary folders for the package can be created by adding a package named edu.fiu.cis to the source packages folder.

The <default package> is the package that has no name. Avoid using it. It is better to always place your servlets in a named package. Strange things can happen if you place servlets in the default package. The only files that should be placed here are configuration files, like those for Hibernate and Log4j.

There are several templates for creating files in NetBeans. When creating a servlet, there are two choices. An empty class file can be created. It is then up to the developer to add all the code for the servlet and to create the servlet mapping for the servlet. There is also a template for a servlet. When this template is used, the default methods for a servlet are defined and a servlet mapping is added to the *web.xml* file.

When the NetBeans wizard is used to create a servlet, there are options for defining the servlet mapping. By using the wizard, it will not be necessary to edit the *web.xml* file to define a servlet mapping. If the template is not used to create the servlet, then the servlet definition and servlet mapping will need to be added to the *web.xml* file manually.

2.3.2   Including Source Files in a WAR File

Developing locally and deploying on a remote server is a common practice for creating web applications. By default, the .java files are not added to the WAR file when the web project is built. In order to be able to modify servlets on the remote server, the source files need to be added to the WAR. To have them added to the WAR file, right-click on the name of the project in the project window and select properties.

From the properties screen, select Build -> Packaging. Edit the *Exclude From WAR File* box and remove **/*.java,. This will allow the .java files to be included in the WAR file.

When the WAR file is uploaded to the remote servlet engine, it can be deployed without modification. This is the standard way that web applications are created: develop locally, run remotely.

2.3.3   Web Application Files

A Project in NetBeans is an abstraction of a web application. When the project is built, the corresponding web application structure is created. However, not all of the directories are visible from the project view, but they are visible from the *Files* view.

The *web* subdirectory of *build* contains the actual web application directory for your project.

The *dist* directory contains the WAR file.

The *.class* files for your servlets are located in the *build* directory. Open the *web* subdirectory of *build*. In the WEB-INF is located the *classes* directory, which contains the `.class` files for the servlets.

Do not edit files from this tab. Whenever the project is built, the WAR file is created and these files are recreated. The files from the project folders are copied to the files in the web application. Any changes that were made directly to files in the web application folders will be lost when the project is rebuilt. Always edit files in the project folders.

Try It   http://netbeans.org

If you have not already done so, download a copy of the latest NetBeans package.

Add a package to the *Source Packages* folder and add a servlet to the package.

Define a servlet mapping for the servlet, so that it can be accessed from the web.

Edit the *index.jsp* page in the *Web Pages* folder. Add a relative URL to the servlet. To make a relative URL to the servlet from this page, create a hypertext link that contains the URL pattern from the servlet mapping, except remove the leading slash from it.

Build and run the web application. The *index.jsp* page will appear in the browser. Follow the link to the servlet.

2.4   Summary

Typical web applications have an edit page, a confirm page and a process page. The edit page contains visible form elements where the user can enter information. The confirm page has two buttons: one for sending the data back to the edit page and one for sending the data to the process page. The process page shows the results of processing the user's data. The form tag has an attribute, named *action*, which allows the form to send the data to any other page. The page could be in the current directory, in a different directory on the same server or on a different server. All data that is in a named form element will be sent to the URL that is in the action attribute. It is important that the element has a name or it will not be added to the query string.

Only the edit page has visible form elements for the user to enter data. The confirm page only shows the data as plain text: plain text is never sent to the next page when a button is clicked. In order for the data to be sent, it must be in a named form element. There is a non-visible form element, whose type is *hidden*, that can be used to store the data that was received by the current page. When a button is clicked, the data will be sent to the next page. If the current JSP places the data that it receives into the hidden fields, then the user's data can be passed on to the next page.

Some pages in web applications need to send data to one of two pages: for example, the confirm page. There are two buttons on the confirm page: one that sends the data back to the edit page and one that sends the data on to the process page. Using a simple JSP to solve this problem requires two separate forms in the page; each form would have a separate copy of the hidden fields. Such a solution is difficult to read and difficult to modify. There is a better solution for this situation: use a separate program to determine the next page based on the button that the user clicks.

Such a program is known as a controller. Instead of hard coding the name of the next page into the action attribute, all JSPs send the data to the controller. It is important that the buttons in the forms are named, so that the controller will know which button the user clicked. The controller will calculate the URL of the next JSP and send the user's data to that page.

Controllers can be written as JSPs or as servlets. The first example of a controller was developed as a JSP; however, it is better to write the controller as a servlet, since it has no HTML in it. It is easier to debug Java code if it is in a servlet.

Since servlets are Java programs, the details of creating, compiling, and accessing servlets were covered. Creating and compiling servlets is the same as creating and compiling any Java program. Accessing the servlet is more difficult because it must be placed in a web application. The *web.xml* file is used to create a URL mapping that can be used to access the servlet. If this URL mapping is not created in the *web.xml* file, then the servlet cannot be accessed from the web.

2.5   Chapter Review

Terms

1. Form's Action Attribute
   a. Relative
   b. Absolute
2. Controller
   a. JSP
   b. Servlet
3. Query String

Java

1. _jspService
2. javax.servlet.http.HttpServletRequest
   a. getParameter
   b. getRequestDispatcher
3. javax.servlet.http.HttpServletResponse
4. javax.servlet.ServletException
5. javax.servlet.RequestDispatcher
   a. forward

Tags

1. JSP
   a. `${param.element_name}`
   b. `<% java code %>`
2. INPUT
   a. HIDDEN

Questions

1. What is contained in the request object that is sent to the `_jspService` method?
2. What is contained in the response object that is sent to the `_jspService` method?
3. How often is the servlet for a JSP generated?
4. How often is the `.class` file for a servlet generated?
5. How can data be entered in a form on one page and be sent to a different page?
6. How is a parameter in the query string retrieved from Java code?
7. What is the purpose of the nested if block in a controller?
8. Write the statements that belong in a controller that will forward the request and response to the JSP named "Example.jsp".
9. What are the advantages of using a JSP over a servlet?
10. What are the advantages of using a servlet over a JSP?
11. Where does the `.class` file for a servlet belong in a web application?
12. Assume that a form has two text boxes named `firstName` and `lastName`.
    a. Write the query string if the user enters *Fred* for the `firstName` and *Flintstone* for the `lastName`.
    b. Write the query string if the user enters *John Quincy* for the `firstName` and *Adams III* for the `lastName`.
    c. Write the query string in the event that the user enters *Laverne & Shirley* for the `firstName` and leaves the `lastName` blank.
    d. Write the EL statements that will display the values for the first name and last name.
13. A confirmation page was covered in this chapter that could send data to one of two pages. There were two techniques discussed for achieving this. Summarise the differences between these two techniques.
14. Summarise the differences in how the Tomcat engine handles a JSP and a servlet.
15. Assume there is a class named `MyJavaExample` in a package named `book.webdev`. Create a servlet definition and servlet mapping for this class as follows.
    a. Create a servlet definition of `MyExample` for this class in web.xml.
    b. Associate the URL `/book/webdev/MyExample` with the short name that was just created in the web.xml.

Tasks

1. Another form element is a password text box. Its type is PASSWORD.

```
<input type="password" name="secretCode">
```

Create a JSP that has a text box, a password text box and a button. Send the data from the form to a second JSP in which the values from the text box and the password text box are displayed.

2. Create a form with three text boxes and a button. Initialise the text elements with corresponding data from the query string. Send the data to a second page that will display the values that are sent to it. The second page should have hidden fields and a button so that the data can be sent back to the first page.

   a. Implement this design without using a controller.

   b. Implement this design with a JSP controller.

   c. Implement this design with a servlet controller.

3. Create a page with three text boxes and three buttons. Create three more distinct JSPs. Each button on the first page will send the data from the form to a different page.

   a. Implement this design with a JSP controller.

   b. Implement this design with a servlet controller.

   c. How could this design be implemented without using a controller and without embedding code in the first JSP?

3   Java Beans and Controller Helpers

With the introduction of a controller servlet, it is now possible to add all the power and convenience of Java to the development process. It is possible to create auxiliary classes in the web application that will simplify development.

One of the most powerful classes that can be added to a web application is one that contains all the data that was entered by the user. All of the data from the user is available from the request object, but the request object also contains a lot of other information that is not related to the user's data. It will be a better design to create a new class that only contains the data. Such a class is known as a *bean*.

With the introduction of a bean, it is a simple matter to add validation to the web application. One type of validation is *default validation*. In default validation, the user's data must meet criteria. If the data does not meet the criteria, then a default value is used in place of the data that the user entered.

While servlets are very powerful tools for implementing dynamic content on the web, they do have a limitation: member variables. Member variables are useful when designing object-oriented programs, but they are dangerous to use in a servlet. In order to circumvent this limitation, an auxiliary class will be added to the web application that is created by the controller and can use member variables.

With the addition of these new classes, the servlet from the last chapter will be reorganised. It will still perform the same functions, but it will be redesigned to use a class for the data and a class that does the work of the controller. The JSPs for the web application will also need some minor changes.

3.1   Application: Start Example

In order to demonstrate the new features clearly, the web application from the last chapter will be modified with the addition of a new text element and the addition of a button on the process page that will allow the user to edit the data again.

These are the changes that will need to be made to the web application.

1. The edit page will have a new text element added.
2. There will be an additional hidden field in the confirm page.
3. There will be a new form, hidden fields and a button on the process page.

The first controller in this chapter will be identical to the servlet controller from the last chapter (see Listing 2.7), except that it is in a different package.

1. For organisation, the controller for this example has been placed in a package named ch3.startExample.
2. In the *web.xml* file of the web application, the controller has been mapped to the URL /ch3/startExample/Controller.
3. The JSPs for the web application have been placed in the directory named /ch3/startExample.

Figure 3.1 shows the location of the files for the Start Example controller.

Just like the servlet controller from the last chapter, this controller has been mapped to the directory where the JSPs are located.

```
...
<servlet>
  <servlet-name>
    StartExampleCh3
  </servlet-name>
  <servlet-class>
    ch3.startExample.Controller
  </servlet-class>
</servlet>
<servlet-mapping>
  <servlet-name>
    StartExampleCh3
  </servlet-name>
  <url-pattern>
    /ch3/startExample/Controller
  </url-pattern>
</servlet-mapping>
...
```

The edit page is similar to Listing 2.1, but will have an additional input field for a property named *aversion*.

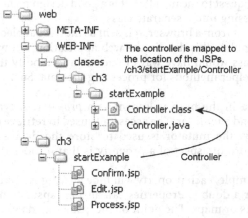

Figure 3.1 The location of files for the Start Example.

```
Aversion:
<input type="text" name="aversion"
                    value="${param.aversion}">
```

The confirm page is similar to Listing 2.6, but will echo the new property and have an additional hidden field for the new property.

```
The value of the aversion that was sent to
this page is: <b>${param.aversion}</b>
...
<input type="hidden" name="aversion"
                     value="${param.aversion}">
```

The Process page is similar to Listing 2.3, but will echo the new property and will have a form with a button, for returning to the edit page, and two hidden fields.

```
Thank you for your information. Your hobby of
<b>${param.hobby}</b> and aversion of
<b>${param.aversion}</b> will be added to our
records, eventually.
...
<form action="Controller">
  <input type="hidden" name="hobby"
                       value="${param.hobby}">
  <input type="hidden" name="aversion"
                       value="${param.aversion}">
  <p>
  <input type="submit" name="editButton"
                       value="Edit">
</form>
```

3.2 Java Bean

Controllers are all very similar. They have two basic tasks: process the user data and forward the request to the next JSP. It is a good design principle to encapsulate all the data processing into a separate class.

When data is sent from a browser, it is sent as individual pieces of data. It would be easier to manipulate this data in the web application if it were all placed into one class. This class would have ways to access and modify the data and would have additional helper methods for processing the data. Such a class is known as a *bean*.

A piece of data in the bean is known as a *property*. A typical property will have an *accessor* and a *mutator*. The accessor is used to retrieve the data associated with the property, the mutator is used to store the data associated with the property. An important aspect of a property is that it hides the implementation of the data.

In the next example, each property will hide a string variable, but it could also hide an integer or a double. Properties can also encapsulate more complex data structures like lists or maps. The point of encapsulating data in a property is that when the implementation for the data changes, no other classes that use the property will need to be changed.

In a web application, the data can be accessed from the controller and the JSPs. Soon, the data will also be accessed by a database. In this type of application, it is essential to have a central class for the data that uses a standard way to retrieve the data; a bean is such a class. In the future, if the data changes, then only the bean will need to be updated, not all the classes that use the data.

The standard format of a bean requires that the names of the accessor/mutator pair have a fixed syntax.

1. The mutator will be of the form setXxx.
2. The accessor will be of the form getXxx.
3. *set* and *get* are in lowercase.
4. The first letter after set or get is uppercase. All letters after that can be uppercase or lowercase.

The accessor/mutator pair should operate on the same type.

1. The mutator has a parameter that must have the same type as the return value of the accessor.
2. The accessor returns a value that must have the same type as the parameter to the mutator.

The next listing shows a complete property named *hobby*. It makes no difference what the name of the variable is in the bean, since the variable is protected. What makes this a property is that there are methods named *getHobby* and *setHobby* that operate on the same type.

```
protected String hobby;
public void setHobby(String hobby) {
    this.hobby = hobby;
}
public String getHobby() {
    return hobby;
}
```

3.2.1 Creating a Data Bean

Beans should be used to store the elements coming from the form. The names of the properties in the bean should correspond with the names of the form elements in the JSPs. If the form has an input element named *hobby*, then the bean should have a property with an accessor named getHobby and a mutator named setHobby.

The bean for our web application will have two properties: hobby and aversion. These correspond to the input elements that are in the JSPs for this web application. For each input element that contains data to be processed, create a corresponding property in the bean.

Java Bean: Request Data

When encapsulating data, the first step is to recognise what the data is. In a web application, the user enters the data in form elements. In our application, all the data is entered in the edit page. A bean will be created which has properties that correspond to the input elements that are in the edit page.

```
. . .
Hobby:
<input type="text" name="hobby"
                     value="${param.hobby}">
<br>
Aversion:
<input type="text" name="aversion"
                     value="${param.aversion}">
. . .
```

There are two input elements in the edit page that contain data to be processed: hobby and aversion. Table 3.1 shows the relationship between the input elements in the form and the corresponding properties in a bean.

A bean that encapsulates the web application data will need to have properties with these accessors and mutators. The next listing contains a bean with a property for the hobby and aversion. Note that in the JSP, the names are all lowercase, but in the bean, the first letter after *get* or *set* is uppercase.

```
package ch3.dataBean;

public class RequestData {

    protected String hobby;
    protected String aversion;

    public RequestData() {
    }

    public void setHobby(String hobby) {
        this.hobby = hobby;
    }

    public String getHobby() {
        return hobby;
    }

    public void setAversion(String aversion) {
        this.aversion = aversion;
    }

    public String getAversion() {
        return aversion;
    }
}
```

Table 3.1 The relationship between the form element name and the accessor/mutator names.

Element Name	Accessor Name	Mutator Name
name="hobby"	getHobby	setHobby
name="aversion"	getAversion	setAversion

3.2.2   Using the Bean in a Web Application

Now that the bean class exists, it must be incorporated into the web application. It must be added to the controller and accessed in the JSP.

The controller is in charge of all of the logic in the web application, so it is the controller's responsibility to create the bean. Once the bean has been created, it must be filled with the data from the request and placed somewhere so that the JSPs will have access to it.

Each JSP is primarily HTML, with some data to display from the controller. A special syntax is used in a JSP for accessing the data from a bean.

Creating and Filling the Bean

The controller will create the bean. In this example, the name of the bean class is *RequestData*, which is in the *ch3.dataBean* package.

```
RequestData data = new RequestData();
```

The most important thing that the controller can do is to get the new data that was just sent from the user and copy it into the bean. The controller must call the mutators for the properties in the bean in order to fill them with the data from the request.

```
data.setHobby(request.getParameter("hobby"));
data.setAversion(request.getParameter("aversion"));
```

We are calling getParameter to retrieve the data from the request parameters and then calling the bean's mutators to copy the data to the bean.

Making the Bean Accessible to the JSPs

The controller is a separate class from the JSPs. The bean has been created as a local variable in the controller. The last detail to work out is how to let the JSP access this bean.

There is an object which is maintained by the servlet engine that can hold arbitrary data for the web application. This object is known as the *session*; the data in it can be accessed by the controller and by all of its JSPs. If the controller places the bean in this object, then it can be retrieved in all of the JSPs. From inside the controller, the session can be retrieved with the method getSession.

Additional information can be added to the session by using the method setAttribute. This method associates a simple name with an object. In our application, it will be used to associate a name with the bean that holds the data. For example, if a new bean has already been created and named *data*, then it can be added to the session with the following statement.

```
request.getSession().setAttribute("refData", data);
```

The second parameter is the bean, which contains the data; the first parameter is an arbitrary name. Figure 3.2 is a representation of how the session is changed after a call to the setAttribute method.

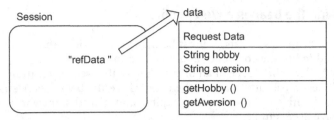

Figure 3.2 The effect of calling getSession().setAttribute("refData", data).

Two steps are required to make the bean accessible to a JSP.

1. Retrieve the session object for the request with the `getSession` method.
2. Call the `setAttribute` method to associate a name with the bean.

3.3   Application: Data Bean

All the previous steps can now be put together to create an application that uses a bean to encapsulate the request data. In addition to these new steps, it is necessary to know the details that were introduced in Chapter Two: the location of the JSPs, the visible URL for the controller, the package of the controller and the package for the bean.

1. The JSPs for the web application have been placed in the `/ch3/dataBean` directory.
2. In the *web.xml* file of the web application, the controller has been mapped to the URL `/ch3/dataBean/Controller`. Notice that the path in the URL is the same as the path to the JSPs. This allows the controller to use a relative reference in the address for the JSPs.
3. The controller for this example has been placed in a package named `ch3.dataBean`. It is not necessary that the name of the package resemble the path to the JSPs. This was done just as an organisational tool. By keeping the package and the path similar, it is easier to remember that they correspond to the same servlet.
4. The bean is in the same package as the controller.

Figure 3.3 shows the location of the files for the Data Bean Controller.

The location of the controller and the location of the JSPs are needed in order to create the servlet definition and the servlet mapping in the *web.xml* file.

```
. . .
<servlet>
    <servlet-name>ControllerBean</servlet-name>
    <servlet-class>ch3.dataBean.Controller</servlet-class>
</servlet>
<servlet-mapping>
    <servlet-name>ControllerBean</servlet-name>
    <url-pattern>/ch3/dataBean/Controller</url-pattern>
</servlet-mapping>
. . .
```

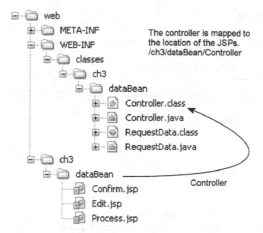

Figure 3.3 The location of the files for the Data Bean Controller.

3.3.1 Controller: Data Bean

There are now five tasks that a controller performs. In Listing 3.1, identify the sections of code that implement these five tasks:

1. creating the bean
2. making the bean accessible to the JSPs
3. copying the request parameters into the bean
4. decoding the button name into an address
5. forwarding the request and response to the JSP.

```
package ch3.dataBean;

import java.io.IOException;
import javax.servlet.RequestDispatcher;
import javax.servlet.ServletException;
import javax.servlet.http.HttpServlet;
import javax.servlet.http.HttpServletRequest;
import javax.servlet.http.HttpServletResponse;

public class Controller extends HttpServlet
{

  protected void doGet(HttpServletRequest request,
     HttpServletResponse response)
     throws ServletException, IOException
  {
    RequestData data = new RequestData();
    request.getSession().setAttribute("refData", data);

    data.setHobby(request.getParameter("hobby"));
    data.setAversion(request.getParameter("aversion"));
```

```
   String address;

   if (request.getParameter("processButton") != null)
   {
     address = "Process.jsp";
   }
   else if (request.getParameter("confirmButton") != null)
   {
     address = "Confirm.jsp";
   }
   else
   {
     address = "Edit.jsp";
   }

   RequestDispatcher dispatcher =
       request.getRequestDispatcher(address);
   dispatcher.forward(request, response);
  }
}
```

Listing 3.1 A controller that uses a data bean.

3.3.2 Accessing the Bean in the JSP

All the details for adding a bean to the controller have been covered. The controller has even made the bean available to the JSPs. The last step is for the JSPs to access the data.

In a JSP, EL can be used to access the bean that was stored in the session. The bean is accessed by the name that was used in the call to the setAttribute method in the controller. In our example, the name *refData* was used by the controller when adding the bean to the session. The bean was added to the session with the call to setAttribute:

```
request.getSession().setAttribute("refData", data);
```

The second parameter is the bean, which contains the data; the first parameter is an arbitrary name. Place the name in an EL statement and the bean will be retrieved. Do not use quotes around the name in the EL statement.

```
   ${refData}
```

In addition to accessing the entire bean, EL can access every public accessor that is in the bean. The servlet engine translates all EL statements into Java code. Table 3.2 shows the equivalent Java code for the EL statements in the edit page.

Table 3.2 EL statements and the equivalent Java code.

EL Statement in JSP	Equivalent Java in Controller
${refData.hobby}	data.getHobby()
${refData.aversion}	data.getAversion()

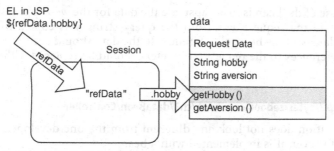

Figure 3.4 ${refData.hobby} accesses data.getHobby() in controller.

Figure 3.4 demonstrates how the EL in the JSP can access the public accessor from the bean.

3.3.3 JSPs: Data Bean

All references to the data should use the bean and not the request parameters. This is possible since all the data from the query string was copied into the bean in the controller. In the JSPs, replace all occurrences of ${param.hobby} with ${refData.hobby}, and replace all ${param.aversion} with ${refData.aversion}.

In the edit page, use the bean to initialise the input elements with any data that was passed in the query string.

```
Hobby:
<input type="text"  name="hobby"
                    value="${refData.hobby}">
<br>
Aversion:
<input type="text"  name="aversion"
                    value="${refData.aversion}">
```

In the confirm and process pages, use the bean to retrieve the values for the hobby and aversion that were sent in the query string.

```
The value of the hobby that was sent to
this page is: <b>${refData.hobby}</b>
<br>
The value of the aversions that was sent to
this page is: <b>${refData.aversion}</b>
```

Use the bean to initialise the hidden elements with any data that was passed in the query string.

```
<input type="hidden"  name="hobby"
                      value="${refData.hobby}">
<input type="hidden"  name="aversion"
                      value="${refData.aversion}">
```

The purpose of the bean is to encapsulate the data for the web application. In the controller, all the request data from the query string was copied to the bean. Once the data is in the bean, all references to the data should use the bean. In the JSPs, all references to the request parameters should be replaced with references to the bean.

 Try It   http://bytesizebook.com/book/ch3/dataBean/Controller

This application does not look any different from the one developed in the last chapter. However, it is implemented with a bean.

3.4   Application: Default Validation

So far, there has not been much of a motivation for using a bean, other than demonstrating the advanced features of Java. However, a bean is a powerful class. The bean can be enhanced to validate that the user has entered some data. This will use default validation.

Default validation is used to fill in fields with default values, if the user leaves out some data. This is not the most powerful way to do validation, but it is simple and offers a good introduction to two topics at once: validation and enhancing the bean.

A new bean and controller will be created to demonstrate default validation. In order to keep the code organised better, each new controller and bean will be created in a new package. If the JSPs are changed, then they will also be placed in a new directory, while the names of the JSPs will remain the same: Edit.jsp, Confirm.jsp and Process.jsp. If the JSPs are the same as another example, then those JSPs will be used.

3.4.1   Java Bean: Default Validation

This bean is similar to the last example, but the accessors now do default validation. For each property, a helper method has been added that will test if the user has entered data into the input field. If the data is empty, then a default value will be supplied.

For example, there is a helper method in the bean that tests if the hobby element is valid. A simple validation is used: the hobby cannot be null or empty.

```
. . .
public boolean isValidHobby() {
  return hobby != null && !hobby.trim().equals("");
}
. . .
```

This helper method is called by the accessor for the hobby property. If the hobby does not pass the validation, then the accessor will return a default string, instead of null or empty. If the hobby passes the validation, then the value that the user entered will be returned by the accessor.

```
...
public String getHobby() {
  if (isValidHobby()) {
    return hobby;
  }
  return "No Hobby";
}
...
```

A similar helper method has been added for the aversion property, which is called from the accessor for the aversion.

The validation has been placed in the accessor, but it could easily have been placed in the mutator. It is a matter of personal preference. If the validation is done in the mutator, then the actual value that the user entered will be lost. By placing the validation in the accessor, the user's invalid data is still in the bean. It is conceivable that the validation test could change and that an invalid value today could become a valid value tomorrow. Because of this, I prefer to place the validation in the accessor.

3.4.2 Controller: Default Validation

The only differences between the controller for this example and the *Data Bean* controller of Listing 3.1 are the name of the bean, the URL for the controller and the name of package. Since nothing has changed in this example as far as the JSPs are concerned, this controller will use the same JSPs that were used in the last example.

The next listing shows the part of the controller that has changed. Notice that the URL for the JSP must include a path. This is necessary because the controller is being mapped to /ch3/defaultValidate/Controller, while the JSPs are the ones from the previous application and are already located in the /ch3/dataBean folder.

```
...
String address;
if (request.getParameter("processButton") != null)
{
  address = "/ch3/dataBean/Process.jsp";
}
else if (request.getParameter("confirmButton") != null)
{
  address = "/ch3/dataBean/Confirm.jsp";
}
else
{
  address = "/ch3/dataBean/Edit.jsp";
}
...
```

Notice that the name of the web application is not included in the URL. Web applications can only forward to URLs that are within the web application, so the name of the web application is always assumed and should not be included in the URL that is used to forward to a JSP.

The following excerpt from the *web.xml* file shows the servlet mapping for this controller. The URL pattern does not correspond to a physical directory in the web application, but this is irrelevant; the URL can still be used to access the controller. The servlet engine will intercept the URL for the controller and route it to the correct location. This demonstrates the point that the URL pattern can be any string at all.

```
...
<servlet>
  <servlet-name>DefaultController</servlet-name>
  <servlet-class>ch3.defaultValidate.Controller</servlet-class>
</servlet>
<servlet-mapping>
  <servlet-name>DefaultController</servlet-name>
  <url-pattern>/ch3/defaultValidate/Controller</url-pattern>
</servlet-mapping>
...
```

Figure 3.5 shows the location of the files for the Data Bean Controller. There are no new JSPs for this example, it uses the JSPs from the previous example.

By making a few modifications to the bean, and minor modifications to the controller, the web application now does default validation. This is a simple example of how a bean is the perfect place for extending the capabilities of the web application.

 Try It   http://bytesizebook.com/book/ch3/defaultValidate/Controller

This application will supply default values if the user leaves either input field empty.

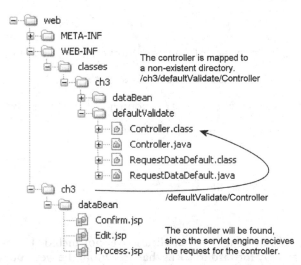

Figure 3.5 The location of the files for the Default Validate Controller.

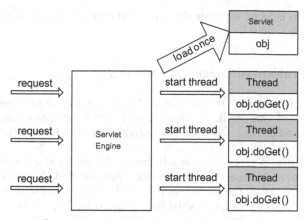

Figure 3.6 Each request is handled in a new thread.

When the application starts, the default values have already been supplied by the bean. Erase the values that are there and click the confirm button. You will see that on the next page the default values have been provided by the bean again.

3.5 Member Variables in Servlets

In object-oriented design, member variables are powerful tools. By using member variables, the number of parameters that must be passed to methods can be reduced. Member variables also allow for encapsulation of data: access to the underlying variable can be limited through the use of methods. However, using member variables in servlets is dangerous and can lead to bugs.

3.5.1 Threads

Consider the process of filling out a form on a web site: the user visits a web site that has a form; the user fills in the data on the form; the user clicks the submit button on the form. If there were multiple requests at the same time, then the server would process each set of data independently: the data from one request would not be mixed up with the data from another. The server ensures that the data is processed independently by using *threads*. A thread is like a separate process on the computer: each thread runs independently of all other threads. Each request to a web application creates a new thread on the server (Figure 3.6).

Multiple requests to a web application are like students taking a midterm exam (Table 3.3).

Table 3.3 Requests compared with an exam.

Student	Servlet Engine
A student asks the teacher for a test.	A request is sent to the servlet engine.
A student receives the test paper.	A thread is started for each request.
Each student works on the exam.	The thread processes the doGet method of the servlet.

Each student is like a separate thread performing the same steps on different data.

3.5.2   The Problem with Member Variables

After a servlet is called for the first time, the servlet engine will load the servlet into memory and execute it. The servlet will stay in memory until the servlet engine is stopped or restarted. Member variables exist as long as the servlet is in memory.

When a request is received from a browser, the server starts a new thread to handle the request. As soon as the request has been handled, the thread is released. The thread is created by the servlet engine and has access to the servlet's member variables. The member variables exist before the thread starts and will continue to exist after the thread has ended.

Member variables in the servlet can be accessed by all of the threads. If two threads attempt to save a value to a member variable, only the value written by the last thread will be stored.

Continuing the analogy of the midterm exam, using a member variable is like writing an answer on the board in the front of the room. This might not seem like a bad idea until you realise that the board can only hold one answer to each question; only the response of the last student who answers the question will be recorded. Only the last student who writes the answer on the board will receive credit for that question.

The problem with member variables makes them dangerous to use in a servlet. Think of member variables in a servlet as being more like static variables in a simple Java program. Because of this, it is better to avoid using member variables in a servlet.

It is possible that the simple example of $x = x + 1$ can return the wrong result, if enough simultaneous requests are made. Consider the steps that are taken by a computer in order to complete this task:

1. read x from memory into the CPU
2. increment the value in the CPU by 1
3. write the value from the CPU back to x, in memory.

Consider two different requests, A and B. Each would try to increment x, and the steps from Table 3.4 would be needed.

Assuming that both threads are being executed on the same processor, all that is guaranteed is that request A performs these tasks in the order A1, A2, A3 and that request B performs these tasks in the order B1, B2, B3. However, there is no

Table 3.4 Two threads executing the same commands.

Thread A	Thread B
A1 read x	B1 read x
A2 increment	B2 increment
A3 write x	B3 write x

Table 3.5 The values of shared variable x.

Step	Value in CPU	Value in x
A1: read x	0	0
A2: incr x	1	0
B1: read x	0	0
B2: incr x	1	0
A3: write x	1	1
B3: write x	1	1

rule that states that request A will complete all of its steps before request B begins its steps. Since the two requests are in different threads, it is up to the CPU to schedule time for each request.

The CPU might perform these steps in the order A1, A2, B1, B2, A3, B3. In this case, both requests will wind up with the same value for x, since they both read the value of x before either request writes the new value of x. It is important to understand that arithmetic only occurs in the CPU and that the results need to be written back to memory. Table 3.5 shows the values of x as it is changed by each thread.

Both threads incremented x and both threads received the same value for x. This is the type of error that occurs when member variables are used incorrectly in a servlet.

In an actual case, this error happened in a chat program. From time to time, the comments made by one user would be attributed to a different user. This occurred because the user name was being stored in a member variable. If enough people were on line at the same time, the error would occur.

3.5.3 Local versus Member Variables

If two users on different machines access the servlet at the same time, then each one will have its own doGet running in its own thread. Variables that are local to the doGet procedure are private variables that cannot be accessed by a different thread. However, member variables are shared by all the threads.

Consider a controller that has a member variable, x. Assume that the doGet method has a local variable, y. If the doGet method increments both x and y, then what values will they have after three requests have been made?

Figure 3.7 demonstrates how these variables will be changed. Each new request will create a separate thread to run the doGet method. Each thread will have its own local copy of the variable y. There will only be one instance of the variable x and each thread will access that one instance. The value of x after three requests will be 3. The value of y for each request will be 1.

The servlet is loaded and executed by the servlet engine the first time the servlet is called. After that, the servlet resides in memory and handles requests from browsers. Each request is handled in a different thread. This means that the member variables of the servlet are created and initialised when the servlet is first loaded and executed. Each request will share the member variables. Local variables inside the doGet method are created each time the method is called.

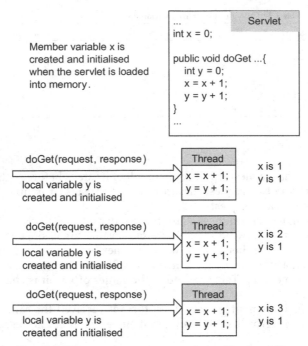

Member variable x is
created and initialised
when the servlet is loaded
into memory.

Figure 3.7 How a servlet processes member and local variables.

3.6 Application: Shared Variable Error

Programmers must resist the desire to create member variables in servlets to
avoid passing parameters to methods. Even though object-oriented design pro-
motes the use of member variables, it can cause intermittent errors when used in
a servlet.

It is difficult to create an example that always produces incorrect answers, but
with enough requests, most servlets that use member variables will have errors.
Of course, it is possible to use member variables if the intent is to share data across
all requests. In this case, care must be taken to synchronize all access to the shared
variable. This example demonstrates that something as simple as adding 1 to a
shared variable can produce incorrect answers.

3.6.1 Controller: Shared Variable Error

The controller for this application is very simple. It always transfers control to the
same JSP. The only work that it performs is to increment a member variable by 1.
In order to cause an error each time a request is processed, the work has been
placed in a helper method.

```
...
protected void doGet(HttpServletRequest request,
                     HttpServletResponse response)
```

```
throws ServletException, IOException {

    String address = jspLocation() + "Edit.jsp";

    incrementSharedVariable();

    request.setAttribute("accessCount", accessCount);
    request.getRequestDispatcher(address)
        .forward(request, response);
}
...
```

Describing the error is easier than causing the error in a servlet. Such an error will only occur if two requests are made very close to each other. Usually, this will occur in a servlet that receives many requests. There is a low probability that this error will occur, but, with enough requests, it can happen.

There is a static method in the thread class that tells the CPU to stop processing the current thread for a period of time. The result of this is that the CPU will allow other threads to run and then will return to this thread after the specified time has elapsed. The name of this method is `sleep`. By using it, we can force the CPU to stop processing the current thread and to start processing another thread. It is not possible to know which thread will be selected by the CPU; however, if we put the current thread to sleep for a long enough time, then we can be assured that the CPU will access all other threads before returning to this one.

In this example, the value of the shared variable is copied into a local, private variable; the local variable is then incremented and the thread is put to sleep; the thread copies the local variable back to the shared variable when it wakes up.

This mimics the action of the thread copying the value of a variable into the CPU; the thread incrementing the value and being interrupted by the CPU; the thread writing the value in the CPU back to memory when it regains control.

The advantage of doing this is to be able to set the length of time that the thread sleeps. Instead of losing control for a few milliseconds, we can force the thread to sleep for many seconds. This will give us slow humans the ability to cause this error every time.

```
...
public int accessCount = 0;
...
public void incrementSharedVariable() {
    int temp = accessCount;
    temp++;
    System.out.println(temp);
    try {
      Thread.sleep(3000);
    } catch (java.lang.InterruptedException ie) {

    }
    accessCount = temp;
}
...
```

If two threads are started within a few seconds of each other, this arrangement will force the execution of the statements similar to what was outlined above: A1,

A2, B1, B2, A3, B3. To see the effect, open two browsers and execute the servlet in each one. Be sure to start both requests to the servlet within a few seconds of each other. It is important that this is done in two different brands of browsers since the servlet engine will only allow one thread per browser brand.

 Try It   http://bytesizebook.com/book/ch3/sharedVariable/error/Controller

Open two different browsers, not just two instances of the same browser, as Tomcat does not allocate a new thread to the same servlet from the same browser. After doing this, you will see that both instances display the same number, even though both of them were incrementing the same shared variable.

Synchronizing

There are two solutions to this problem: synchronize access to the shared variable and avoid using member variables in servlets. The simpler solution is to avoid using member variables in servlets; however, it is possible to avoid this problem by using a synchronization block.

```
. . .
public void incrementSharedVariable() {
    synchronized (this) {
        int temp = accessCount;
        temp++;
        System.out.println(temp);
        try {
          Thread.sleep(3000);
        } catch (java.lang.InterruptedException ie) {
        }
        accessCount = temp;
    }
}
. . .
```

A synchronization block forces the CPU to give the thread all the time it needs to complete the block, without being interrupted. It is best to keep the synchronized block as short as possible so that the CPU is not limited in how it allocates time segments to threads. By synchronizing the access to the shared variable, there is no error.

This was an example where the programmer wanted to have shared access to a member variable. In this case, synchronization fixed the error. However, there are very few instances where shared access to a member variable is needed.

Even with synchronization, never place the request object in a member variable in a servlet; otherwise all active threads will have access to the parameters of the thread that set the member variable last. This would be a bad idea if this were an application for Swiss bank accounts.

 Try It   http://bytesizebook.com/book/ch3/sharedVariable/Controller

Open two different browsers, not just two instances of the same browser, as Tomcat does not allocate a new thread to the same servlet from the same browser. After doing this, you will see that both instances display different numbers.

Notice that the requests take longer to complete. Instead of taking around three seconds to complete both requests, it now takes six seconds. The CPU must allow the thread to sleep and wake up before it gives access to the second thread. This is another reason for not using synchronized, shared variables in servlets.

When to Use Member Variables in Servlets

The simple answer to the question is to never use member variables in servlets. There will never be synchronization issues if there are no member variables in servlets.

Another way to answer the question of using member variables is to ask the question, "Should this data be shared amongst all requests?" If the answer is "Yes", then it is safe to use a synchronized member variable. If the answer is "No", then use local variables inside methods and pass the data to other methods via parameters.

3.7 Reorganising the Controller

Member variables are useful; it would be nice to be able to use them in a controller. For instance, controllers communicate with the browser through the request and response objects. Any helper method that needs to know information about the request or that needs to add information to the response would need to have these objects passed to it as parameters. It would be easier to place these two objects into member variables, so that they could be accessed by every method in the controller.

The problem with member variables is only limited to classes that extend *HttpServlet*. However, member variables can be used in every class that does not extend *HttpServlet*. For this reason, a helper class will be created that will be used to store the request and response objects. This helper class can have helper methods, too. These helper methods will have direct access to the request and response objects. Even a doGet method can be added to the helper class, so that the controller only needs to call doGet in the helper.

In addition to the request and response objects, the helper class will have a member variable for the bean that contains all of the user's data. This will make it easier for the controller to process the data. A helper method named getData will be added so that the data in the bean can be accessed from the JSPs using EL.

From now on, whenever a controller is created, a helper class will also be created. Most of the work that could be done in the controller will be done in the helper class, instead. It will be easier to do the work of the controller in the helper class because of the member variables.

There are two types of variables that can be added to the helper class. Some of the variables that are added are not specific for a controller, but are common to all controllers. For example, the request and response objects have the same structure for all controllers. On the other hand, some variables are unique to a controller, like the bean that encapsulates the request data.

This is a perfect place to use inheritance. Those variables that are common to all controllers can be placed in a base class, while the ones that are specific to a controller will be placed in a class that extends the base class. The base class will

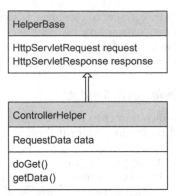

Figure 3.8 ControllerHelper will inherit from HelperBase.

be called `HelperBase` and the extended class will typically be called
`ControllerHelper`.

Figure 3.8 shows the relationship between the two classes, the member variables
in each and the helper methods in each.

3.7.1   Creating the Helper Base

The helper base will contain the member variables that are common to all controllers, like the request and response objects. These objects have the same structure
regardless of the controller that is using them. Helper methods will be added to
the class to facilitate access to these variables. There needs to be a helper method
that sets the request and response objects. These should be set as soon as the helper
base is created. The most logical place to set them is in the constructor for the
helper base class. The helper base will not have a default constructor, it will only
have a constructor that has parameters for the request and response objects.
Whenever a new helper base object is constructed, the current request and response
objects will need to be passed to the constructor.

```java
package ch3.reorganised;

import javax.servlet.http.HttpServletRequest;
import javax.servlet.http.HttpServletResponse;

public class HelperBase {

    protected HttpServletRequest request;
    protected HttpServletResponse response;

    public HelperBase(HttpServletRequest request,
                      HttpServletResponse response) {
        this.request = request;
        this.response = response;
    }

}
```

For the current example, the helper base class will be placed in the same package as the controller. In the future, as more features are added to the helper base class, it will be placed in a more centrally located package.

3.7.2   Creating the Controller Helper

The main motivation for using a controller helper is to be able to use member variables. There are two types of member variables: those that are created in the controller helper and those that are created in the helper base.

The controller helper will be placed into the session. This means that the member variables in it can be made visible to the session. In order to make a member variable visible from the session, an accessor for the variable needs to be added to the controller helper. The member variables in the controller helper can be accessed from a JSP just like the member variables in a bean are accessed: by using an accessor.

The controller helper will do all the work for the controller. The controller will still receive the request from the browser, but will then delegate the work to the controller helper. For this reason, the controller helper will have a `doGet` method that does all the work that the controller used to do. The controller will only create the controller helper and call its `doGet` method.

Controller Helper Variables

The controller helper will contain variables that are specific to the current controller, like the bean that contains the request data. The bean will have a different structure for each controller, since each bean will contain different properties that encapsulate the data that the user enters. For this reason, it cannot be placed in the `HelperBase`. In the future, additional member variables will be added to the controller helper.

```
protected RequestDataDefault data =
   new RequestDataDefault();
```

Initialise Helper Base Variables

The controller helper will extend the helper base and must initialise the request and response variables that are stored in it. The constructor for the controller helper will have parameters for the request and response objects. The constructor must call the base class constructor with these parameters. The call to `super(request, response)` must be the first statement in the constructor. The call to the base constructor will set the values of the request and response objects in the helper base class.

```
public ControllerHelper(HttpServletRequest request,
                        HttpServletResponse response) {
   super(request, response);
}
```

Making Variables Visible from the Session

There needs to be a helper method that allows the data to be retrieved from the
JSPs, using EL. Remember that EL statements are translated into calls to accessors,
so there should be an accessor in the controller helper that returns the bean. This
accessor only needs to return the type Object because the EL uses reflection to
determine the methods an object has. Without this method, the bean would not
be accessible from the JSPs.

```
public Object getData() {
  return data;
}
```

Doing the Work of the Controller

The ControllerHelper will also have a doGet method that is similar to
the code that has been in previous controllers. It does not need the request
and response objects passed to it, since it can access them directly from the helper
base class.

Five basic steps were performed by the doGet method in the servlet controller
from Listing 2.7: create the bean, make the bean accessible, fill the bean, translate
the button name and forward to the next page.

This method does not need to create a bean, since the bean has been added to
the controller helper as a member variable and is created when the controller
helper is constructed.

Instead of placing the bean in the session, the controller helper will place itself
in the session. In conjunction with the getData accessor, the bean will still be
accessible from the JSPs.

The remaining steps for a controller are performed just like the previous
controller.

```
protected void doGet()
    throws ServletException, IOException
{
  request.getSession().setAttribute("helper", this);

  data.setHobby(request.getParameter("hobby"));
  data.setAversion(request.getParameter("aversion"));

  String address;

  if (request.getParameter("processButton") != null)
  {
    address = "Process.jsp";
  }
  else if (request.getParameter("confirmButton") != null)
  {
    address = "Confirm.jsp";
  }
  else
```

```
{
  address = "Edit.jsp";
}

RequestDispatcher dispatcher =
    request.getRequestDispatcher(address);
dispatcher.forward(request, response);
}
```

Complete Controller Helper

The next listing shows the complete code for a simple controller helper. It is using the bean from the *DefaultValidate* application – the controller helper has imported the class for the bean. The JSPs for the application will be rewritten in the next section. Since a relative reference is being used in the address for the JSP, it is assumed that the controller will be mapped to the directory that contains the JSPs.

```java
package ch3.reorganised;

import java.io.IOException;
import javax.servlet.RequestDispatcher;
import javax.servlet.ServletException;
import javax.servlet.http.HttpServletRequest;
import javax.servlet.http.HttpServletResponse;

import ch3.defaultValidate.RequestDataDefault;
public class ControllerHelper extends HelperBase {

  protected RequestDataDefault data =
    new RequestDataDefault();

  public ControllerHelper(HttpServletRequest request,
                          HttpServletResponse response) {
    super(request, response);
  }

  public Object getData() {
    return data;
  }

  protected void doGet()
    throws ServletException, IOException
  {
    request.getSession().setAttribute("helper", this);

    data.setHobby(request.getParameter("hobby"));
    data.setAversion(request.getParameter("aversion"));

    String address;

    if (request.getParameter("processButton") != null)
    {
```

```
   address = "Process.jsp";
  }
  else if (request.getParameter("confirmButton") != null)
  {
    address = "Confirm.jsp";
  }
  else
  {
    address = "Edit.jsp";
  }

  RequestDispatcher dispatcher =
      request.getRequestDispatcher(address);
  dispatcher.forward(request, response);
 }

}
```

The controller helper looks very similar to the controller from previous examples. At this point, there does not seem to be a justification for going to all of this trouble. However, this reorganisation will simplify the implementation of features that will be added to the controller.

3.7.3   JSPs: Reorganised Controller

The only difference between the JSPs for this example and the JSPs from the previous example is how the data is retrieved from the session. The servlet controller from earlier in the chapter placed the bean in the session and accessed the bean from the JSP. The current example placed the controller helper into the session. This requires an extra step to access the data.

The controller helper is added to the session under the name of *helper*. Any public accessors in the controller helper can be accessed from the JSP using EL. In particular, the getData accessor can be accessed from the bean using ${helper. data}. This will return the bean that contains the data.

Once the bean is accessible, then all its public accessors are accessible. In particular, the getHobby accessor could be called to retrieve the hobby that the user entered. The EL statement that would do this is ${helper.data.hobby} (Figure 3.9).

To modify the JSPs for this example, replace all ${refData.hobby} with ${helper.data.hobby} and replace all ${refData.aversion} with ${helper.data.aversion}.

In the edit page, use the helper to access the bean, then access the bean to initialise the input elements with any data that was passed in the query string.

```
Hobby:
<input type="text" name="hobby"
                   value="${helper.data.hobby}">
<br>
Aversion:
<input type="text" name="aversion"
                   value="${helper.data.aversion}">
```

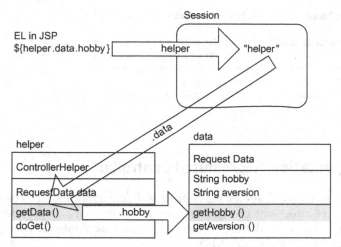

Figure 3.9 EL statement that uses the helper to access the hobby from the data bean.

In the confirm and process pages, use the helper to access the bean, then access the bean to retrieve the values for the hobby and aversion that were sent in the query string.

```
The value of the hobby that was sent to
this page is: <b>${helper.data.hobby}</b>
<br>
The value of the aversions that was sent to
this page is: <b>${helper.data.aversion}</b>
```

In the confirm and process pages, use the helper to access the bean, then access the bean to initialise the hidden elements with any data that was passed in the query string.

```
<input type="hidden" name="hobby"
                     value="${helper.data.hobby}">
<input type="hidden" name="aversion"
                     value="${helper.data.aversion}">
```

3.7.4 Controller: Reorganised Controller

The last detail is to modify the controller so that it uses the controller helper. The controller only has to construct a controller helper and call its doGet method.

```
package ch3.reorganised;

import java.io.IOException;
import javax.servlet.ServletException;
import javax.servlet.http.HttpServlet;
import javax.servlet.http.HttpServletRequest;
import javax.servlet.http.HttpServletResponse;
```

```
public class Controller extends HttpServlet {

    protected void doGet(HttpServletRequest request,
                         HttpServletResponse response)
    throws ServletException, IOException {
        ControllerHelper helper =
            new ControllerHelper(request, response);
        helper.doGet();
    }
}
```

3.8 Application: Reorganised Controller

With the above modifications, the *Default Validate* application can be rewritten. The `HelperBase`, `ControllerHelper` and `Controller` were developed in the last three sections. All the Java files have been placed into the package named `ch3.reorganised` (Figure 3.10).

In *web.xml*, the controller has been mapped to */ch3/reorganised/Controller*, which is the directory where the JSPs have been placed. Even though the controller is using a helper, the controller is still the class that is visible from the web, because it is the class that extends *HttpServlet*. The controller helper, helper base and bean classes should not be added to the *web.xml* file. They are not visible from the web, so they do not need entries in the *web.xml* file.

```
. . .
<servlet>
    <servlet-name>Reorganised</servlet-name>
    <servlet-class>ch3.reorganised.Controller</servlet-class>
</servlet>
<servlet-mapping>
    <servlet-name>Reorganised</servlet-name>
    <url-pattern>/ch3/reorganised/Controller</url-pattern>
</servlet-mapping>
. . .
```

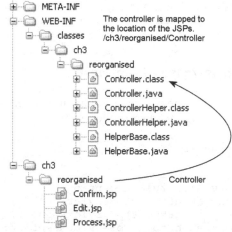

Figure 3.10 The location of files for the Reorganised Controller.

Try It   http://bytesizebook.com/book/ch3/reorganised/Controller

This controller behaves exactly like the *DefaultValidate* controller. The only difference is that the controller has been reorganised using a controller helper class and a helper base class.

3.9   Model, View, Controller

There are three major components in a web application: the bean, the JSPs and the controller. These components are know as the *Model, View, Controller* [MVC].

Model

> The model defines the data that will be used in the application. It also defines the operations that can be performed on the data. In a web application, the bean is the model.

View

> The view displays the data to the user. The view does not do any of the processing of the data, it only presents the data. There are usually multiple views in an application. In a web application, each JSP is a separate view.

Controller

> The controller is the program that ties the views and the models together. In a web application the controller servlet is the controller.

The model is where the data processing will be done. The most important aspect of a web application is data processing. The model encapsulates the data and all the methods that work on it.

The controller is important because it is the program that is handling the request from the browser and sending a response back to the server. The controller will delegate responsibility to the model whenever it can.

The views are simple. They contain HTML and a few directives to display the data from the model. It is best not to add code to the view.

3.10   Summary

This chapter introduced Java beans, which are used to encapsulate the data that is sent from a request. The basic structure of a bean was covered, as well as how a bean can be incorporated into a web application. To demonstrate the power of a bean, the additional feature of default validation was added.

One of the shortcomings of a servlet is the problem with using member variables. This restriction goes against one of the basic concepts of object-oriented design. This problem was discussed in detail and two solutions to the problem were offered: avoid using member variables or use synchronization blocks. Synchronization blocks should only be used when data needs to be shared amongst all requests. For most situations, member variables should be avoided in servlets.

A helper class was introduced that can use member variables to simplify the tasks of the controller. The helper class contained a member variable for the bean that encapsulates the request data. A base class was introduced for member variables that are the same for all controllers. The first variables that were added to this class were for the request and response objects. Together, these classes allow easy access to all the objects that are needed in an application.

In the future, every controller will have a controller helper that is extended from the base class. All request and response processing will be done in the helper class.

The addition of the bean to a web application adds the final component of the MVC structure. The model is the bean; the views are the JSPs; the controller is the servlet that extends HttpServlet.

3.11   Chapter Review

Terms

1. Java Bean
2. Property
3. Accessor
4. Mutator
5. Default Validation
6. Default Value
7. Variables
   a. Member
   b. Local
8. Thread
9. Synchronization
10. Controller Helper
11. Helper Base
12. MVC

New Java

1. `request.getSession().setAttribute`
2. `super`
3. `synchronized`

Tags

1. `${param.name}`
2. `${bean.property}`
3. `${helper.bean.property}`

Questions

1. When discussing threads, the steps A1, A2, A3 must execute in order, and the steps B1, B2, B3 must execute in order. However, there is no restriction on how the A steps relate to the B steps. Other than the sequence A1, A2, B1, B2, A3, B3 explained above, what other sequences will cause both threads to obtain a value of 1 for x?

2. What would be the name of the mutator and accessor in a bean for form elements with the following names?
   a. fun
   b. moreFun
   c. tOoMuChFuN
   d. wAYTOOMUCHFUN

3. What would be the name of the form element that would correspond with the following accessors in a bean?
   a. getBetter
   b. getOutOfHere
   c. getOFFMYCLOUD

4. What methods in the helper and the bean are called when the EL statement ${helper.data.hobby} is executed?

5. What determines if a member variable should be declared in the helper base or in the controller helper?

6. What method must be added to the controller helper in order to allow a member variable to be accessed from a JSP?

Tasks

1. Create a bean that encapsulates the data in a form with elements named name, city and country.
   a. Add default values to the accessors for city and two-letter country code. Use a city and country of your choice for the default values. Use the default values if user leaves the city or the country blank.
   b. Change the validation in the last question so that the country must be GB, US or DE. If the country is GB, then the city must be London, Oxford or Leeds. If the country is US, then the city must be New York, Los Angeles or Miami. If the country is DE, then the city must be Berlin, Frankfurt or Baden-Baden. Add additional countries and cities of your choice. If the country is not valid, then choose a default country and city. If the country is valid, but the city is not valid, choose a default city for that country.

2. In a servlet,
   a. Write the statements that will add a bean named preferences to the session attributes.
   b. Write the statements that will copy the request parameters into a bean object named fruit that has properties named apples and bananas with data from the query string. Assume that the form elements in the query string have the same names as the bean properties.

3. In a JSP,

   a. Write the EL statements that will display the values of the query string parameters named `bookName` and `bookAuthor`.

   b. Write the EL statements that will display the values of session attributes named `salesManager` and `accountant`.

   c. Write the EL statements that will display the values of the bean properties named `car` and `boat`. Assume that the bean has been added to the session attributes with the name `vehicles`.

   d. Write the EL statements that will display the values of the bean properties named `car` and `boat`. Assume that the bean has been added to the helper and that the helper has been added to the session attributes. Assume that there is a `getData` method in the helper that returns the bean.

4. Create a new controller application that accepts the data from question 1. Create a bean and a controller helper for this application.

4 Enhancing the Controller

The previous chapter introduced the idea of a helper class that has easy access to all the objects that are used in a controller application: the bean, the request, the response. This chapter builds on this framework and adds features to the helper class and its base class.

Many tasks are common to all controller applications. These tasks include specifying the location of the JSPs, eliminating hidden fields, filling a bean, using a logger and decoding a button name into an address. Other common capabilities will be added to the controller application in future chapters.

Some of these tasks require specific information about the current controller application, so they will be added to the controller helper class. Others are common to all controller applications, so they will be added to the helper base class.

Up until now, all the features that have been used are part of the normal servlet engine. From now on, additional features will be added to the servlet engine by including *Java Archive* [JAR] files. JAR files are actually *zip* archives with the extension *.jar* that can be read by the *Java Virtual Machine* [JVM]. Typically, a developer who wants to add a feature to the servlet engine will package all the necessary class files in a JAR. Then, anyone who wants to incorporate the new feature into the servlet engine only has to place the JAR into a specific directory in the web application where the servlet engine can find it. This directory is the *lib* subdirectory of the WEB-INF directory.

4.1 Logging in Web Applications

When debugging a Java application, it can be useful to display error messages when some exception fires. A standard technique is to use System.out.

```
System.out.println("Something bad happened");
```

In a servlet, this is not a very useful technique. In a typical Java application, System.out is routed to the monitor, so the error will display on the current monitor. However, a servlet is not connected to a monitor; it is run by the servlet engine. The servlet engine is not connected to a monitor either; the servlet engine routes System.out to a log file that is owned by the system administrator and cannot be accessed by a typical developer.

Instead of using `System.out`, it is better to create a log file that the developer can read.

4.1.1   Logging with Log4j

There is a package named Log4j that can be used to open and write to a log file. To implement it, add the following jar file to the *lib* directory of the web application. This file can be downloaded from *http://bytesizebook.com/jar* or the most recent version of the JAR can be retrieved from *http://logging.apache.org/log4j/docs/download.html*.

```
log4j-1.2.11.jar
```

One of the nicest features of a Log4j logger is that an error message can be given an error level. The log file also has a level; it will only record error messages that have the same level or a more severe level. Those messages that have a less severe error level will be not be written to the log file. This feature allows the developer to add error messages that will only display when trying to trace an error. By changing the level of the log file to a more severe level, the less severe messages will not be written to the log file.

There are five error levels for a log file: `Level.FATAL`, `Level.ERROR`, `Level.WARN`, `Level.INFO`, `Level.DEBUG`. These error levels range from the level that records the fewest number of messages to the level that records the highest number of messages.

There are five error methods that a logger can use to write to a log file: `fatal()`, `error()`, `warn()`, `info()`, `debug()`. For each of these methods, a message will be written to the file, only if the level of the log file includes that type of message. For instance, `warn()` will only write to the log file if the level of the log file is `Level.WARN`, `Level.INFO` or `Level.DEBUG`; `debug()` will only write to the log file if the level of the file is `Level.DEBUG`.

4.1.2   Configuring Log4j

There are many ways to configure Log4j; one way is to use an initialisation servlet. An initialisation servlet is different from a normal servlet. The initialisation servlet should only have its code executed once. It should never be called by the user; it should only be called by the servlet engine. To prevent users from executing the servlet, it will not have a `doGet` method.

Log File Location

One advantage of using a servlet to initialise Log4j is that the location of the actual log file can be specified using a relative reference from the root of the current web application. This allows the log file to be made portable; whenever the web application is deployed, the log file will be deployed with it. In order to retrieve the path to the root of the web application on the current computer, use the two methods `getServletContext().getRealPath()`.

The log file should never be placed in a location that can be viewed from the web. By placing the log file in the WEB-INF directory, it cannot be accessed from the web. Use the following command to specify that the log file is located in a file named *error.log* located in the *logs* subdirectory of WEB-INF. Be sure that the file already exists and is writable by the servlet engine.

```
getServletContext().getRealPath("/WEB-INF/logs/error.log")
```

Loggers

Log4j uses a class named `Logger` to encapsulate the process of writing messages to a log file. There could be many different loggers that write to the same log file. In web applications that use many different packages, it is common that many loggers will write to one log file.

There is a default logger that should be initialised when using Log4j. This logger is known as the root logger. This logger is always available. This is the logger that will record all messages that are written to any other logger. This is the only logger that needs to be defined. By defining the root logger, all messages from all packages can be recorded.

Once Log4j has been initialised, any application can retrieve a logger and write to it. The logger can be given a name, so that different parts of the same application can write to the same logger.

Helper Methods

To simplify the initialisation of Log4j, two helper methods will be created. One helper method is used to open the actual file that will contain the error messages. The other helper method will configure the object that is used to write to the file.

In order to associate an actual file with the logger, there is a class named `Appender`. An appender is created with the name of the file that will hold the error messages and the pattern to be used for each message.

The name of the file will be passed to the method. The name will be translated into a path that is relative to the root of the web application. The pattern can include many things, like the date, the method that threw the error, the error message, etc.

```
private FileAppender getAppender(String fileName) {
  RollingFileAppender appender = null;
  try {
    appender = new RollingFileAppender(
      new PatternLayout("%-5p %c %t%n%29d - %m%n"),
      getServletContext().getRealPath(fileName),
      true);
    appender.setMaxBackupIndex(5);
    appender.setMaxFileSize("1MB");
  } catch (IOException ex) {
    System.out.println(
      "Could not create appender for "
      + fileName + ":"
      + ex.getMessage());
  }
  return appender;
}
```

To initialise a logger, retrieve the logger from Log4j, using the static methods `Logger.getLogger(name)` or `Logger.getRootLogger()`. These will create the logger or return it if it had been created already. Log4j keeps track of all the loggers that have been opened.

The next steps are to set the level and the appender. A helper method has been added to the servlet for these steps.

```
private void initLogger(String name,
                        FileAppender appender,
                        Level level)
{
  Logger logger;
  if (name == null) {
    logger = Logger.getRootLogger();
  } else {
    logger = Logger.getLogger(name);
  }
  logger.setLevel(level);
  logger.addAppender(appender);
  logger.info("Starting " + logger.getName());
}
```

Init Method

In each servlet, there is a method that is executed when it is loaded into memory: init. Servlets are loaded into memory by the servlet engine when they are accessed for the first time. They remain in memory until the web application shuts down. Whenever an action needs to be executed once, then it can be placed in the init method.

With the aid of the helper methods, it is a simple matter to configure the root logger. By passing a null value as the first parameter, the helper method will create the root logger.

```
FileAppender appender = getAppender(logPath);
if (appender == null ) return;
initLogger(null, appender, Level.ERROR);
```

It is also possible to define additional loggers that can be configured differently from the root logger. By using separate loggers, it is possible to limit the number of messages from one logger, while allowing many messages from another.

For instance, in a later section of the chapter, a new package will be introduced that automates copying the request parameters to the bean. A separate logger could be opened for this package with a different level. This new logger could be set to Level.DEBUG, while the root logger is set to Level.ERROR. The new package could generate a lot of information that could be useful while debugging and the other packages in the web application would only write error messages to the log file.

```
private static final String logPath =
    "/WEB-INF/logs/error.log";
public void init() {
  FileAppender appender = getAppender(logPath);
  if (appender == null ) return;
  initLogger(null, appender, Level.ERROR);
  initLogger("org.apache.commmons.beanutils",
             appender, Level.DEBUG);
}
```

Initialisation Servlet

Putting this all together yields the initialisation servlet for Log4j. This servlet has been placed in the *shared* package. This is a package which will be used throughout the book that will contain classes that will be used by many different controllers. The complete `InitLog4j` servlet can be found in the Appendix.

```java
package shared;

import java.io.IOException;
import javax.servlet.http.HttpServlet;
import org.apache.log4j.FileAppender;
import org.apache.log4j.Level;
import org.apache.log4j.Logger;
import org.apache.log4j.PatternLayout;
import org.apache.log4j.RollingFileAppender;

public class InitLog4j extends HttpServlet {

  private static final String logPath =
    "/WEB-INF/logs/error.log";

  public void init() {
    ...
  }

  private FileAppender getAppender(String fileName) {
    ...
  }

  private void initLogger(String name,
                          FileAppender appender,
                          Level level)
  {
    ...
  }
}
```

Since this servlet does not have a `doGet` method, there is no way to call it from the web. The servlet needs to be called by the web application when the web application starts. This can be accomplished by modifying the *web.xml*.

A servlet definition will be created for the servlet in the *web.xml* file. There is a tag named `load-on-startup` that tells the servlet engine to start the associated servlet whenever the web application starts.

```xml
...
<servlet>
  <servlet-name>InitLog4j</servlet-name>
  <servlet-class>shared.InitLog4j</servlet-class>
  <load-on-startup>1</load-on-startup>
</servlet>
...
```

By removing the doGet method from the servlet, adding an init method and configuring the servlet to load when the servlet engine starts, the initialisation servlet will only be run once and cannot be accessed by the user. No servlet mapping will be created for the initialisation servlet.

4.1.3   Retrieving the Logger

The helper base class has been renamed HelperBaseCh4 and has been placed in the *shared* package. Each of the next three chapters will add features to the helper base, so there will be a distinct helper base for each chapter: HelperBaseCh4, HelperBaseCh5 and HelperBaseCh6. They have been placed into the *shared* package because they do not contain specific details for any controller helper and can be accessed from any package.

A variable for a logger will be added to the application. Since the logger is the same for all controllers, it will be placed in the helper base class. It will be declared as a member variable that will be initialised when the helper base class is created. The helper base class now has three member variables: request, response, logger (Figure 4.1). Each is initialised in the constructor.

To initialise the logger, call the static method Logger.getLogger with an arbitrary name. This will create a new logger that is inherited from the root logger, so it will use the same appender that the root logger uses. It is also possible to change the level of the new logger, without changing the level of the root logger.

```
. . .
protected HttpServletRequest request;
protected HttpServletResponse response;
protected Logger logger;

public HelperBaseCh4(HttpServletRequest request,
    HttpServletResponse response) {
  this.request = request;
  this.response = response;
  logger = Logger.getLogger("bytesizebook.webdev");
  logger.setLevel(Level.DEBUG);
}
. . .
```

Once it is retrieved into a member variable, the logger can be accessed from any method in the controller helper and helper base classes. There are five methods to write errors with a specific level:

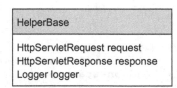

Figure 4.1 Add the logger to the helper base class.

1. `logger.debug("message");`
2. `logger.info("message");`
3. `logger.warn("message");`
4. `logger.error("message");`
5. `logger.fatal("message");`

Use these to write a message with a given severity level to the log file. Only those messages that have the same or higher severity as the level of the logger will be written to the file.

The next few sections will all use the logger to write error messages to the log file.

4.2   Eliminating Hidden Fields

In the *Reorganised Controller* example from Chapter Three, the controller helper is saved in the session and can be accessed from a JSP using the EL statement of `${helper}`. The controller helper has a member variable for the bean that contains the user's data. Because there is also a `getData` method, the data in the bean can also be retrieved in a JSP using the EL statement of `${helper.data}`. The fact that the helper is in the session has an added benefit: the JSPs no longer need hidden fields to pass data from one page to the next.

The session attributes exist as long as the user does not close the browser and continues to interact with the controller. The information that is in the controller helper is available for the JSPs to access. Furthermore, the information will still be available the next time the controller is called during the same session. The controller helper for the next request only needs to retrieve the data that is in the session (Figure 4.2).

Consider how the data is stored in the session and retrieved from the session.

1. The controller helper has a bean that contains the data that was entered by the user.
2. The controller helper writes itself to the session so that the JSPs can access it. The data bean can also be accessed.

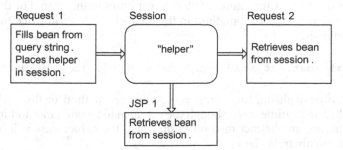

Figure 4.2 The data is always available from the session.

3. The hidden fields were used to store this data and send it back to the application when a form button was clicked.

4. The data that is in the session was used to initialise the values in the hidden fields. This means that the data that the hidden fields are sending back to the controller is identical to the data that is already in the session.

5. Since the data is in the session and the session exists from request to request, the hidden fields are no longer needed.

6. The controller helper for the next request can retrieve the data from the session, instead of from the query string.

4.2.1 Retrieving Data from the Session

Each time a new request is made, the controller helper is added to the session. If there is already a controller helper in the session, then it should be retrieved and its data should be copied into the current controller helper. A method will be added to the helper base class to do this: addHelperToSession. Every time this method is called, the current controller helper will be saved in the session. This method will have two parameters that control how the session is accessed.

There may be times when the application creates a new helper, but does not want to retrieve the previous one from the session. For this reason, the method will have a parameter that will control if the old helper in the session is accessed. If it is not accessed, then the data from the previous helper will not be copied into the current helper.

There may be times when helpers from different applications are saved in the session at the same time. To allow this, there is an additional parameter to the addHelperToSession method that specifies the name that is used to save the object in the session.

Helper Base: Eliminating Hidden Fields

Three modifications need to be made to the helper base class to eliminate the need for hidden fields.

If there is a controller helper in the session with the correct name, then its values will be copied to the current helper. This requires an additional method named copyFromSession. This method should not be defined in the base class, since it needs to know the names of all the properties in the bean. For this reason, it is declared as an abstract method in the base class; this will force the derived class to define it.

```
protected abstract void copyFromSession(Object helper);
```

Through polymorphism, the copyFromSession method in the derived class will be called at runtime, even though the call is made from a method in the base class. By having an abstract method in the class, the helper base will have to be declared as an abstract class.

```
public abstract class HelperBaseCh4 {
   ...
}
```

The next listing contains the code for the `addHelperToSession` method that
checks the session for previous data and adds the current helper to the session.
There are two parameters to this method: the name to use to retrieve the data and
a parameter that indicates if any previous data in the session should initialise the
current helper. The method makes a polymorphic call to the `copyFromSession`
method, which will be resolved at runtime to a method in the derived controller
helper.

```
...
public void addHelperToSession(String name,
                               SessionData state) {
  if (SessionData.READ == state) {
    Object sessionObj =
       request.getSession().getAttribute(name);
    if (sessionObj != null) {
      copyFromSession(sessionObj);
    }
  }
  request.getSession().setAttribute(name, this);
}
...
```

The first parameter to this method is a string that identifies the object that is
placed in the session. This name should be unique. If the same name is used for
different controllers that are running at the same time, then each controller will
erase the data from the other controller. By having unique names, more than one
object can be stored in the session. Each controller would use its name to retrieve
its object from the session.

With that said, all of the controller helpers in this book will always use the name
helper for the session object. The reason for this is that each controller that is
developed is an extension of the controllers before it. These controllers are not
intended to run at the same time. If these controllers were designed to run at
the same time, then each one should use a different name when adding data to
the session.

The second parameter to this method is an enumeration type named
`SessionData` and has the values READ and IGNORE (Figure 4.3). When the
old helper in the session should be used to initialise the current helper, call

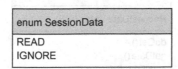

Figure 4.3 The `SessionData` enumeration.

addHelperToSession with the value SessionData.READ. If this is the
start of a new request and the old session helper should not be used to initialise
the current helper, then call addHelperToSession with the value Session-
Data.IGNORE.

Controller Helper: Eliminating Hidden Fields

There are two modifications to the controller helper to eliminate the need for
hidden fields. The copyFromSession method is defined and the doGet method
must be modified so that it always updates the session with itself and checks the
session for old data.

The copyFromSession method must be defined in every controller helper
that extends the helper base class. The helper base is now an abstract class. Every
class that extends it must implement its abstract method. The helper base and
controller helper class diagrams are listed in Figure 4.4. Both classes define the
copyFromSession method. In the base class, it is an abstract method. In the
extended class, it must be implemented.

For example, the controller that will be developed in this chapter defines a
copyFromSession method that sets the bean for the controller helper to the
bean that was found in the session.

```java
public void copyFromSession(Object sessionHelper) {
  if (sessionHelper.getClass() == this.getClass()) {
    data = ((ControllerHelper)sessionHelper).data;
  }
}
```

It is necessary to test that the controller helper that is in the session has the same
type as the controller helper for the current application. It is possible that there is

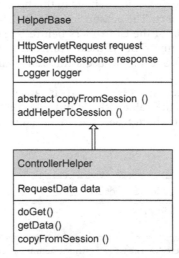

Figure 4.4 The copyFromSession method is defined in the helper base and controller helper.

a helper from a previous application in the session that was stored with the same name as the helper for the current application. By testing the type, a class cast exception is avoided.

The doGet method in the controller helper will be modified to call the addHelperToSession method. It should be called every time a request is made so that any previous values can be retrieved and to add the current bean to the session. For now, call this method with SessionData.READ.

```
...
protected void doGet()
throws ServletException, IOException
{
  addHelperToSession("helper", SessionData.READ);
...
```

By calling this method for each request, the JSPs no longer need to have hidden fields. This simplifies the JSPs. However, hidden fields still have an advantage over the session data: hidden fields never expire. There may be times when a hidden field will be more useful than using the session.

4.3   Specifying the Location of the JSPs

In the *Data Bean* controller, from Chapter Three, the JSPs were in a directory that was visible from the web and the controller was mapped to that directory; a relative reference could be used to specify the address of the JSPs, since the controller was mapped to the same directory.

```
if (request.getParameter("processButton") != null)
{
  address = "Process.jsp";
}
else if (request.getParameter("confirmButton") != null)
{
  address = "Confirm.jsp";
}
else
{
  address = "Edit.jsp";
}
```

In the *Default Validate* controller, from Chapter Three, the JSPs were in a visible directory that was different from the directory where the controller was mapped; a path had to be added to the address of the JSP, since the controller was not mapped to the directory of the JSPs.

```
if (request.getParameter("processButton") != null)
{
  address = "/ch3/dataBean/Process.jsp";
}
else if (request.getParameter("confirmButton") != null)
{
```

```
  address = "/ch3/dataBean/Confirm.jsp";
}
else
{
  address = "/ch3/dataBean/Edit.jsp";
}
```

In this example, if the location of the JSPs were changed, this would require modifying several lines of code. A more efficient solution is to encapsulate the path to the JSPs in a helper method. By adding a method to the bean that generates the location of the JSPs, it is easy to modify the application in the future if the JSPs are moved (Figure 4.5).

The method has one parameter that is the file name of the next JSP. The method will append this name to the path of the JSPs. By adding the path in a separate method, it will be easier to move the JSPs in the future.

```
protected String jspLocation(String page) {
  return "/ch3/dataBean/" + page;
}
```

The path should not include the name of the web application. The controller cannot access paths outside the web application, so the name of the web application is assumed.

The address of each JSP that is used in the bean must use this method to generate the address of the JSP.

```
if (request.getParameter("processButton") != null)
{
    address = jspLocation("Process.jsp");
}
else if (request.getParameter("confirmButton") != null)
{
    address = jspLocation("Confirm.jsp");
}
else
{
    address = jspLocation("Edit.jsp)";
}
```

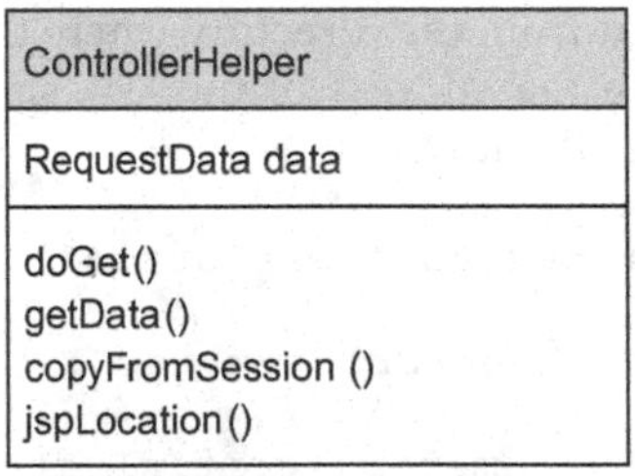

ControllerHelper
RequestData data
doGet() getData() copyFromSession () jspLocation()

Figure 4.5 The jspLocation method is added to the controller helper.

Table 4.1 The relationship between the servlet mapping and the location of the JSPs.

URL Pattern	JSP Location
/ch2/servletController/Controller	/ch2/servletController/Edit.jsp
/ch3/startExample/Controller	/ch3/startExample/Edit.jsp
/ch3/dataBean/Controller	/ch3/dataBean/Edit.jsp

In the future, if the location of the JSPs is changed, then only the return value of this method needs to be changed in order to update the controller helper.

Let's see how to use this method when the JSPs are in a visible directory, a hidden directory and the same physical directory as the controller.

4.3.1   JSPs in the Directory Where the Controller Is Mapped

If the JSPs are in a visible directory and the controller is mapped to that directory, then return the parameter that was passed to the jspLocation method.

```
protected String jspLocation(String page) {
  return page;
}
```

This will look for the JSP in the same directory where the controller is mapped.

The controller's *.class* file is not visible from the web, which is why a servlet mapping is created in the *web.xml* for the controller. The servlet mapping defines a URL that is visible from the web that can be used to access the controller. If the directory of this URL is also a physical directory in the web application, then the JSPs can be placed in that directory and a relative reference can be used to specify the URL of the JSPs. This is the technique that has been used for all controllers before the *Default Validate* controller (Table 4.1).

In each case, the path that was used in the URL pattern for the controller is the same as the path to the edit page. Since the directory for the servlet mapping and the directory for the JSPs are the same, the URL of the JSP can be specified by using the name of the JSP only.

4.3.2   JSPs in a Different Visible Directory

If the JSPs are in a visible directory, but not in the same directory as where the controller is mapped, then append the name of the page to the path to the JSPs. This path must start with a slash, which represents the root of the web application. Do not include the name of the web application in the path.

For example, in the *Default Validate* controller, the controller was mapped to the URL /ch3/defaultValidate/Controller, but the JSPs were located in the /ch3/dataBean/ directory. The method would return this path:

```
protected String jspLocation(String page) {
  return "/ch3/dataBean/" + page;
}
```

4.3.3   JSPs in a Hidden Directory

If the JSPs are not in a visible directory, then it will always be necessary to return the full path to the JSPs.

The WEB-INF directory cannot be accessed from the web. By placing the JSPs in this directory they cannot be accessed directly from the web, they can only be accessed through the servlet. The servlet has access to all the files and directories in the web application.

For example, if the JSPs are located in WEB-INF as

```
WEB-INF/Edit.jsp
WEB-INF/Confirm.jsp
WEB-INF/Process.jsp
```

then they cannot be accessed from the web. By setting the base path to /WEB-INF/ in the *jspLocation* method, the servlet will be able to access the JSPs.

```
protected String jspLocation(String page) {
  return "/WEB-INF/" + page;
}
```

4.3.4   JSPs in the Controller's Directory

We can take this concept one step further and place the JSPs in the same physical directory as the controller.

```
protected String jspLocation(String page) {
  return "/WEB-INF/classes/ch3/defaultValidateHidden/" + page;
}
```

This has advantages and disadvantages. One advantage is that applications will be easier to develop. It will not be necessary to change to different directories to edit the files that are in the application. One disadvantage is that if there are JSP developers and servlet developers, then they would each have access to all the files. This might not be acceptable. It might be better to place the JSPs in one directory and the servlet in another directory.

4.3.5   Where Should JSPs Be Located?

By creating the *jspLocation* method in the controller, it is easy to modify the location of the JSPs. However, this raises the question of where the JSPs should be placed. The answer to this question depends on your development needs.

Single Developer

If there is only one developer who is maintaining the JSPs and the controller, then it is easier to place the JSPs in the same directory as the controller's *.class* file. This is the approach that will be used for the remainder of this book.

HTML Developer and Controller Developer

> If there are separate developers for HTML and for the controller, then the JSPs should be kept in a separate directory from the controller's *.class* file. This would allow the system administrator to allow different access permissions to the different directories.

Visible versus Hidden

> It is recommended to have the JSPs in a hidden directory. The intent of the controller is that all requests should be made to the controller and that the controller will forward the request to the proper JSP. If the JSPs are in a directory that is visible from the web, then it would be possible for a user to circumvent the controller and access the pages directly; this could result in unexpected results.

4.4 Controller Logic

Every controller needs to translate the button that the user clicked into the address for the next JSP. Each controller has a series of nested if statements that do this translation.

```
. . .
if (request.getParameter("processButton") != null)
{
  address = "Process.jsp";
}
else if (request.getParameter("confirmButton") != null)
{
  address = "Confirm.jsp";
}
else
{
  address = "Edit.jsp";
}
. . .
```

This is the logic for the simplest controller. However, in addition to calculating the next address, there will usually be tasks to perform when different buttons are clicked. The following listing is an example of a more complicated controller.

```
if (request.getParameter("processButton") != null)
{
  hibernateHelper.updateDB(data);
  request.setAttribute(
      "database",
      hibernateHelper.getListData(RequestData.class));
  address = jspLocation("Process.jsp");
}
else if (request.getParameter("confirmButton") != null)
{
```

```
  fillBeanFromRequest(data);
  String address;
  if (isValid(data)) {
    address = jspLocation("Confirm.jsp");
  } else {
    address = jspLocation("Edit.jsp");
  }
}
else
{
  address = jspLocation("Edit.jsp");
}
```

A more organised solution would be to write a separate method for each button. In the method, the next address would be calculated and the tasks for that button would be executed (Listing 4.1).

```
public String processMethod() {
  hibernateHelper.updateDB(data);
  request.setAttribute(
      "database",
      hibernateHelper.getListData(RequestData.class));
  return jspLocation("Process.jsp");
}

public String confirmMethod() {
  fillBeanFromRequest(data);
  String address;
  if (isValid(data)) {
      address = "Confirm.jsp";
  } else {
      address = "Edit.jsp";
  }
  return jspLocation(address);
}

public String editMethod() {
  return jspLocation("Edit.jsp");
}

protected void doGet()
throws ServletException, java.io.IOException
{
  updateSession("helper", SessionData.READ);

  if (request.getParameter("processButton") != null)
  {
    address = processMethod();
  }
  else if (request.getParameter("confirmButton") != null)
  {
    address = confirmMethod();
  }
  else
```

```
{
  address = editMethod();
}

request.getRequestDispatcher(address)
    .forward(request, response);
}
```

Listing 4.1 A more organised controller helper.

4.4.1 Java Annotations

Java annotations are new in JDK 1.5. Annotations are used to mark up the Java code. Before there were annotations, separate configuration files were used to define how a package would be initialised. With annotations, the statements that were in a configuration file can now be placed in the Java code itself. Annotations make it easier to configure a package.

Annotations start with the @ symbol. There are annotations for classes, for methods and for variables. Each annotation can have optional parameters. The annotation must precede what it modifies.

Extending Listing 4.1 and using annotations, it is now possible to automate the nested if block and place it into the helper base class. The idea is to mark each method with an annotation that associates the name of the button with the method and to replace the nested if block with a call to a method that loops through the button names in the annotations, looking for the one that matches the user's choice.

```
@ButtonMethod(buttonName="processButton")
public String processMethod() {
  hibernateHelper.updateDB(data);
  request.setAttribute(
      "database",
      hibernateHelper.getListData(RequestData.class);
  return jspLocation("Process.jsp");
}


@ButtonMethod(buttonName="confirmButton")
public String confirmMethod() {
  fillBeanFromRequest(data);
  String address;
  if (isValid(data)) {
    address = "Confirm.jsp";
  } else {
    address = "Edit.jsp";
  }
  return jspLocation(address);
}


@ButtonMethod(buttonName="editButton", isDefault=true)
public String editMethod() {
  return jspLocation("Edit.jsp");
}
```

```
protected void doGet()
throws ServletException, java.io.IOException {
  updateSession("helper", SessionData.READ);

  String address = executeButtonMethod();

  request.getRequestDispatcher(address)
     .forward(request, response);
}
```

The annotations must precede the method that they modify. The annotations contain information about the method. In this example, the annotation is named @ButtonMethod. The intent of the annotation is to associate the name of a button with the method, so that the method can be called whenever that button is clicked. The executeButtonMethod will determine which method to call.

Two attributes can be included in the annotation: *buttonName* and *isDefault*. Set the *buttonName* attribute to the name that appears in the form element in the JSP for the button. The name of the button in the form element must agree with the *buttonName* attribute.

For example, the following form element is a submit button with a name of *confirmButton*.

```
<input type="submit" name="confirmButton"
                      value="Confirm">
```

In order to associate the above button with a method in the controller helper, annotate a method with the ButtonMethod annotation and set the value of the *buttonName* attribute to *confirmButton*.

```
@ButtonMethod(buttonName="confirmButton")
public String confirmMethod() {
   ...
}
```

Set the *isDefault* attribute to the boolean value *true* if this is the method that should be called when no button has been clicked. One of the button methods should be marked as the default. Do not include *true* in quotes, it must be a boolean value.

4.4.2   Executing the Correct Button Method

The work of calling the correct method is relegated to the helper base class. A new method named executeButtonMethod will be added to the helper base class (Figure 4.6).

Reflection is used to retrieve all the methods in the controller helper and look for those that are marked with the ButtonMethod annotation. If an annotated method is found and its ButtonName attribute is found in the query string parameters, then the method is executed. The essential details are contained in the next listing.

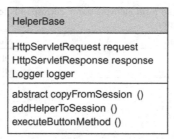

Figure 4.6 The `executeButtonMethod` method is added to the helper base class.

```
Method[] methods = clazz.getDeclaredMethods();
for(Method method : methods) {
  ButtonMethod annotation =
      method.getAnnotation(ButtonMethod.class);
  if (annotation != null) {
    if (request.getParameter(annotation.buttonName())
           != null)
    {
      result = invokeButtonMethod(method);
      break;
    }
  }
}
```

The innermost if should look familiar. It is testing for the presence of a button name in the query string. This is exactly what the nested if in the first controller did. This method automates this by using a loop. In order to handle a new button in the controller helper, all that is needed is an annotated method that performs the tasks for that button.

4.5 Filling a Bean

In all controllers up to this point, the mutators for each property in the bean needed to be called in order to copy the data from the request into the bean.

```
data.setHobby(request.getParameter("hobby"));
data.setAversion(request.getParameter("aversion"));
```

Wouldn't it be nice if someone would write a Java package that would automate this process?

There is an extension to Java that allows all the information from the request to be sent to the bean. This extension will call the mutators automatically.

It is important that the name of the form element corresponds to the name of the mutator. To determine what the name of the form element should be, take the name of the mutator and remove the word *set*, then change the first letter to lowercase. If the names do not correspond correctly, then the data will not be copied from the request to the bean.

Table 4.2 The form element name corresponds to the name of the mutator.

Element Name	Mutator
value	setValue
longName	setLongName

Table 4.2 shows the relationship between the name of a form element and the name of the corresponding mutator.

In order to have the mutators called automatically for all data that is in the query string, include the following JAR files into the *lib* directory of the web application. These can be downloaded from http://bytesizebook.com/jar or the latest versions can be downloaded from http://jakarta.apache.org/commons/.

```
commons-collections-2.1.1.jar
commons-logging-1.0.4.jar
commons-beanutils.jar
```

The magical method that calls all the mutators is named populate and is located in the org.apache.beanutils.BeanUtils package. It has two parameters: the bean to fill and a map that contains the data from the query string.

```
org.apache.commons.beanutils.BeanUtils.
    populate(data, request.getParameterMap());
```

The method can throw several exceptions, so it is best to place the call inside a method that can catch any errors.

```
public void fillBeanFromRequest(Object data) {
  try {
    org.apache.commons.beanutils.BeanUtils.
        populate(data, request.getParameterMap());
  } catch (IllegalAccessException iae) {
    logger.error("Populate - Illegal Access.", iae);
  } catch (InvocationTargetException ite) {
    logger.error("Populate - Invocation Target.", ite);
  }
}
```

If there is an exception, a message is written to the logger. In addition to these messages, if BeanUtils encounters an error, it will also write a message to the log file via its own logger org.apache.commons.beanutils.ConvertUtils. This logger was also declared in the *InitLog4j* servlet.

This method receives the data as an Object. This means that the method does not have access to any specific information about the bean. All that this method knows is that an object has been passed to it. For this reason, the method can be added to the helper base class (Figure 4.7).

Now that the session is being used to retrieve previous values entered by the user, the values from the request only need to be added to the bean when the values

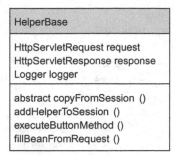

Figure 4.7 The fillBeanFromRequest method is added to the helper base class.

change. In other words, the only time that this method needs to be called is when there are visible form elements that can be changed by the user. In the current example, this only happens when the user clicks the button named *confirmButton*. Using annotations, the only method that needs to call fillBeanFromRequest is the method that corresponds to the confirm button. No other pages have visible form elements.

```
@ButtonMethod(buttonName="confirmButton")
public String confirmMethod() {
  fillBeanFromRequest(data);
  return jspLocation("Confirm.jsp");
}
```

4.6   Application: Enhanced Controller

All of the above enhancements will now be combined into a controller application.

1. The controller and controller helper classes will be placed in the *ch4.enhanced* package.
2. The JSPs will be placed in the same directory as the controller.
3. It makes no difference what the URL pattern is for the controller, since the controller specifies the path to the JSPs. For simplicity, the controller has been mapped to */ch4/enhanced/Controller*.
4. Classes that are shared by many controllers have been placed in the *shared* package.

Figure 4.8 shows the directory structure and file locations for this application.

4.6.1   JSPs: Enhanced Controller

The JSPs are similar to the JSPs from the *Reorganised Controller* in Chapter Three, except all of the hidden fields have been removed from the process and confirm pages. All the JSPs have been placed in the controller's directory.

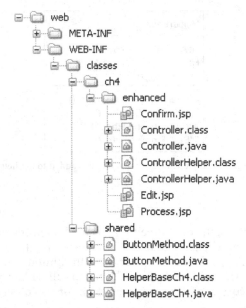

Figure 4.8 The location of files for the Enhanced Controller.

4.6.2   ControllerHelper: Enhanced Controller

The controller helper is extended from the helper base class from this chapter. The complete listing for the helper base class for Chapter Four is in the Appendix. The controller helper will do the following:

1. use a bean to encapsulate the data from the user;
2. use a logger to record any errors;
3. eliminate hidden fields;
4. use a method to specify that the JSPs are in the same directory as the controller;
5. use annotations to execute a method based on the button the user clicked;
6. automatically copy the query string data into the bean.

The complete listing of the controller helper is in Listing 4.2.

```
package ch4.enhanced;

import java.io.IOException;
import javax.servlet.http.HttpServletRequest;
import javax.servlet.http.HttpServletResponse;
import javax.servlet.ServletException;
import shared.ButtonMethod;
import shared.HelperBaseCh4;
import org.apache.log4j.Level;
import org.apache.log4j.Logger;
```

```java
import ch3.defaultValidate.RequestDataDefault;

public class ControllerHelper extends HelperBaseCh4 {

  private RequestDataDefault data =
    new RequestDataDefault();

  public ControllerHelper(HttpServletRequest request,
                          HttpServletResponse response) {
    super(request, response);
  }

  public Object getData() {
    return data;
  }

  public void copyFromSession(Object sessionHelper) {
    if (sessionHelper.getClass() == this.getClass()) {
      data = ((ControllerHelper)sessionHelper).data;
    }
  }

  protected String jspLocation(String page) {
    return "/WEB-INF/classes/ch4/enhanced/" + page;
  }

  @ButtonMethod(buttonName="editButton", isDefault=true)
  public String editMethod() {
    return jspLocation("Edit.jsp");
  }

  @ButtonMethod(buttonName="confirmButton")
  public String confirmMethod() {
    fillBeanFromRequest(data);
    return jspLocation("Confirm.jsp");
  }

  @ButtonMethod(buttonName="processButton")
  public String processMethod() {
    return jspLocation("Process.jsp");
  }

  protected void doGet()
  throws ServletException, IOException
  {
    addHelperToSession("helper", SessionData.READ);

    String address = executeButtonMethod();

    request.getRequestDispatcher(address)
      .forward(request, response);
  }

}
```

Listing 4.2 Enhanced Controller Helper.

The application uses the bean that was developed in the *Default Validate* controller, RequestDataDefault. The class for the bean is imported so that it is easier to reference the class.

The ButtonMethod class is needed to annotate the methods that are associated with button names. This class will be used by all controllers that are developed later in the book. It has been placed in a package named *shared*. This package will be used to hold classes that might be used by all controllers. The HelperBaseCh4 class has also been added to the *shared* package, as it can be used by all controllers. Both of these classes have been imported in the controller helper.

The jspLocation method returns the full path for each JSP. This means that the JSPs for this application should be placed in the directory of the controller. It also means that the JSPs cannot be accessed directly from the web; they can only be accessed through the controller.

Each button that the user can click has a corresponding method that has been annotated with the name of the button. The edit method has also been set as the default method, in the case that the user does not click a button.

The copyFromSession method is the implementation of the abstract method that was declared in the helper base class. The copyFromSession method is needed to copy session information into the current controller helper. There is only one member variable in the controller helper that needs to be copied. The parameter is passed as an object, so it must be cast to the type of the current class in order to access the data variable. If the parameter is not the correct type, then the data in the session will be ignored.

4.6.3   Controller: Enhanced Controller

The controller is simplified; it only needs to create the controller helper and call its doGet method (Listing 4.3).

```
package ch4.enhanced;

import java.io.IOException;
import javax.servlet.ServletException;
import javax.servlet.http.HttpServlet;
import javax.servlet.http.HttpServletRequest;
import javax.servlet.http.HttpServletResponse;

public class Controller extends HttpServlet {

    protected void doGet(HttpServletRequest request,
                         HttpServletResponse response)
    throws ServletException, IOException {
        ControllerHelper helper =
            new ControllerHelper(request, response);
        helper.doGet();
    }
}
```

Listing 4.3 Enhanced Controller Helper.

Try It   http://bytesizebook.com/book/ch4/enhanced/Controller

This application looks the same as the others, but it is now using a controller helper.

4.7   Libraries in NetBeans

JAR files are added to the *Libraries* folder of a NetBeans project. When the project is built, all the JAR files are copied into the corresponding *lib* directory of the web application structure.

4.7.1   Libraries

To add JAR files to your web application, follow these steps.

1. Download the JAR files to your computer.
2. From an open NetBeans project, right-click on the project name in the Projects tab.
3. Select Properties.
4. Select Libraries.
5. Click the Add Jar/Folder button.
6. Navigate to the directory where the downloaded JAR files are.
7. Select all the JAR files you want to include in the web application.

Every JAR that is added to the Libraries folder will be added to the CLASSPATH variable, automatically.

4.8   Summary

From now on, all controllers will have a helper class to facilitate performing the controller's tasks. All controller applications perform similar tasks. Some of these tasks use objects that are the same for all controllers; these objects can be stored in the base class. Other tasks require the details of the current application; these belong in the helper class. In this chapter, many of these common tasks were explored.

There are tasks that are common to all controllers: creating a logger, eliminating hidden fields, automating the controller logic and filling the bean. These tasks have been implemented so that they do not access any of the individual data members of the bean, so they can be placed in the base class. All controller helpers that are extended from the base class will have access to these features. The base class has been placed in the *shared* package, so that all future controller helpers can have access to it.

The tasks that require the knowledge of the current application are specifying the location of the JSPs and copying the data from one bean to another. The copyFromSession method is needed so that hidden fields can be eliminated; the data from the session must be copied into the current bean. These tasks were added to the controller helper.

4.9   Chapter Review

Terms

1. Logger
2. Logger Path
3. Logger Name
4. Logger Initialisation Servlet
5. Initialisation Parameter
6. Session
7. Annotations
8. ButtonMethod Annotation
   a. buttonName
   b. isDefault
9. Default Value
10. Filling a Bean

New Java

1. `Logger.getLogger`
2. `Logger.fatal`
3. `Logger.error`
4. `Logger.warn`
5. `Logger.info`
6. `Logger.debug`
7. `Level.FATAL`
8. `Level.ERROR`
9. `Level.WARN`
10. `Level.INFO`
11. `Level.DEBUG`
12. `addHelperToSession(name, SessionData)`
13. `jspLocation`
14. `exceutButtonMethod`
15. `request.getParameter(btnMethod.buttonName()) != null`
16. `fillBeanFromRequest`
17. Enumerations
    a. SessionData {READ, IGNORE}

Tags

1. `<load-on-startup>`
2. `<init-param>`
3. `<param-name>`
4. `<param-value>`

Questions

1. How are additional packages added to a web application?
2. Why was a method added to the servlet that returns the path to a JSP?
3. Explain how the level of the logger controls the number of messages that are written to the log file.
4. Explain how hidden fields can be removed from an application.
5. Explain what the parameters to `addHelperToSession` do.
6. What should `jspLocation` return if the JSPs are located in the directory where the servlet is mapped?
7. What should `jspLocation` return if the JSPs are located in the same directory as the servlet class?
8. Explain what the `ButtonMethod` annotation does. Explain what the parameters do.
9. Explain what `executeButtonMethod` does.
10. Write the Java code that will test if the button named *confirmButton* is in the query string.
11. Write the Java code that will copy the data from the query string into the bean.

Tasks

1. Use a logger, named *com.bytesizebook.test*, to write five different messages to the log file. Each message should have a different error level.
2. For the *InitLog4j* servlet, look up the PatternLayout class and investigate the constructor. Determine what each character means in the layout. Devise a new layout for your error messages.
3. Implement the *Enhanced Controller* in your own web application. Modify the JSPs to use your own fields, with names other than *hobby* and *aversion*. Create a bean that corresponds to your data. Modify the controller helper so that it uses your bean and your data.

5 Hibernate

Two very important processes are needed in any web site: data validation and data persistence. Both of these can be automated with a package named Hibernate.

Default validation was introduced in Chapter Three. Required validation will be introduced in this chapter. Validation is so important that there is a part of standard Java that can simplify it: regular expressions. Hibernate will use regular expressions to perform sophisticated required validation on string data.

Data persistence is the process of saving data to a database. Hibernate makes this a simple task by letting the developer work only with the bean and not with SQL statements. When data is retrieved from the database, it will be in the form of a collection of beans.

5.1 Required Validation

Default validation is used to supply a value for a property that the user left blank. It is up to the developer to choose a reasonable default value, because not all properties have an obvious default. An area code could have a default value of the local area code, but a bank account number does not have a good default value. In the latter case, it is better to inform the user that something is missing and allow the user to supply the missing data; this is known as *required validation*.

In our application, if there is invalid data, then the user will remain on the edit page. Only when all the data is valid can the user proceed to the confirm page (Figure 5.1).

Required validation should be done every time the user enters new data. It should also be done before data is entered into a database. Since the session is being used to store data, there is the possibility that the session expires and all the data is lost. In such a case, it would be a mistake to enter empty data into the database.

One of the most powerful tools for performing required validation on string data is regular expressions.

5.1.1 Regular Expressions

Validation is such a common task that there is an entire language dedicated to declaring patterns that can be used to test the format of a string. This language is

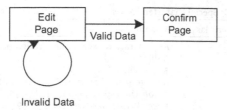

Invalid Data

Figure 5.1 The application will remain on the edit page until valid data is entered.

known as *regular expressions*. Regular expressions are strings that contain wild-cards, special characters and escape sequences. For example, a regular expression can be used to test if a string is a valid zip code, user ID or social security number. A regular expression can also be used to test if a string matches an integer or a double, but this can be done more easily by parsing the string to the desired type and catching an exception if the parsing fails.

A sequence of regular expression characters is known as a pattern. The following patterns can be used to test for a valid Zip Code, SSN and User ID, respectively.

Zip Code: \d{5}(?:-\d{4})?

SSN: \d{3}([-]?)\d{2}\1\d{4}

User ID: [a-zA-Z]{3,5}[a-zA-Z0-9]?\d{2}

These probably look very strange and cryptic now, but soon they will be very clear.

Character Classes

Square brackets define a *character class*. The character class pattern will match any single character that is in the brackets. For instance, the class [xyz] will match *x*, *y* or *z*, but only one of them. If the class starts with ^, then it will match all characters that are not listed inside the brackets.

A hyphen can be used to include a range of characters: [a-z] will match any lowercase letter. More than one hyphen can be used: [a-zA-Z] will match any letter. The order of letters is based on the ASCII numbering system for characters. This means that [a-Z] (lowercase *a* - uppercase *Z*) will not match any letters because lowercase *a* has a higher ASCII number than uppercase *Z*. [A-z] will match all letters, but will also match some additional symbols, since the symbols [\]^_' have ASCII numbers between uppercase *Z* and lowercase *a*.

[abc] *a, b* or *c* (simple class)

[^abc] any character except *a, b* or *c* (negation)

[a-zA-Z] *a* through *z* or *A* through *Z*, inclusive (range)

Predefined Character Classes

Some character classes are used so often that there are special characters and escape sequences for them. Table 5.1 lists the special classes with their meaning.

Table 5.1 Special character classes.

Character Class	Meaning
.	Any character, except line terminators
\d	A digit: [0-9]
\D	A non-digit: [^0-9]
\s	A whitespace character: [\t\n\x0B\f\r]
\S	A non-whitespace character: [^\s]
\w	A word character: [a-zA-Z_0-9]
\W	A non-word character: [^\w]

Repetition

Table 5.2 lists special characters and operators that indicate that the previous pattern could be repeated or that the previous pattern is optional.

Alternation

Character classes allow for the selection of a single character, but do not allow for the choice amongst different words. In this case the operator | is used to indicate alternation. For example yes|no would match the word *yes* or the word *no*. This can be extended for as many choices as are needed: yes|no|maybe will match the word *yes*, *no* or *maybe*, but only one of them.

Grouping and Capturing

It is possible to use parentheses to group several patterns into one pattern. A group can then have repetition sequences applied to it. For example, (a[0-5]b)+ will match *a0b*, *a1b*, *a5ba0ba4b* and many more.

There are two types of parentheses: (pattern) and (?:pattern). The first type will capture what was matched inside the parentheses; the second is non-capturing and is only used for grouping.

If the capturing parentheses are used, then the pattern that was matched can be retrieved later in the regular expression. Retrieve a captured value with

Table 5.2 Repetition symbols.

Repetition Symbol	Meaning
*	Matches zero or more occurrences of the preceding pattern. This means that the preceding pattern might not be in the pattern or it might appear repeatedly, in sequence.
?	Matches zero or one occurrence of the preceding pattern. This means that if the pattern is in the string, then it appears once, but that it might not be there at all.
+	Matches one or more occurrences. This is like *, except that the pattern must appear at least once.
{m,n}	Specifies a range of times that the pattern can repeat. It will appear at least *m* times in sequence, but no more than *n* times. The character ? is the same as {0,1}.
{m}	Specifies that the preceding pattern will match exactly *m* times.
{m,}	Specifies that the preceding pattern will match at least *m* times. The character * is the same as {0,}. The character + is the same as {1,}.

\1 ... \9. The number refers to the order that the parentheses in the regular expression were evaluated. Up to nine different patterns can be captured and accessed in a regular expression.

If the string *aabyesbb* were matched against the pattern `([ab]+)(yes|no).*`, then \1 would be *aab* and \2 would be *yes*.

Ignoring Case

It is possible to ignore the case of the letters that are being tested. For example, if the word *yes* is a valid response, then all variations of case should also be accepted, like *YES* and *Yes*. Entering all the possible combinations could be done like `[yY][eE][sS]`, but there is an easier way. If the regular expression starts with the symbols `(?i)`, then the case of the response will not be considered. The expression `(?i)yes|no` is the same as `[yY][eE][sS]|[Nn][Oo]`.

Examples Explained

It is now possible to explain the meaning of the patterns that were mentioned at the start of this section. Three patterns were introduced: one for a zip code, one for a social security number and one for a user identification number.

A zip code has two formats: five digits or five digits, a hyphen and four more digits. The pattern for the zip code was `\d{5}(?:-\d{4})?`. This indicates that the pattern starts with five digits. The 5 within the braces indicates that the previous pattern should match five times. The previous pattern is a digit. Together, this means that there should be five digits.

A non-capturing parenthesis is used to group the next part of the pattern. The question mark at the end of the closing parenthesis indicates that the entire group is optional. The pattern within the group is a hyphen followed by four digits.

A social security number is nine digits. Typically, the digits are written in two different ways: as nine digits or as three digits, a hyphen, two digits, another hyphen and four more digits.

The pattern for the social security number was `\d{3}(-?)\d{2}\1\d{4}`. The pattern starts with three digits. After the first three digits, there is a capturing group. Whatever matches inside the parentheses will be remembered and can be recalled later in the pattern as \1. Inside the group is an optional hyphen.

The next part of the pattern matches two more digits. After the digits is the symbol for the grouped pattern from earlier in the regular expression: \1. Whatever was matched earlier must be matched again. If a hyphen was used earlier in the expression, then a hyphen must be used here. If a hyphen was not matched earlier, then a hyphen cannot be entered here. The last part of the pattern matches four more digits.

The use of the capturing group is very powerful. This guarantees that there are either two hyphens in the correct places or there are no hyphens. The placement of the ? is very important: try to determine what would happen if the pattern used `([-])?` instead of `([-]?)`.

An example of a user identification number might be from three to five letters followed by three digits or three to six letters followed by two digits. A simple solution would be to use alternation and define two separate patterns:

`[a-zA-Z]{3,5}\d{3}|[a-zA-Z]{3,6}\d{2}.`

However, both of these patterns begin and end with the same sequences, the only difference is the character where letters become digits. By placing an optional character that can be a letter or a digit at this point, the pattern can be rewritten as follows:

```
[a-zA-Z]{3,5}[a-zA-Z0-9]?\d{2}.
```

When writing regular expressions in Java, each \ character must be written as double backslashes, \\. In a traditional regular expression, there would only be one backslash, but in Java there must be two. This is necessary so that the escape sequence is passed to the regular expression and not intercepted by Java. Escape sequences in Java are one backlash character. So it is necessary to escape the escape in order for Java to ignore something like \d. If you leave the \d in a pattern, Java will complain that it is an illegal escape sequence. By placing a back-slash before the escape sequence, Java will translate the \\ into a single \ and send it to the regular expression.

 Try It   http://bytesizebook.com/book/ch5/TestRegEx

This servlet tests several strings to see if they match the above patterns. It is also possible to enter a string and test it against any of these patterns.

5.1.2   Hibernate Validation

Required validation is such a common task that someone has gone to all the trouble to create a package that automates the process. This package is named *Hibernate*.

It is not part of the standard servlet engine, so the following JAR files must be placed in the *lib* directory of the web application in order to enable Hibernate. Download these from http://hibernate.org or from the book's Web site.

```
hibernate3.jar                          hibernate-validator.jar
hibernate-annotations.jar               ejb3-persistence.jar
```

Hibernate can be configured with a separate file or with Java annotations. Java annotations will be used in this book. Java annotations were introduced in the last chapter.

Annotating a Bean for Hibernate

Using annotations, it is a simple task to mark some methods as requiring valida-tion. The methods to mark are the accessors. Two annotations are used for validat-ing string properties: `Pattern` and `NotNull`.

The `@Pattern` annotation has a required attribute named `regex` that is a regular expression. If the complete string returned from the accessor matches the regular expression, then the property is valid, otherwise it is invalid.

There is an optional attribute named `message` that is the error message that will be created if the property is not valid. The default message is "must match `regex`".

The @NotNull annotation tests that the property has a value. If the value returned from the accessor is not null, then the property is considered valid, otherwise it is invalid.

There is an optional attribute named message that is the error message that will be created if the property is not valid. The default message is "may not be null".

By default, the entire string must match the regular expression. If the regular expression only needs to match a substring, then the characters . * can be added to the beginning and end of the pattern. The . * at the start indicates that there can be any other characters before the pattern. The . * at the end means there can be other characters after the pattern.

In our example, the only validation that will be needed is that the hobby and aversion cannot be null or empty. Each accessor will have the Pattern and NotNull annotations. To be non-empty, a test can be made for a non-space character anywhere in the string. The pattern . * \ \ S . * will match any characters, followed by a non-space character, followed by more characters. The characters before and after the non-space character are optional. The double-backslash is needed in the expression because the string is being written in a Java file.

The default error message will be used for the NotNull annotation and a new message will be defined for the Pattern annotation.

```
@Pattern(regex=".*\\S.*", message="cannot be empty")
@NotNull
```

Both of these annotations must be valid in order for the property to be valid. If there is more than one annotation for validation on the accessor, then the validation for the property is the logical AND of the result of each validation.

Place these annotations in the bean directly before the accessor for each property that is being validated.

```
...
public void setHobby(String hobby) {
    this.hobby = hobby;
}

@Pattern(regex=".*\\S.*", message="cannot be empty")
@NotNull
public String getHobby() {
    return hobby;
}
public void setAversion(String aversion) {
    this.aversion = aversion;
}

@Pattern(regex=".*\\S.*", message="cannot be empty")
@NotNull
public String getAversion() {
    return aversion;
}
...
```

Creating the Error Messages

When using required validation, it is important to be able to display an error message for any data that is invalid. It is a simple task to create an array of these messages using Hibernate.

Each message that Hibernate generates is of a type named `InvalidValue`. This type has properties for the name of the property that generated the error and the message that was created.

An array of validation messages is created by using the Hibernate `ClassValidator` class. A `ClassValidator` object is constructed by passing it the class object of the bean. Once the object has been created, use the `getInvalidValues` method to retrieve an array of error messages.

```
InvalidValue[] validationMessages;
ClassValidator requestValidator =
       new ClassValidator(data.getClass());
validationMessages =
       requestValidator.getInvalidValues(data);
```

For each annotated property in the bean, if the user enters invalid data then an error message for it will be placed in the array.

5.1.3   Implementing Required Validation

The array of validation messages that is created by Hibernate does not lend itself to easy access in a JSP. In order to find the error message for a property, a linear search would need to be performed. It would be better if there were direct access to the errors, so that the error for a property could be retrieved using the name of the property. To this end, the interface to the error messages will be enhanced. A map named `errorMap` will be created from the array of validation messages. A map can be accessed using a string, instead of an integer. This map will be used by the JSPs to access the error messages.

In order to make the error messages more accessible, the following will be added to the helper base class.

1. `errorMap`
2. `setErrors()`
3. `isValid()`
4. `getErrors()`

None of these changes requires knowledge of the specific application, so all the features will be added to the helper base class in the `shared` package (Figure 5.2). The helper base class for this chapter is named `HelperBaseCh5` and can be found in the Appendix.

java.util.Map

What is a map?

Think of a map of a city: it contains symbols that represent real things. For instance, on a map, the symbol in Figure 5.3 represents a school. It is just a symbol,

```
HelperBase

HttpServletRequest request
HttpServletResponse response
Logger logger
Map errorMap

abstract copyFromSession ()
addHelperToSession ()
executeButtonMethod ()
fillBeanFromRequest ()
setErrors ()
getErrors ()
isValid ()
```

Figure 5.2 The error map and methods are added to the helper base class.

but if you live near the school, then seeing the symbol on the map will bring the actual school into your awareness. There are other symbols for parks, railroad tracks, etc. So, a map is a collection of simple symbols that represent other objects.

In Java, there is a data structure that is called a Map. It is called a Map because it is like a map. In the Map, one object can be associated with another object. Usually, a simple object is associated with a more complicated object. In this way, the more complicated object can be retrieved using the simple object.

We have already seen something similar to a Map; when the controller helper places itself into the session, it is placed into a data structure like a Map.

```
request.getSession().setAttribute("helper", this);
```

The session has a method named setAttribute that associates a simple object with a more complicated object: the string *helper* is associated with the object this. In the JSP, the more complicated object can be retrieved by using the simpler object.

```
${helper}
```

From a JSP, EL can be used to access the complicated object that was placed into the session. By using the string *helper*, the EL statement can retrieve the object this.

Figure 5.3 A symbol for a school on a topographic map.

The Java `Map` is contained in the package `java.util`. It has two primary methods: `put` and `get`. The method `put` is used to associate one object, know as a key, with another object, known as a value. The method `get` is used to retrieve the value, by passing it a key.

A `Map` is an interface: it cannot be instantiated. In order to create a `Map`, it is necessary to create one of the concrete classes that implement the `Map` interface. One such class is `HashMap`: it implements the `Map` interface using a hash table.

When creating a `Map`, generics from Java 1.5 should be used. The type of the key and the type of the value should be indicated when the `Map` is created. This allows values to be retrieved from the `Map` without casting them and allows for syntax checking.

As an example, a `Map` will be instantiated, a bean will be instantiated, the bean will be placed in the map and the bean will be retrieved from the map. The `Map` will have a key that is a string and a value that is a bean.

```
java.util.Map<String, MyBean> myMap
    = new java.util.HashMap<String, MyBean>();
MyBean bean = new MyBean();
myMap.put("theBean", bean);
MyBean anotherBean = myMap.get("theBean");
```

A `Map` is like a database: a simple key is used to retrieve a complicated value. All of the complicated data can be saved in one collection and can be retrieved easily.

errorMap

A map will be added to the helper base class that will associate the name of a property with the error message for that property. The map can be used for random access into the error messages. By using the map, it will be easy to retrieve one error message at a time in the JSP.

```
java.util.Map<String, String> errorMap =
        new java.util.HashMap<String, String>();
```

This map will be filled from within the `setErrors` method, described next.

setErrors

The `setErrors` method sets the validation messages and fills the error map. The first part of the method sets the validation messages, as was explained above. The second half of the method creates the error map by looping through the array of messages and adding an entry to the map. The property name is used as the key to the map and the error message is the value in the map. It is important to clear the old error map and only fill the map if there are validation messages.

```
public void setErrors(Object data) {
   InvalidValue[] validationMessages;
   ClassValidator requestValidator =
          new ClassValidator(data.getClass());
   validationMessages =
          requestValidator.getInvalidValues(data);

   errorMap.clear();
   if (validationMessages.length != 0) {
       for(InvalidValue msg : validationMessages) {
           errorMap.put(msg.getPropertyName(),
                         msg.getMessage());
       }
   }
}
```

The InvalidValue class has accessors for retrieving the key and the value for a message. These methods cannot be accessed from a JSP, which is why they are being used to add values to the error map. As will be seen shortly, any map can be accessed easily from a JSP.

isValid

The isValid method will return true if all the validations succeed; otherwise it will return false. This is the method that must be called in order to do required validation. It will set the error messages and the error map, by calling setErrors, and return a boolean value indicating if there are any errors. If the error map is empty, then there are no errors, so the data must be valid.

```
public boolean isValid(Object data) {
   setErrors(data);
   return errorMap.isEmpty();
}
```

getErrors

The getErrors method will return the error map variable, so that the errors can be retrieved in a JSP. The errorMap has been added as a member variable to the helper base class, in order for the errors to be accessible from the JSP, there must be an accessor that returns it. The only purpose for this accessor is so that the error messages can be retrieved from a JSP.

```
public java.util.Map getErrors() {
   return errorMap;
}
```

Setting the Error Messages

Required validation should be done every time the user enters new data. In our application, this happens when the user clicks the confirm button on the edit page. Required validation should be done in the controller helper in the method that corresponds to the confirm button.

```
@ButtonMethod(buttonName="confirmButton")
public String confirmMethod() {
    fillBeanFromRequest(data);
    String address;
    if (isValid(data)) {
        address = jspLocation("Confirm.jsp");
    } else {
        address = jspLocation("Edit.jsp");
    }
    return address;
}
```

Call isValid in this method to test if the data is valid and return a different address based on the result. If the data is valid, return the address of the confirm page, otherwise, return the address of the edit page. In this way, the user cannot proceed to the confirm page until the data is valid.

This is an example where the confirm page should not be in a directory that is accessible by the user. If it were, then a user would be able to call the confirm page directly, thereby circumventing the validation.

The method isValid indicates if the data is valid, but it also creates the array of validation messages and the error map. If isValid is not called, then the error messages will not be created.

Retrieving Error Messages

The error messages can be retrieved from the edit page using EL. Since there is a method named getErrors in the helper, it can be accessed from the JSP as ${helper.errors}. This returns a map. An individual message in a map can be retrieved by placing the name of the property in quotes inside square brackets as ${data.error["hobby"]}. Additionally, the dot notation can be used: ${data.error.hobby}.

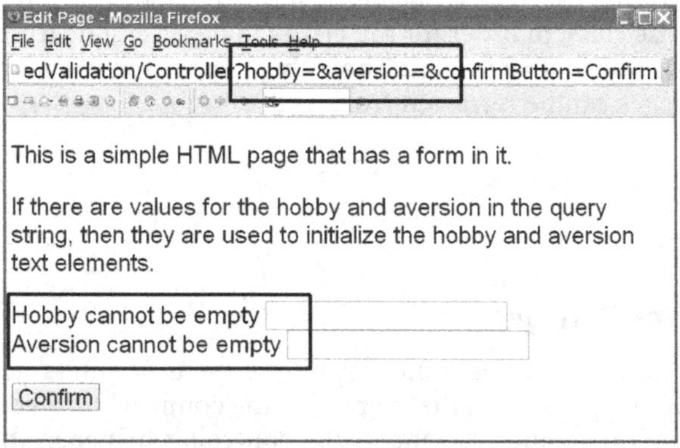

Figure 5.4 A JSP can access the error in the error map.

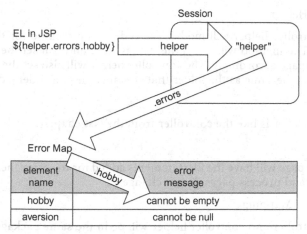

Figure 5.5 Accessing an error message from a JSP.

```
Hobby ${helper.errors.hobby}
<input type="text" name="hobby"
                    value="${helper.data.hobby}">
<br>
Aversion ${helper.errors.aversion}
<input type="text" name="aversion"
                    value="${helper.data.aversion}">
```

When isValid is not called in the doGet method, then all of these references to the error messages will return null, which will be displayed as an empty string by EL. When isValid is called and there is an error for the hobby property, then the reference will return the error message for the hobby (Figure 5.4). The message that is displayed is the message that was defined in the annotation for the hobby.

Figure 5.5 shows how EL can be used to access an error message from a JSP.

5.2 Application: Required Validation

An application that performs required validation can be created by incorporating the above changes into our application.

Bean

> The bean will have the validation annotations added to the accessors for the hobby and aversion.

Helper Base

> The helper base class, in the shared package, will have the error map and the methods for the interface to the errors added to it. The complete helper base class for Chapter Five can be found in the Appendix.

Controller Helper

> The controller helper will modify the code in the method for the confirm button. The method will test if the data is valid and will set the address of the next page accordingly. The controller helper will also set the path of the JSPs to be the same as the folder that contains the controller's class.

Controller

> The controller is like the controller from the last chapter.

JSPs

> The edit page will have the EL statements added for the error messages. The confirm and process pages do not change.

Location and Mapping

> The controller and controller helper will be in the same package. The JSPs will be in the same folder as the controller. Since the controller helper will specify the location of the JSPs, the controller can be mapped to any URL.

 Try It   http://bytesizebook.com/book/ch5/requiredValidation/Controller

Leave the hobby and aversion empty and you will not be able to proceed beyond the edit page. If one field is empty, then one error message appears. If both fields are empty, then both error messages appear.

5.3   POST Requests

If the user is entering personal data, like a bank account number, there is a small problem with the application: the bank account number will be saved in the URL in the history file of the browser. This means that any other user of the computer could see the user's bank account number by browsing through the history file. Now, if the password were also entered, then there is a big problem. There is a simple way to fix this problem.

5.3.1   POST versus GET

Up to this point, every servlet has used one type of request: GET. This is the default type of request. Whenever a hypertext link is followed or a URL is typed into the location box of a window, then a GET request is made. However, when a button on a form is clicked, there is a choice of request types: GET or POST. The POST request is identical to a GET request, except for the location of the data from the form.

Format of GET Requests

A GET request sends the data from the form via the URL. Until now, every form has used this method to send data to the server. Below is an example of a GET request from the edit page from Chapter Three.

```
GET /?hobby=hiking&confirmButton=Confirm HTTP/1.1
Host: tim.cs.fiu.edu:9000
User-Agent: Mozilla/5.0 (Windows; U; ...
Accept: image/png,image/jpeg,image/gif,text/css,*/*
Accept-Language: en,es;q=0.8,fr;q=0.5,en-us;q=0.3
Accept-Encoding: gzip,deflate
Accept-Charset: ISO-8859-1,utf-8;q=0.7,*;q=0.7
Keep-Alive: 300
Connection: keep-alive
Referer: http://localhost:8085/book/ch5/request_get.jsp
```

Many request headers provide information about the browser that made the request. The data from the form has been placed in the URL in the first line of the request.

Format of POST Requests

A POST request sends the data from the form as part of the request. When POST is used, the data will not appear in the URL, but will be attached to the end of the request.

```
POST / HTTP/1.1
Host: tim.cs.fiu.edu:9000
User-Agent: Mozilla/5.0 (Windows; U; ...
Accept: image/png,image/jpeg,image/gif,text/css,*/*
Accept-Language: en,es;q=0.8,fr;q=0.5,en-us;q=0.3
Accept-Encoding: gzip,deflate
Accept-Charset: ISO-8859-1,utf-8;q=0.7,*;q=0.7
Keep-Alive: 300
Connection: keep-alive
Referer: http://localhost:8085/book/ch5/request_post.jsp
Content-Type: application/x-www-form-urlencoded
Content-Length: 34

hobby=hiking&confirmButton=Confirm
```

The headers are mostly the same as for a GET request, except there are two additional ones: Content-Type and Content-Length. These extra headers indicate the type and amount of additional content that follows the headers. The data from the form is formatted the same way as in a GET request. The only difference is that the data follows the request headers, after a blank line.

What does the word *post* mean? It means *to send*, but it also means *after*. That is a precise definition of a POST request: it posts the data, post the request.

Method Attribute

The method of a form can be changed to POST by adding the method attribute to the opening form tag. If the method of a form is set to POST, then all buttons clicked in that form will generate POST requests to the server.

```
<form method="POST" action="Controller">
  <p>
    If there are values for the hobby and aversion
    in the query string, then they are used to
    initialize the hobby and aversion text elements.
```

```
<p>
  Hobby ${helper.errors.hobby}
  <input type="text" name="hobby"
                      value="${helper.data.hobby}">
  <br>
  Aversion ${helper.errors.aversion}
  <input type="text" name="aversion"
                      value="${helper.data.aversion}">
<p>
  <input type="submit" name="confirmButton"
                       value="Confirm">
</form>
```

This is the same form that was used in the *Required Validation* example, except that the method has been changed to POST.

Motivation for POST

The only other difference between GET and POST is how they are created.

1. There are three ways that a GET request is generated:
   a. The user types a URL into the browser.
   b. The user follows a hypertext link.
   c. The user clicks a button in a form, whose method is GET.
2. A POST request is only generated when the user clicks a button on a form, whose method is POST.

The fact that POST can only be generated as a result of clicking a button on a form allows the conclusion that if a POST request is made, then it cannot be the first access to the application. The first access would be made by following a hypertext link or by typing a URL into the location box of a browser; both of these techniques use a GET request.

There are several reasons for using POST.

Hides Data

The data from a POST request cannot be seen in the URL. This is useful when the data contains a password.

More Data

There is no limit to the amount of data that can be transmitted using a POST request. A file can be opened to store all the data from a POST request; as more data is received over the network, the data can be written to the file. GET requests always have a limit to the amount of data that can be sent, because there is a limited amount of space for storing the URL.

More Secure

Since the data is not in the URL, the data will not be saved in the browser's history file. Since an unlimited amount of data can be sent, there is no danger of hacking the server by a buffer overrun attack.

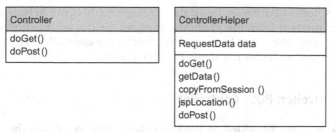

Figure 5.6 The controller and controller helper classes have a doPost method.

Handling POST

In a servlet, there is another method that can be overridden: doPost. It has the exact same signature as the doGet method. It will be called if a form changes its method to POST and submits data to the servlet.

```
public class Controller extends HttpServlet {

    protected void doGet(HttpServletRequest request,
                         HttpServletResponse response)
    throws IOException, ServletException {
    ...
    }

    protected void doPost(HttpServletRequest request,
                          HttpServletResponse response)
    throws IOException, ServletException {
    ...
    }
}
```

A doPost method will be added to the helper, too. Like its doGet method, this will be called from the controller. Since the request and response objects are already declared in the helper base, this method does not need any parameters.

```
protected void doPost()
throws ServletException, java.io.IOException {
    ...
}
```

Figure 5.6 demonstrates that the controller and controller helper classes will each have a doPost method.

5.4   Application: POST Controller

The *Required Validation* example will be redesigned using doGet and doPost. Just as the doGet method was handled, the controller will defer the doPost method to the controller helper. In the controller helper, these methods will be designed to perform different tasks: the `doPost` method will behave exactly like the `doGet` method from the previous example; the `doGet` method will handle all GET requests like they are the first request to the controller. The JSPs will be modified so that all forms use the POST method.

5.4.1   Controller: POST Controller

A new method will be added to the controller: `doPost`. It has the exact same signature as the `doGet` method. To be consistent with how the `doGet` method is handled, the controller will defer the `doPost` to the controller helper.

```
protected void doPost(HttpServletRequest request,
                      HttpServletResponse response)
throws IOException, ServletException {
    ControllerHelper helper =
        new ControllerHelper(request, response);
    helper.doPost();
}
```

If a controller does not handle the `doPost` method, then an error will be generated whenever a POST request is made (Figure 5.7).

A similar error would occur if a GET request was made and there was not a `doGet` method.

5.4.2   ControllerHelper: POST Controller

If all the forms in an application use the POST method, then the `doGet` and `doPost` methods can perform different tasks in the web application. The `doGet` method can be used to show the welcome page only. Such a technique could be used if the user had to log into the site using a username and password. The `doPost` method can be used to process the user's data that has been entered via a form. Since the only way that a POST request can be made is from a form, the developer can assume that the user has entered data already.

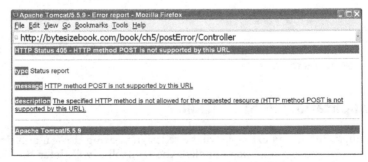

Figure 5.7 An error will occur if the `doPost` method is not created.

doPost

The `doPost` method will perform all the same tasks as the previous `doGet` method: check for data in the session; execute the method for the button; forward to the next JSP. Except for the name of the method, this is identical to the previous `doGet` method.

```
protected void doPost()
throws ServletException, java.io.IOException {
  addHelperToSession("helper", SessionData.READ);

  String address = executeButtonMethod();

  request.getRequestDispatcher(address)
    .forward(request, response);
}
```

doGet

The `doGet` method will assume this is the first access to the application: it will **not** check if there is previous data in the session, when placing the bean in the session, and it will **always** display the edit page.

Since this is being treated as a first request to the application, the data in the session should be ignored. In the call to `addHelperToSession` set the second parameter to `SessionData.IGNORE`; the current controller helper will be added to the session, but any previous data will not be read from the session.

```
protected void doGet()
throws ServletException, java.io.IOException {
  addHelperToSession("helper", SessionData.IGNORE);

  String address = editMethod();

  request.getRequestDispatcher(address)
    .forward(request, response);
}
```

Many web sites will give the user the opportunity to start over. Whenever I book an airline reservation, I will look for several different options. The site that I use allows me to click a button to start over. When I do that, all of the previous flight information that I obtained is removed, so that I can begin a new search.

The simplest way to implement such a feature is to use a GET request when all the old information should be ignored and to use a POST request when information should be carried from request to request.

5.4.3 JSPs: Updating the JSPs with POST

The final change to be made is to change all the form elements in the JSPs so that they use the POST method.

```
<form method="POST" action="Controller">
```

It is important that all of the form tags use the POST method. If one is omitted, then the user will be redirected to the edit page, regardless of the button that is clicked. The only time a form should use the GET method is when all the old data should be ignored and new data is to be entered into the edit page.

 Try It   http://bytesizebook.com/book/ch5/postServlet/Controller

Notice that as you navigate from page to page the URL does not change, but the data is still transmitted to each page. Instead of placing the data in the URL like a GET request does, the POST request adds it to the end of the request from the browser.

Next, instead of clicking a button, click in the URL window in the browser and hit the enter key: you will always be taken to the edit page and the old data will be destroyed.

5.5   Saving a Bean to a Database

The next feature that will be added to the servlet engine will be the ability to save a bean to a relational database. The package that will be used is Hibernate. We have already seen how Hibernate can be used to validate input, now it will be used to save data to a database.

Structured Query Language [SQL] is a standard language for accessing a relational database. The details of SQL are beyond the scope of this book, so this would seem to indicate that accessing a relational database from our web application would not be possible. However, there is Hibernate! The beauty of Hibernate is that a relational database that uses SQL can be accessed without learning SQL.

Hibernate focuses on the data. If a bean is sent to Hibernate, it will generate all the SQL statements to save the bean in the database. Hibernate can also generate all the SQL for creating the database tables from a bean. Hibernate can also take a bean and update it in the database or remove it entirely. By creating a bean in a web application, most of the work of saving it to a database can be handled by Hibernate, without knowing one statement of SQL.

5.5.1   Hibernate JAR Files

Saving data to a database is a complex process, so it stands to reason that a lot of JAR files will need to be added to the servlet engine in order to enable this feature. As of Hibernate 3.2, the JAR files that are needed at runtime are listed in Table 5.3.

Table 5.3 JAR files needed for Hibernate.

antlr-2.7.6.jar	asm-attrs.jar
asm.jar	c3p0-0.9.0.jar
cglib-2.1.3.jar	commons-collections-2.1.1.jar
commons-logging-1.0.4.jar	dom4j-1.6.1.jar
ehcache-1.1.jar	ejb3-persistence.jar
hibernate3.jar	hibernate-annotations.jar
jdbc2_0-stdext.jar	jta.jar
log4j-1.2.11.jar	xerces-2.6.2.jar

With the Hibernate distribution, there are optional JAR files for the cache, SAX parser, etc. View the README file in the *lib* directory of the Hibernate distribution for more information. Hibernate can be downloaded from http://hibernate.org. All of the JAR files listed here can also be obtained from http://bytesizebook.com.

From Table 5.3, the following have been added for features that were used in Chapters Three and Four:

commons-collections-2.1.1.jar

commons-logging-1.0.4.jar

log4j-1.2.11.jar

In addition to these files, it is also necessary to have a JAR file for the type of database that will be accessed. In this book, we will use the following JAR for MySQL. There is a short section in the Appendix which contains instructions on how to connect to MySQL; mysql-connector-java-5.0.4-bin.jar.

5.5.2   JAR File Modifications and Deployment

A servlet engine is a complex piece of software that uses many packages from many different sources. This always introduces the problem of memory leaks caused by one package maintaining static pointers to the classes in another package.

In Tomcat releases prior to 6, a memory leak was caused whenever a JSP used expression language. In those releases, the commons-el JAR needs to be modified to remove the leak. In Tomcat 6, a different JAR file has been used to implement the expression language and the leak has been fixed.

There are also memory leaks that are annoying, but not fatal. These will cause a leak the first time a class is loaded, but will not leak more memory after that. These leaks usually involve a static variable that references an object. Often, the leak can be removed by using a weak reference to the static object.

ZIP Files

The JAR files for all the web applications in the book have been placed into two ZIP files that can be downloaded from http://bytesizebook.com. One file contains the Hibernate related JAR files. The other file contains the non-Hibernate related JAR files. Both ZIP files should be unpacked in the *lib* directory of the web application.

1. http://bytesizebook.com/hibernate.zip (6 MB)

2. http://bytesizebook.com/non-hibernate.zip (1 MB)

5.5.3   Hibernate Persistence: Configuration

It is also necessary to configure Hibernate. There are several options for configuring Hibernate which can be used individually or can be combined. Two of the options are to use Java or to use XML.

1. Each of the configuration options can be defined inside a Java program. For the first example, this is the technique that will be used, so that none of the details for Hibernate are hidden in some other configuration file.
2. An XML file can be created. Each property has its own XML tag. Such a file of properties is placed in the class path of the web application and the file will be read automatically when Hibernate is configured.

Programmatic Configuration

One common mistake when using configuration files is placing them in the wrong location. When this happens, the configuration could be correct, but the program cannot find the file. To a novice, it will look like the configuration is wrong. For this reason, the first example will configure Hibernate in the controller helper, where there is no possible problem of finding the configuration directives. Once the initialisation works, it will be a simple matter to move the code into a separate configuration file.

There is a Java class named `Properties` that implements the `Map` interface. The key and value must be strings. This class is used to set the configuration for Hibernate.

The following properties are used to configure Hibernate. The first set will be the same for everyone connecting to the MySQL database. The second set of properties contain the URL, username and password for accessing the database. These must be updated with your information.

```
Properties props = new Properties();
props.setProperty("hibernate.dialect",
                  "org.hibernate.dialect.MySQLDialect");
props.setProperty("hibernate.connection.driver_class",
                  "com.mysql.jdbc.Driver");
props.setProperty("hibernate.c3p0.min_size", "1");
props.setProperty("hibernate.c3p0.max_size", "5");
props.setProperty("hibernate.c3p0.timeout", "300");
props.setProperty("hibernate.c3p0.max_statements",
                  "50");
props.setProperty("hibernate.c3p0.idle_test_period",
                  "300");

props.setProperty("hibernate.connection.url",
                  "jdbc:mysql://SERVER:PORT/DATABASE");
props.setProperty("hibernate.connection.username",
                  "USERNAME");
props.setProperty("hibernate.connection.password",
                  "PASSWORD");
```

These statements will be placed in a method named `initHibernate` in the controller helper.

HibernateHelper Class

There are many methods that are used to access Hibernate. All of these methods have been encapsulated into a helper class named `HibernateHelper` (Figure

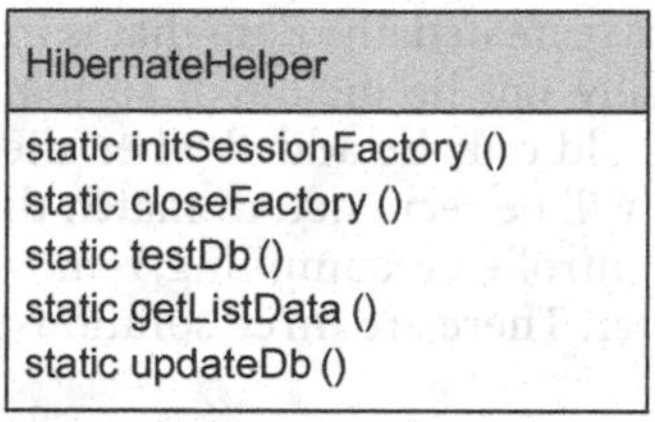

```
HibernateHelper

static initSessionFactory ()
static closeFactory ()
static testDb ()
static getListData ()
static updateDb ()
```

Figure 5.8 The `HibernateHelper` class.

5.8). The complete listing of this class is in the Appendix. There are methods for initialising, closing, saving, deleting, etc. This helper class can be downloaded from http://bytesizebook.com. It should be placed into a package named `shared`.

These methods are exactly the same for all web applications, except for the names of the tables that are accessed. A helper class has been created that contains all of these methods. Since they are the same for all web applications, they have been created as static methods. Whenever a method is to be called that uses Hibernate, the method will be in the Hibernate helper class.

The method for initialising Hibernate is `initSessionFactory`. It has two parameters: the initialisation properties and the class object for the bean. Since these two parameters may change from web application to web application, the call to this method should be made from the controller helper.

```
HibernateHelper.initSessionFactory(
                props,
                RequestDataPersistent.class);
```

If there are multiple tables in the servlet, they can all be sent to the method by adding a new argument for each.

```
initSessionFactory(props,
                table1.class,
                table2.class,
                table3.class);
```

The Hibernate helper class maintains a list of database tables that can be accessed by Hibernate. Whenever `initSessionFactory` is called, the class objects are added to the list, if they are not already in it. If one is added to the list, then Hibernate is closed and reinitialised. If the class objects are already in the list, then Hibernate already has the ability to access them, so no initialisation needs to be done.

Creating the SQL Tables

Hibernate has the ability to create a table in the database from your bean. This is amazing: no SQL needs to be coded in order to create the table. This is controlled by an additional property.

Whenever the tables are recreated, the data that is in them is erased. Therefore, this property should usually not be included, so that the data in the database does not get erased. It should only be added when the structure of the bean has changed, so that the table will be recreated to match the new structure. However, adding statements to the controller, recompiling, removing statements and recompiling is a recipe for disaster. There are three solutions for avoiding this unhappy situation.

1. Manually create the database tables in MySQL before running the servlet the first time.
2. Add the property to a separate XML file, when the tables need to be created. The next time the servlet engine starts, it will read the value of this property from the file and create the tables. Remove the property from the XML file after the servlet is running.
3. Add an initialisation parameter to the *web.xml* file and read it during servlet initialisation. Conditionally include the property whenever the initialisation parameter is true.

I prefer the third choice: use the *web.xml* file. By using the *web.xml* file, the initialisation parameter is written in code, so there is no question of forgetting its syntax. It is easy to remember the syntax of the parameter in the *web.xml* file: it will be either `true` or `false`.

Initialisation Parameters in web.xml

The `servlet` tag has already been used in the `web.xml` file. Initialisation parameters are added to this tag, using a nested `init-param` tag.

The `init-param` tag has two nested tags. Define the name of the initialisation parameter with the `param-name` tag. Define the value of the parameter with the `param-value` tag.

Add a parameter named `create` to the `servlet` tag. It will have a value of `true` or `false`. If the value is set to `true`, then the controller will add the property for creating the database tables when Hibernate is configured. All other values will be interpreted to mean that the tables should not be created.

```
<servlet>
  <servlet-name>PersistentController</servlet-name>
  <servlet-class>ch5.persistentData.Controller</servlet-class>
  <init-param>
    <param-name>create</param-name>
    <param-value>false</param-value>
  </init-param>
</servlet>
```

Reading Initialisation Parameters

The value of an initialisation parameter is retrieved from a servlet using the `getInitParameter` method of the servlet. This method returns a string, so the value must be cast to **boolean** in order to store it in a variable.

```
boolean create =
   Boolean.parseBoolean(getInitParameter("create"));
```

If the create parameter in the *web.xml* is set to true, then the boolean variable will be set to true. If the parameter does not exist or has any value except true, then the variable will be set to false.

Conditionally Creating the Tables

After reading the initialisation parameter from the *web.xml* file, the boolean variable can be used to conditionally call a method from the Hibernate helper that will create the table. In this method, the additional property for creating the table will be added to the other properties that initialise Hibernate. The developer does not need to remember what the property is. By including true in the *web.xml* file, the table will be created. The method that creates the table has the exact same parameters as the initSessionFactory method.

```
if (create) {
   HibernateHelper.createTable(
                   props,
                   RequestDataPersistent.class);
}
```

Set the initialisation parameter to true and restart the web application. The tables will be recreated. Afterwards, reset the parameter to false, so that the next time the web application is restarted, the tables will not be recreated and the new data will not be lost.

Initialising Hibernate in the Controller Helper

The controller helper will declare a public method that encapsulates all the commands to initialise Hibernate: setting the necessary properties, conditionally creating the table and calling the initSessionFactory method. The method will have a **boolean** variable passed to it that indicates whether the tables should be created in the database.

```
static public void initHibernate(boolean create) {
   Properties props = new Properties();
   props.setProperty("hibernate.dialect",
                      "org.hibernate.dialect.MySQLDialect");
   props.setProperty("hibernate.connection.driver_class",
                      "com.mysql.jdbc.Driver");
   props.setProperty("hibernate.c3p0.min_size", "1");
   props.setProperty("hibernate.c3p0.max_size", "5");
   props.setProperty("hibernate.c3p0.timeout", "300");
   props.setProperty("hibernate.c3p0.max_statements",
                      "50");
   props.setProperty("hibernate.c3p0.idle_test_period",
                      "300");
```

```
props.setProperty("hibernate.connection.url",
                  "jdbc:mysql://SERVER:PORT/DATABASE");
props.setProperty("hibernate.connection.username",
                  "USERNAME");
props.setProperty("hibernate.connection.password",
                  "PASSWORD");

if (create) {
  HibernateHelper.createTable(
                  props,
                  RequestDataPersistent.class);
}

HibernateHelper.initSessionFactory(
                  props,
                  RequestDataPersistent.class);
}
```

This method does not use any non-static members in the controller helper, so it is declared as a static method. This allows it to be called without instantiating a controller helper.

Using *init* in the Controller

Hibernate is initialised with many properties, like username and password. These properties should be set once, when the servlet is first loaded into memory. Recall from the *Log4j* servlet in Chapter Four, that the init method in a servlet is executed when it is loaded into memory. An init method will be added to the controller (Figure 5.9).

In the method, read the parameter from the *web.xml* file that controls whether the database tables are created. Pass this parameter to the method in the controller helper that initialises Hibernate. By calling it from init, the initialisation will only occur once.

Since the method that initialises Hibernate was declared as a static method in the controller helper, it can be called from the controller without having to instantiate a controller helper object.

```
public void init() {
  boolean create =
      Boolean.parseBoolean(getInitParameter("create"));
  ControllerHelper.initHibernate(create);
}
```

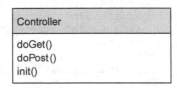

Figure 5.9 An init method is added to the controller.

5.5.4 Closing Hibernate

Closing Hibernate is imperative. If the web application closes without releasing the resources that Hibernate uses, there will be a memory leak in the servlet engine. The `closeFactory` method has been added to the Hibernate helper class to close Hibernate.

```
public void closeFactory(SessionFactory factory) {
   ...
}
```

The difficult part is to know when to call this method. Each servlet in the web application uses the same static helper class to make connections to the database server. If one servlet closes Hibernate, this means that it will be closed for all servlets.

Since the Hibernate helper class only has static members and methods, the class will exist until the web application is stopped. Static variables will not be garbage collected until the class is removed from memory. There is no method that is called when a class is removed from memory. However, it is possible to detect when the web application is stopped.

There is an interface named `ServletContextListener` that has two methods that will be called when the web application starts and when the web application stops. By adding a class to the web application that implements the interface and configuring the *web.xml* file to call this class, Hibernate can be closed only when the web application is stopped.

This is also the place for the web application to close any other resources that it is using. In addition to closing hibernate, the web application should deregister the SQL drivers that it is using.

```
try {
  Enumeration<Driver> enumer = DriverManager.getDrivers();
  while (enumer.hasMoreElements()) {
    DriverManager.deregisterDriver(enumer.nextElement());
  }
} catch (java.sql.SQLException se) {
  se.printStackTrace();
}
```

Servlet Context Listener

The context listener interface only has two methods: one that is called when the web application starts and one that is called when the web application stops. Define a class that implements this interface. There is nothing to do when the web application starts, but close Hibernate when the web application stops. By closing Hibernate when the web application stops, all the resources for Hibernate will be released.

```
package shared;

import java.sql.Driver;
import java.sql.DriverManager;
```

```
import java.sql.SQLException;
import java.util.Enumeration;
import javax.servlet.ServletContextEvent;
import javax.servlet.ServletContextListener;

public class WebappListener implements ServletContextListener
{
  public void contextInitialized(ServletContextEvent sce)
  {}

  public void contextDestroyed(ServletContextEvent sce)
  {
    try {
      Enumeration<Driver> enumer = DriverManager.getDrivers();
      while (enumer.hasMoreElements()) {
        DriverManager.deregisterDriver(enumer.nextElement());
      }
    } catch (java.sql.SQLException se) {
      se.printStackTrace();
    }
    shared.HibernateHelper.closeFactory();
  }
}
```

Calling the Listener

The context listener must be called by the servlet engine when the web application starts. This is done by adding some tags to the *web.xml* file. The only parameter that is needed is the class for the above listener class.

```
<listener>
<listener-class>shared.WebappListener</listener-class>
</listener>
```

When the web application starts, it will load the listener class into memory and the `contextInitialized` method will be called. The listener class will remain in memory as long as the web application is running. When the web application receives a command to stop, it will first call the `contextDestroyed` method.

5.5.5   Persistent Annotations

Hibernate operates through beans. Hibernate will create the table in the database based on the structure of the bean. Most of the information that Hibernate needs can be derived from the standard structure of the bean, but there are a few details that have to be configured. These additional details could be added to a separate configuration file, but Hibernate supports annotations from Java 1.5. By using annotations, the additional configuration parameters can be placed in the bean class. The advantage of this is that the configuration information is physically located next to what it modifies.

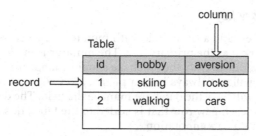

Figure 5.10 A table has columns and rows.

A table in a database is organised in columns, just like a table in a spreadsheet. By default, a column will be created for each property that is in the bean. Each row in the table represents all the data for one bean object (Figure 5.10).

The tables that are based upon a bean need a column that identifies each row uniquely. In other words, the value that is stored in that column is different for each row in the table. For instance, a student ID or a bank account number would be examples of such a column. This column is known as a *primary key*.

Once the primary key for a row has been created, it is important that it never changes. For this reason, it is better to create a separate column that has nothing to do with the data that is being entered by the user. Most relational databases have the ability to generate a primary key automatically. By allowing the database to manage the primary key, there is never a concern that two rows in the database will have the same value for the primary key. Hibernate has annotations for declaring the primary key.

There are four annotations that are used to give Hibernate additional information about the structure of the table that it creates for the bean.

1. `@Entity`
2. `@Id`
3. `@GeneratedValue`
4. `@Transient`

Creating a Separate Table

The `@Entity` annotation precedes the definition of the bean class. It indicates that the class will be represented in the database as a separate table. The name of the table in the database will be the same as the name of the bean class.

```
. . .
@Entity
public class RequestDataPersistent
. . .
```

This annotation is located in the `javax.persistence` package.

Creating a Primary Key

For the primary key, add a `Long` field with mutators and accessors. Use the `@Id` annotation to mark it as the primary key. The mutator is made protected to limit how the field is modified. Only the database should change the value of this field.

Our examples will not always have a primary key like an account number or student ID, so we will have the database manage the field. The database will create a unique value for each new row that is added to the table; this is controlled with the `@GeneratedValue` annotation.

```java
protected Long id;

@Id
@GeneratedValue
public Long getId() { return id; }

protected void setId(Long id) { this.id = id; }
```

The `@GeneratedValue` annotation is telling the database to assign numbers to the id and to be sure that they are unique. This precedes the accessor for the primary key of the table. It indicates that the database will generate the primary key when a row is added to the database.

Both of these annotations are located in the `javax.persistence` package.

PersistentBase Class

All of the beans that are marked with the `Entity` annotation should have a primary key. For all such examples in this book, the primary key will be generated by the database, by inserting the above code into the bean. As a convenience, there is a base class named `PersistentBase` that contains this annotated property. Instead of typing the above code into the bean, if the bean extends this class, then the primary key will be created for it.

```java
...
@Entity
public class RequestDataPersistent
    extends shared.PersistentBase
{
...
```

Transient Fields

By default, any property in the bean that has an accessor will have a column created for it in the database table. There will be situations where a property does not need to be saved in the database. In such cases, if the property is preceded by the `@Transient` annotation, then Hibernate will not create a column in the table for the property and will ignore the property when the bean is saved to the table.

Any method name that begins with *is* or *get* is considered an accessor and Hibernate will try to create a column for it and try to save it to the database.

As an example of a field that does not need to be saved in the table, consider the isValidHobby method from the *Default Validation* example in Chapter Three. This is an accessor, since it begins with *is*, but it should not be saved to the database. Hopefully, the only data that is saved to the database is valid. If this method is in a bean that is being saved to a database, then it should be marked as transient.

```
@Transient
public boolean isValidHobby() {
  return hobby != null && !hobby.trim().equals("");
}
```

This annotation is located in the javax.persistence package.

5.5.6 Accessing the Database

Hibernate uses sessions and transactions to manage the access to the database. A session in Hibernate is used to connect to the database. Sessions are obtained from the session factory that was created in initSessionFactroy. A transaction is used to update data in the database.

In its simplest format, the way that the database is accessed is to obtain a session, obtain a transaction, do the work in the database, send the transaction to the database and close the session.

```
session = factory.openSession();
Transaction tran = session.beginTransaction();

someDatabaseProcess();

tran.commit();
session.close();
```

The details of the session and transaction are the same, regardless of the type of work that is being done in the database: retrieving, saving, deleting. There is a separate method in the Hibernate helper class for each operation in the database. The details of these methods can be found in the listing of the Hibernate helper class in the Appendix.

Testing the Connection

When Hibernate is configured and a session factory is created in the initSessionFactory method, there is the possibility that the session factory was not created. If the information to connect to the database is incorrect or the format of the bean is incorrect, the creation of the session factory will fail.

A method has been added to the Hibernate helper class that tests if the session factory has been created. If it hasn't, then the method will create an error page containing the error that occurred. In order to send this page back to the browser, the response object will be passed to the method.

```java
public boolean testDB(HttpServletResponse response)
throws IOException, ServletException {
  if (!isSessionOpen()) {
    writeError(response);
  }
  return isSessionOpen();
}
```

There are several overloaded versions of this method in the Hibernate helper class. The one that does all the work is an example of creating an HTML error page in Java and sending it back to the browser, instead of forwarding the request to a JSP that displays the error message. The response object is all that is needed to send a page back to the browser. The entire page must be coded in Java. This means that all the HTML statements must be enclosed in quotation marks, since they are plain text.

```java
public void writeError(HttpServletResponse response,
                       String title,
                       Exception ex)
throws java.io.IOException, ServletException
{
  java.io.PrintWriter out = response.getWriter();
  response.setContentType("text/html");
  out.println("<html>");
  out.println("  <head>");
  out.println("    <title>" + title + "</title>");
  out.println("  </head>");
  out.println("  <body>");
  out.println("<h2>" + title + "</h2>");
  if (ex != null) {
    if (ex.getMessage() != null) {
      out.println(
        "<h3>" + ex.getMessage() + "</h3>");
    }
    if (ex.getCause() != null) {
      out.println(
        "<h4>" + ex.getCause() + "</h4>");
    }
    StackTraceElement[] trace = ex.getStackTrace();
    if (trace != null && trace.length > 0) {
      out.print("<pre>");
      ex.printStackTrace(out);
      out.println("</pre>");
    }
  } else {
    out.println("Hibernate must be initialized");
  }
  out.println("  </body>");
  out.println("</html>");
  out.close();
}
```

The response object contains all the information that is needed to communicate with the browser. The most important piece of information is the stream that is used to send data to the browser. This stream can be retrieved from the response object with a call to the `getWriter` method.

When a servlet generates a response to send to the browser, it is the servlet's responsibility to inform the browser of the content that is being sent. The default content is *text/plain*. In order to have all browsers interpret the content correctly, the content type must be set as *text/html*. The content type is set with the `setContentType` method in the response object.

This example of generating a simple error page entirely from within a servlet makes me very grateful for JSPs.

Retrieving Data

Data is retrieved from a table using the `getListData` method. The method returns a collection of beans. Each bean contains the data from one row in the database table (Figure 5.11). Hibernate generates a bean for each row in the database and places them into a collection. This collection is returned from the method.

This method is overloaded several times in the Hibernate helper class. One version accepts a parameter that is the class object for the bean class. Since this method will be called from the controller helper, the simplest way to retrieve the class object of the bean is from the bean itself: `data.getClass()`.

```
java.util.List list =
    HibernateHelper.getListData(data.getClass());
```

This call to the method returns a list of beans. Each bean in the list represents a row from the table.

Saving Data

The method to save data to the database is `updateDB`, which has a parameter that is the bean containing the data to save. Since this will be called from the controller helper, the bean object to save will be named `data`.

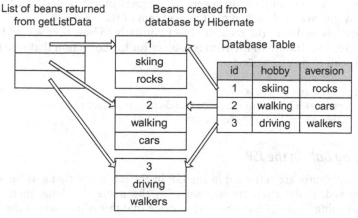

Figure 5.11 A collection of beans is created by Hibernate.

```
HibernateHelper.updateDB(data);
```

Hibernate will determine the type of the bean by using reflection. From the type of the bean, Hibernate will determine the name of the table in the database.

If the bean had been retrieved from the database, then it will replace the data that is in the database. If the bean was not retrieved from the database, then it will be added to the database, even if there is duplicate data in the database. As long as the primary key is null, the bean will be added as a new row in the table. Hibernate uses the primary key to determine if a row has been saved to the database. This is a major reason for allowing Hibernate to manage the primary key.

5.5.7   Making Data Available

Once the data has been retrieved from the database, it needs to be displayed in a JSP. Whether the collection of beans that is retrieved from the database contains all the rows or just some of the rows, the collection must be made available for JSPs and the JSPs must be able to display this data in a readable format.

Placing Data in the Request

The getListData method is used to retrieve data from the database; however, the data will not be available to the JSPs. So far, the only way that an object will be accessible from a JSP is to add it to the session or to add an accessor for it in the controller helper.

The list of rows from the database should not be added to the controller helper as a member variable. Once it is in the controller helper, it would be passed from request to request via the session. This is a waste of resources, since the data is already saved in the database.

The list of rows should not be added directly to the session for the same reason. Furthermore, objects that have been retrieved from the database and then stored directly in the session may cause thread death in the web application.

There is a third way to make an object accessible in a JSP. Arbitrary objects can be placed in the request object by the controller helper and retrieved by the JSPs, just like the session object. However, the request object is destroyed when the request is finished. This will avoid the problem of thread death.

Objects are added to the request object similarly to how they are added to the session. Set an attribute in the request object for the collection that was retrieved from the call to getListData.

```
java.util.List list =
   HibernateHelper.getListData(data.getClass());
request.setAttribute("database", list);
```

Displaying Data in the JSP

Request attributes are retrieved in the JSP in the same way that session attributes are retrieved. If the attribute was set with the name *database*, then it can be retrieved using EL as ${database}. Notice that this is not part of the helper: it is a separate object stored in the request.

The only complication is that this is a collection of data and a loop will be needed to access all the individual beans in the collection. There are two ways that loops can be added to a JSP: using Java and using HTML. In order to separate Java coding from HTML presentation as much as possible, the ability to loop will be added to the JSP using custom HTML tags.

It is a good design principle to reduce the amount of Java code that is exposed in a JSP. The chief justification is so that a non-programmer could maintain the JSPs. If there is Java code embedded in a JSP, then there is always the possibility of an exception. If the JSP throws an exception, then a stack trace will be displayed to the user. Such a page would not instil much confidence in your site by the user. The less Java code that is being maintained by a non-programmer means the less chance of seeing a stack trace.

Another strong reason for not placing Java code in a JSP is so that the application logic is not scattered amongst many different files. When it is time to change the logic of an application, it is preferable to have the code in as few different files as possible.

Looping in a JSP

Using HTML to loop in a JSP means that custom HTML tags must be created. Wouldn't it be nice if someone would create a package of custom tags that would allow looping in a JSP?

There is a package of custom tags that is know as the *Java Standard Template Library* [JSTL]. To install the library, add the following jar files to the *lib* directory of the web application.

```
jstl.jar
standard.jar
```

Add JSTL to a JSP by adding the following tag. It is a directive that informs the JSP that additional HTML tags will be used and that they are defined at the given location. It also indicates that the new HTML tags will be preceded by a given prefix: core. Only include it once in each JSP that uses it, no matter how many JSTL tags are used in the page.

```
<%@ taglib uri="http://java.sun.com/jsp/jstl/core"
           prefix="core" %>
```

JSTL adds HTML tags that can be used in JSPs. These tags allow for looping and conditional testing, without having to expose Java code to the JSP.

One of theses tags is a forEach tag. It has two parameters that are similar to a for statement in Java 1.5. The first parameter is named var and it represents the loop control variable. The second parameter is named items and is the collection that is being looped through. On each pass through the loop the var becomes the next element in the items collection. The value of the control variable can be retrieved in the body of the tag, using EL.

```
<core:forEach var="control" items="collection">
   do something with ${control}
</core:forEach>
```

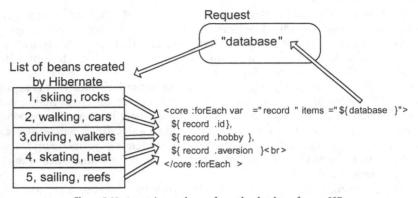

Figure 5.12 Accessing each row from the database from a JSP.

Looping through the Database

In the JSP, use a JSTL loop to access all the rows in the database and display the details. On each pass through the loop, the `var` will be another bean that was retrieved from the database (Figure 5.12).

Every public accessor in the bean can be accessed from a JSP using EL. The bean has three public accessors: `getId`, `getHobby` and `getAversion`. If the name of the loop control variable is *row*, then these can be accessed using EL of `${row.id}`, `${row.hobby}` and `${row.aversion}`.

```
<core:forEach var="row" items="${database}">
  ${row.id},
  ${row.hobby},
  ${row.aversion}<br>
</core:forEach>
```

The above statement will display all the data from the database. Each row will appear on its own line with its id, hobby and aversion displayed.

5.5.8   Data Persistence in Hibernate

There are several methods in Hibernate that can be used to save data to the database: `save`, `update`, `saveOrUpdate`. The save method will always write a new row to the database. The update method will only work if the bean was previously saved to the database, in which case the data in the bean will replace the data in the database. The third method is a combination of these two. If the bean has not been saved previously, then it will be added to the database; otherwise, it will update the bean in the database.

The method that is used by the `updateDB` method in Hibernate helper is the `saveOrUpdate` method. If a bean that has already been saved in the database, then any changes to this bean will update the row in the database, instead of adding a duplicate row.

By placing such a bean in the session, it means that all JSPs will be accessing and modifying the data that was retrieved from the database. When the updateDB method is called, the new data will replace the data that is in the database.

Reading Session Data

Whenever the session is used, care must be taken when the session data is passed to a collection or to a database. Once the bean from the user has been saved into the database, Hibernate will set its primary key. The next time the bean is written to the database, the values that are in the bean will be used to update the row in the database that has the same primary key.

If a bean has been placed in the session, the next time a button is clicked, the bean will be copied into the current application. The primary key will be copied from the session bean into the current bean. If the primary key of the session bean had been set by Hibernate, then the current bean will have a valid primary key, too. When the current bean is sent to the database, it will replace the data in the database, instead of adding a new row (Figure 5.13).

If the user accesses the application via a GET request, then the old data from the session will be discarded. Even if the data that the user enters is identical to the data in the database, the bean will add a new row to the database. The reason for this is that the primary key will be null and can only be set by Hibernate; it is not possible to set the primary key from user input.

In the Post Servlet application, there is a distinction between GET and POST requests. GET requests do not read data from the session; POST requests do. An additional form can be added to a JSP that allows the user to initiate a GET request, thereby starting the application from the beginning.

```
<form method="GET" action="Controller">
  <p>
  <input type="submit" name="editButton"
                       value="New">
</form>
```

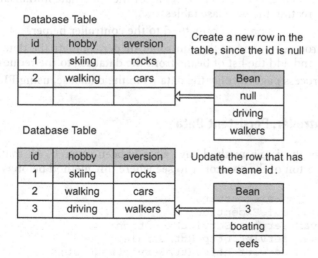

Figure 5.13 Data persistence depends on the primary key.

Contrast this form with the form that is already in the process page. This form uses POST and allows the user to edit the current data.

```
<form method="POST" action="Controller">
  <p>
  <input type="submit" name="editButton"
                        value="Edit">
</form>
```

Both buttons have the same name, they only have different words on the button. The big difference is the type of the request that the forms use. With the GET request, the session will not be read, so a new bean will be used to retrieve the user's data. With the POST request, the old bean will be copied into the current application. The effect of this is that when the bean is saved to the database, it will replace the data that was already saved in the database.

5.6   Application: Persistent Data

The Post Controller example can be extended to save data to the database. The following modifications need to be made.

1. Add the Hibernate JAR files to the *lib* directory of the web application.
2. Initialise Hibernate when the controller is loaded into memory.
3. Add the `WebappListener` class to the `shared` package.
4. Add the statements to the *web.xml* file for starting the listener class.
5. Annotate the bean class as an entity.
6. Add an Id field to the bean, by extending it from `PersistentBase`.
7. If there are any properties in the bean that do not need to be saved, mark them as transient.
8. Add the statements to the *web.xml* file for the Hibernate initialisation parameter for creating the database tables.
9. Add the `initHibernate` method to the controller helper.
10. In the process method of the controller helper, validate the data again, save the data and add the list of beans from the database to the request object.
11. In the process page, display the data from the database, using EL.

5.6.1   Controller: Persistent Data

The details of the `init` method have already been covered. All that is left is to show the skeleton of the controller to see where this method belongs.

```
package ch5.persistentData;
import java.io.IOException;
import javax.servlet.ServletException;
import javax.servlet.http.HttpServlet;
import javax.servlet.http.HttpServletRequest;
import javax.servlet.http.HttpServletResponse;
```

```
public class Controller extends HttpServlet {

  public void init() {
    ...
  }

  protected void doGet(HttpServletRequest request,
      HttpServletResponse response)
      throws IOException, ServletException {
    ...
  }

  protected void doPost(HttpServletRequest request,
      HttpServletResponse response)
      throws IOException, ServletException {
    ...
  }
}
```

5.6.2 ControllerHelper: Persistent Data

The other steps above have been covered in detail, except for modifying the controller helper so that it writes to the database. The data will be saved to the database when the user clicks the process button. The data does not need to be written until this point, because the user has not confirmed that the data is correct.

Be sure to validate the data before it is written to the database. This may seem redundant, but the data is being saved in the session. Sessions expire after a period of inactivity. It is possible that the user entered all the data and then clicked the process button many hours later. In this case, the data would be lost and an empty bean would be added to the database. To avoid this, validate again; if the data is invalid, route the user to an expiration page.

The data retrieved from the database will be made available for JSPs, so it is added to the request object. It is essential that the database is added to the request object and not the session object.

Modify the method that is associated with the process button so that it validates the data, writes to the database and makes the list of data available to the JSPs.

```
@ButtonMethod(buttonName="processButton")
public String processMethod() {
  if (!isValid(data)) {
    return jspLocation("Expired.jsp");
  }
  HibernateHelper.updateDB(data);
  java.util.List list =
    HibernateHelper.getListData(data.getClass());
  request.setAttribute("database", list);
  return jspLocation("Process.jsp");
}
```

The doGet and doPost methods should be modified to test that Hibernate has been configured properly. Wrap the normal statements in these methods with a call to the `testDB` method in the Hibernate helper. If there is an error, the method will send an error page to the browser.

```
protected void doGet()
throws ServletException, java.io.IOException {
  if (HibernateHelper.testDB(response)) {
    addHelperToSession("helper", SessionData.IGNORE);

    String address = editMethod();

    request.getRequestDispatcher(address)
        .forward(request, response);
  }
}

protected void doPost()
throws ServletException, java.io.IOException {
  if (HibernateHelper.testDB(response)) {
    addHelperToSession("helper", SessionData.READ);

    String address = executeButtonMethod();

    request.getRequestDispatcher(address)
        .forward(request, response);
  }
}
```

The other changes to make to the controller helper are to rename all occurrences of the bean class to the name of the annotated bean class and to modify the return value of `jspLocation` to point to the directory of the JSPs.

 Try It   http://bytesizebook.com/book/ch5/persistentData/Controller

Enter some data and navigate to the process page: all the data you entered will be displayed, along with data that is already in the database.

That is all there is to it! Honestly, it may seem a little complicated at first, but that is only because you might not be familiar with what would need to be done if this task were completed using SQL alone. Hibernate generates all the SQL statements that are needed to access the database. It will even create the tables in the database.

5.7   Hibernate Configuration Files

Some of the properties for Hibernate will be the same every time you call it. Instead of placing these in the servlet, they can be placed in a configuration file named `hibernate.cfg.xml`. This is an XML file and will take precedence over the properties added in the `initHibernate` method of the controller helper.

5.7.1   XML File

The statements in the XML file are similar to the statements that were added as properties in Java code. Be sure to update the connection URL, username and password for your database server. If you are using a different type of database, you will need to update the dialect and driver class.

```xml
<?xml version='1.0' encoding='utf-8'?>
<!DOCTYPE hibernate-configuration PUBLIC
"-//Hibernate/Hibernate Configuration DTD 3.0//EN">
<hibernate-configuration>
  <session-factory>
    <property name="dialect">
      org.hibernate.dialect.MySQLDialect
    </property>
    <property name="connection.driver_class">
      com.mysql.jdbc.Driver
    </property>
    <property name="connection.url">
      jdbc:mysql://your-server:your-port/your-database
    </property>
    <property name="connection.username">
      your-user-name
    </property>
    <property name="connection.password">
      your-password
    </property>
    <property name="c3p0.min_size">1</property>
    <property name="c3p0.max_size">5</property>
    <property name="c3p0.timeout">300</property>
    <property name="c3p0.max_statements">50</property>
    <property name="c3p0.idle_test_period">300</property>
  </session-factory>
</hibernate-configuration>
```

5.7.2   File Location

Place this file in the *classes* directory of the web application, since your web application will always have access to it. If you are using NetBeans, then place it in the *Source Packages* folder, under the default package.

5.7.3   Simplified Controller Helper

This file simplifies the initHibernate method of the controller helper.

```java
static public void initHibernate (boolean create) {
  if (create) {
    HibernateHelper
        .createTable(RequestDataPersistent.class);
  }
  HibernateHelper
      .initSessionFactory(RequestDataPersistent.class);
}
```

5.8   Summary

Required validation is used to verify that the user has entered valid data. Regular expressions are a powerful tool for performing complicated validations with simple code.

Hibernate can simplify the process of required validation. It is easy to specify the validation rules using annotations in Hibernate and to generate an array of error messages. Hibernate's array is not as convenient as is needed in a JSP, so a map was created that contains the error messages and can be accessed easily from a JSP. The methods `isValid` and `getErrors` were also added to facilitate generating and retrieving the error messages.

Two types of requests can be made to a servlet: post and get. POST requests can send an unlimited amount of data and the data cannot be viewed in the URL. GET requests are useful for bookmarking a page with the parameters that were needed to find the page. A servlet can handle the two types of requests differently.

Hibernate can be used to save data to a relational database. Once Hibernate has been configured, it is a simple matter to save a bean to a database. Retrieving the data from the database is also a simple task.

Hibernate can use annotations to indicate how the table in the database can be created from the bean. Through the use of annotations, the configuration statements can be placed in the bean instead of in a separate configuration file.

If rows from the database are sent to the JSP, then a loop is needed to display the data. It is better to use a custom HTML tag than to add Java code to the JSP. The JSTL has many useful predefined tags, including a tag that does looping.

Once a servlet has been configured, it is easy to place all of the configuration parameters into a configuration file that can be accessed by all the controllers.

5.9   Chapter Review

Terms

1. Required Validation
2. Regular Expressions
3. Character Class
4. Predefined Character Class
5. Repetition
6. Alternation
7. Grouping
8. Capturing
9. Map
10. Hibernate Validation Messages
11. Java Annotations
12. Error Map
13. Retrieving Error Messages

14. Request Types
    a. GET
    b. POST
15. Initialisation Parameter
16. Primary Key
17. Transient Field

Java

1. Annotations
    a. @Pattern(regex="...", message="...")
    b. @NotNull
    c. @Entity
    d. @Id
    e. @Transient
    f. @GeneratedValue
2. Required Validation
    a. errorMap
    b. setErrors
    c. isValid
    d. getErrors
3. POST Request
4. GET Request
5. Hibernate Helper

New Java

1. `request.setAttribute`
2. Servlet Methods
    a. doPost
    b. init
3. Hibernate Helper
    a. updateDB
    b. getListData
4. JSTL
5. Looping in a JSP

Tags

1. <form method="POST">
2. ${helper.errors.hobby}

3. taglib statement for JSTL
4. forEach in JSTL

Questions

1. If a bean is passed to a method only as an `Object`, what must be done in order to access the public methods in the bean from inside the method?
2. How are the validation errors retrieved from a JSP?
3. Why does the method `setErrors` create a map of error messages, in addition to the Hibernate validation messages?
4. Name two advantages of a POST request over a GET request.
5. Name an advantage of a GET request over a POST request.
6. How is a GET request generated from a browser?
7. How is a POST request generated from a browser?
8. Name an advantage for having two different methods for handling GET and POST requests.
9. What can be done in an application to ensure that whenever a user clicks a button in a form, then a POST request will be made to the controller?
10. What are the three Hibernate properties that must be changed in order to connect to a MySQL server?

Tasks

1. Create regular expressions for the following.
   a. Match one of the following words, ignoring case. Try to create one expression: ned, net, nod, not, ped, pet, pod, pot, red, ret, rod, rot, bed, bet, bod, bot.
   b. A full name.
      i. There must be at least two words.
      ii. Each of the two words must start with an uppercase letter.
   c. A telephone number with the following formats
      i. 999-999-9999
      ii. 999.999.9999
      iii. 999 999 9999
      iv. 9999999999
2. Initialisation Parameters.
   a. Define a servlet tag in *web.xml* for a servlet that will have an initialisation parameter named *interest* with a value of *4.23*.
   b. Write the Java code that would read the value of the initialisation parameter and cast it to a double.
   c. Add an initialisation parameter for the database username for a controller that uses Hibernate to save data. Read the initialisation parameter in the `init` method and use its value as the username when configuring Hibernate.

3. If a bean has properties named make, model and year, then write the code for a JSP that will display all the values for a collection of these beans. Assume that the collection was sent under the name "database".

4. Write an application that accepts city, state, and zip. Validate that the zip code is 5 digits and that the state is FL, GA, NO, LA or MS. Write the data to a database.

5. Write an application that accepts first name, last name and email. Validate that the email has one @ sign in it, and has text before and after the @ sign. Write the valid data to a database and display all the values that are in the database.

6 Advanced HTML and Form Elements

The first time I saw a web page, I was amazed at hypertext links, images, advanced layout, colours and fonts. Of these, hypertext links already existed in another protocol on the web: gopher. Gopher used a series of index pages to navigate a site; the links on one index would take you to another index page or to some text file. Libraries were the principal users of the gopher protocol. A lot of information could be retrieved using gopher; however, it never became popular like the web. It was the remaining features that made the web as popular as it is: images, advanced layout, colours and fonts.

It has been said that a picture is worth a thousand words. This is certainly true for the web. An HTML tag is used to include an image in the current page. This tag is different from all the other tags: it inserts a separate file into the current page at the location of the tag.

There are two aspects of every HTML page: the layout of the page and the style used to display the page. The layout indicates that some text should stand out from the rest of the text, regardless of the browser that is used to display it. The style controls the actual appearance of the text: how much larger than normal text it will be, how many lines precede and follow the text, the type of font that is used to display the text. Many other aspects, like the colour of the text, could also be controlled by the style.

HTML tags have a mix of layout and style. Some tags are very specific about the layout, while others are more specific about the style. Those that indicate a specific layout include tables, lists, and rules. Those that indicate a specific style include italic, bold and underline. Many more tags are more generic about the layout and the style. These tags are intended to be used with a separate file that defines the style to be used for these tags.

A separate syntax is used to describe the style used in a page: *Cascading Style Sheets* [CSS]. By using CSS, the style definition can be saved in one file that can be used by multiple HTML pages; such a file is known as a *style sheet*. By using a style sheet, only one file needs to be edited in order to change the appearance of all pages that use it.

The recommended way to create HTML pages is to use HTML to define the layout of the page and to use a style sheet to control the appearance of the page.

There are other input elements besides the text box. There are elements for entering passwords and many lines of text. There are also elements for displaying checkbox and radio button groups, as well as elements for drop down and multiple selection lists.

Checkbox groups and multiple selection lists are more difficult to initialise with data from the query string. A technique will be introduced to simplify the process. It is also more difficult to save the multiple values, if they are to be saved in a readable format in the database.

6.1 Images

Images are different from other tags. They reference an external file, but the content of the file is displayed in the current file. The tag for embedding an image in a page is <img> and it has an attribute named src for indicating the location of the image file.

```
<img src="happy.gif">
```

When referencing graphics on the web, you must know the complete URL of the source in order to create a link to it. However, depending on where the resource is located, you may be able to speed up the loading of your page by using relative references. The src attribute uses relative and absolute references just like the action attribute in a form.

1. If the resource is not on the same server, then you must specify the entire URL.

```
<img src="http://www.where.com/images/picture.gif">
```

2. If the resource is on the same server, but is not descended from the current directory, then include the full path from the document root, starting with a /.

```
<img src="/not_my_images/picture.gif">
```

3. If the resource is in the same directory as the HTML page that references it, then only include the file name, not the server or the directory.

```
<img src="picture.gif">
```

4. If the resource is in a subdirectory of the directory where the HTML page that references it is located, then include the name of the subdirectory and the file name.

```
<img src="my_graphics/picture.gif">
```

6.2 HTML Design

HTML tags contain layout and style. The basic layout for a tag is whether it is an inline tag or a block tag: inline tags are embedded in the current line, whereas block tags start a new line. A default style has been defined for each HTML tag.

For instance, HTML has a tag for emphasis, <em>. To the HTML designer, the use of this tag meant that the text should indicate emphasis, but did not define what emphasis meant. The only things that the designer knew was that this was an inline tag, so the text would be embedded in the current line, and that the text would look different from normal text, when displayed in the browser. It was up to the browser to implement emphasis: it might underline the text; it might make the text bold; it might invert the colours of the foreground and background. The designer could not specify how the text should be emphasised. There were many such tags that could be used to specify general style, but not to specify the exact appearance.

Other tags are more specific about the style that is used for them. For instance, the italic tag, <i>, indicates that text should be italicised. Most display monitors and browsers can display italicised text, so it is not a bad design to insist that the browser use italics.

There are tags that are more specific about the layout that is used to display them. There are tags for organising data into a list and a table. There is a tag for inserting lines into a page.

Designers liked the ability to specify the exact appearance of the page, so more ways to specify style were added to HTML. A tag to specify the font to be used for text was added. Also, attributes were added to individual tags to specify colour and alignment. However, these additional ways to add style made it difficult to update a web site. These style tags that were placed in the layout tags are now deprecated and should not be used.

6.2.1   Inline and Block Tags

There are two ways that tags are inserted into pages: inline and block. *Inline* tags can be embedded in a line of text. *Block* tags will start on a new line. The emphasis tag, *em*, is an inline tag: it can be used repeatedly in the same sentence. The paragraph tag, *p*, is a block tag: every appearance of the tag will start a new line. If the emphasis tag is used several times in one sentence, there will still be only one sentence in the browser.

```
This <em>is</em> a <em>sentence</em> with several
points of <em>emphasis</em>.
```

If the paragraph tag is used several times in the same line, there will be many lines in the browser.

```
This is a paragraph</p><p>So is this</p><p>And one
more to make a point</p>
```

The above lines of HTML will appear, in most browsers, as Figure 6.1.

6.2.2   General Style Tags

There are many tags in HTML that can be used to add style to a document. These styles are named for the type of text that they represent in a document. There are

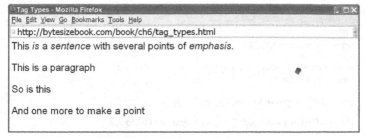

Figure 6.1 Inline and block tags viewed in a browser.

tags for citations, variables, inserted text, deleted text, etc. There is no indication in the tag as to how it will be displayed in a browser; in fact, several of these tags might have the same appearance in a browser. Table 6.1 lists the inline tags and Figure 6.2 shows how they would appear in a browser.

Many of the inline tags seem to do the same thing; for instance, kbd, sample and code all use a fixed space font to display the text. As will be covered soon, through the use of a style sheet, the web designer could define these tags differently. The style could also be changed easily in the future.

There are also different tags defined for blocks of code. These are six tags for headings, one for preformatted text and one for quoted text. Figure 6.3 lists the block tags and how they appear in a browser.

6.2.3   Specific Style Tags

As HTML and display monitors progressed, additional tags were added that could control style directly: the italic tag, <i>, was used in place of the emphasis tag. The emphasis tag still exists, but on most browsers it displays text in italics. Table 6.2 lists the tags for a specific style. The name of the tag indicates how it will appear in the browser.

It would lead to confusion if a designer redefined how these tags appeared. While it is understood that the *em* tag might not show in italics, it is assumed that the *i* tag will use italics. It would be proper to change other characteristics for the *i* tag, but it should always use italics.

Table 6.1 Inline tags and how they appear in a browser.

Tag	Description
acronym	Intended for acronyms, like IBM and MODEM.
cite	Indicates that text is included from another source.
code	Intended to markup code from a program.
del	Indicates that text is to be deleted.
ins	Indicates that text that has been inserted.
dfn	Used to markup text that is a definition.
em	Used to markup text with emphasis.
kbd	Indicates that text is to be entered from the keyboard.
abbr	Used to markup text that is an abbreviation.
samp	Used to markup text that is taken from another source.
strong	Used to markup text that is put forth in a strong way.
var	Used to markup text that represents a variable from a program.

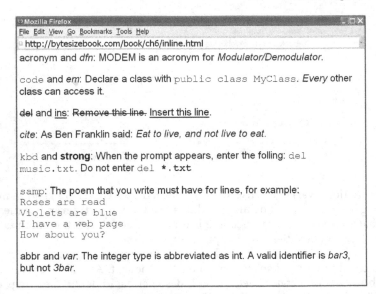

Figure 6.2 Inline tags and how they appear in a browser.

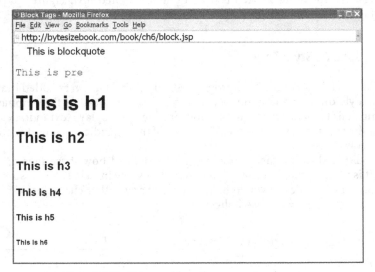

Figure 6.3 Block tags and how they appear in a browser.

Table 6.2 Tags for specific style.

Tag	Style
i	italics
u	underline
b	bold
q	quotes
strike	line through the text
super	superscript
sub	subscript

6.2.4 Layout Tags

There are more ways to lay out a web page than using the paragraph and line break tags. Lists are a useful way to display a table of contents at the top of a page. Tables are used by most news service sites to lay out the material to look like a newspaper page. Horizontal lines can be added to separate sections of text.

Consider the table of contents at the top of a page; such a layout cannot be achieved using paragraph and line breaks. There is no way to indent text or to insert automatic numbering using such simple tags. Think of the web site of any news service: the content is displayed like a newspaper page. Text and images are arranged in columns on the page. There is no way to do this using paragraph and line break tags alone.

Lists

Lists are a good way to organise data in an HTML page. There are three types of lists: ordered, unordered and definition.

Ordered and unordered lists have similar structures. They each use nested `<li>` tags to indicate an item in the list. All the items in the list are enclosed within the paired tags for the list. Ordered lists start with `<ol>` and end with `</ol>`. Unordered lists start with `<ul>` and end with `</ul>`. List items for ordered lists will have a number inserted automatically. List items for unordered lists will have a bullet inserted automatically.

```
<ol>
  <li>First
  <li>Second
  <li>Third
</ol>
<ul>
  <li>Red
  <li>Green
  <li>Blue
</ul>
```

Definition lists start with the `<dl>` tag and end with the `</dl>` tag. Two tags are needed to define each item in a definition list: the term and the definition. The idea of a definition list is that there will be a short term, and then a longer definition of this term. Use the `<dt>` tag to indicate the term, and use the `<dd>` tag to indicate the definition.

```
<dl>
  <dt>Miami
  <dd>
  A city in Florida that has a tropical climate.
  <dt>Maine
  <dd>
  A state in the northeast part of the country.
  <dt>Marne
  <dd>
  A river in France.
</dl>
```

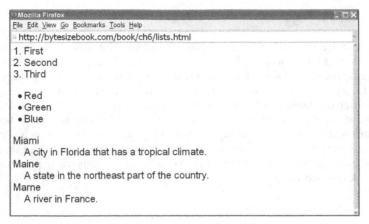

Figure 6.4 The HTML code for lists and how they might appear in a browser.

Figure 6.4 shows how the different lists might appear in a browser.

Tables

Tables are the most sophisticated and most complicated way to layout HTML. Most pages for news agencies use tables to arrange the content on the site. Tables begin with the `<table>` tag and end with the `</table>` tag. Tables use nested `<tr>` tags to indicate rows in the table. Each row has nested `<td>` tags that indicate the data that is in each row. Each `<td>` tag represents one square in the table. The browser will adjust the table so that all rows will display the same number of squares, even if the rows are defined with different numbers of `<td>` tags. The row with the most `<td>` tags determines the number of squares for all the rows in the table.

The default for a `<td>` tag is that it is equivalent to one square in the table. This can be altered with the *rowspan* and *colspan* attributes in the `<td>` tag. The *rowspan* indicates that the `<td>` tag will cover successive squares in different rows, starting in the current row. The *colspan* indicates that the `<td>` will occupy successive squares in the same row. A `<td>` tag can have both *rowspan* and *colspan* attributes.

```
<table border=1>
  <tr>
     <td rowspan=2>
       <img src="/book/images/yoga2.gif"><br>
       <img src="/book/images/yoga2.gif"></td>
     <td colspan=2>
       <img src="/book/images/yoga2.gif">
       <img src="/book/images/yoga2.gif"></td>
  </tr>
  <tr>
     <td rowspan=2 colspan=2>
       <img src="/book/images/yoga2.gif">
       <img src="/book/images/yoga2.gif"><br>
```

```
            <img src="/book/images/yoga2.gif">
            <img src="/book/images/yoga2.gif"></td>
    </tr>
    <tr>
        <td>
            <img src="/book/images/yoga2.gif"></td>
    </tr>
    <tr>
        <td>
            <img src="/book/images/yoga2.gif"></td>
        <td>
            <img src="/book/images/yoga2.gif"></td>
        <td>
            <img src="/book/images/yoga2.gif"></td>
    </tr>
</table>
```

Figure 6.5 shows how a table might appear in a browser. Notice the effect of the *rowspan* and *colspan* attributes.

1. The first cell in the table extends over two rows.
2. The second cell in the first row extends over two columns.
3. The second row is partially filled by the first cell from the first row.
4. The cell in the second row extends over two rows and two columns.
5. The third row is partially filled by the cell from the second row.
6. The fourth row defines all its own cells.

In addition to the <td> tag, there is also the <th> tag. The <th> tag behaves just like a <td> tag, except that the all text in it is centred and is bold.

Figure 6.5 Viewing a table from a browser.

6.3   Cascading Style Sheets

As HTML progressed, more tags were added to control style. However, this soon became unmanageable. Additional attributes were added to the body tag to control the background colour of the page and the text colour of the page. Additional attributes were added to each tag to control alignment; tables could specify borders and padding. Soon, style information was added throughout the layout. If a web site wanted to change the style that was used on every page, there was a lot of tedious editing to do.

While tags like italic had style embedded, it would still be a good design to use the italic tag: a designer would rarely think that all italic text should now be underlined. However, if code was embedded in every page that defined the colour of the text, it is quite reasonable to want to change the colour from time to time: this would be time consuming if the style were embedded in each page.

Style sheets allow the designer to place all the style in a separate file. Many HTML pages can use the same style sheet. The style for all the general styles, like kbd, sample and var, can be redefined using a style sheet.

6.3.1   Adding Style

The simplest way to add style to an HTML page is to include a style sheet. The style sheet is a separate file that contains style definitions. The contents of the file will be covered in the next section. Use a <link> tag in the *head* section of the HTML file to include the style sheet. The <link> tag has three attributes

---

Href

> This contains the URL for the style sheet file. It has the same format as the HREF attribute in the anchor tag, <a>.

Rel

> This will always have a value of *stylesheet.*

Type

> This will have a value of *text/css.*

For example, if the style sheet is named *style.css* and is located in the same directory as the HTML file, then the basic tags for an HTML page might look like the following.

```
<!DOCTYPE HTML PUBLIC "-//W3C//DTD HTML 4.01//EN">
<html>
  <head>
    <link rel="stylesheet" type="text/css"
          href="style.css">
```

```
  <meta http-equiv="content-type"
        content="text/html;charset=utf-8">
  <title>Simple Page</title>
 </head>
 <body>
  <p>
   This is a <i>simple</i> web page.
  </p>
 </body>
</html>
```

Whatever styles are defined in the file, *style.css* would be applied to the web page. Any changes to the style sheet would affect the web page the next time it was loaded into a browser. If the style sheet was referenced from 100 different pages, then every change to the style sheet would immediately affect all 100 pages.

6.3.2 Defining Style

CSS have been defined by W3C. CSS is a recommendation that has been adopted by most web browsers. Each browser is different in its level of compliance with the W3C recommendation. Some features will work one way on one browser and another way on a different browser. The effects will be similar, but will have slight differences.

The best way to define a style sheet is to place it in a separate file from the HTML that it will control. The reason for this is so that the style sheet can be used by many different pages. If the style needs to be changed, then it can be modified in one place and all the pages that reference it will be updated as well.

A style sheet file contains one or more style blocks. A style block contains one or more of the styles that have been defined by W3C. A style block has an HTML tag and a set of curly braces that enclose the styles that will be applied to it.

```
HTML_tag {
    style-name: style-value;
    style-name: style-value;
    style-name: style-value;
}
```

The name of the style block must match an HTML tag. The styles within the block will be applied to all tags that have that name.

Scales

Many of the styles deal with a measurement. Table 6.3 lists many different ways that length can be specified in a style sheet.

Common Styles

There are many styles defined for CSS. Only a few will be used in this book. The basic styles to be used are in the following list.

Table 6.3 CSS Measurements.

Abbreviation	Measurement
px	pixels – dots on the screen. Usually there are 96 to the inch
pt	points – a point is 1/72″ and is usually used to specify a font size
in	inches
cm	centimetres
em	the height of the letter M in the current font
ex	the height of the letter x in the current font
%	percentage of the parent's property

Background-color: Green;

The colour can be a standard colour name or can be a three or six hex digit number (*#036* or *#003568*).

Background-image: Url(fiu.gif);

Enclose the path to the image inside the parentheses. Do not have a space after *url*.

Color: #003399;

The colour can be a standard colour name or can be a three or six hex digit number (*#036* or *#003568*).

Font-family: Bazooka, "Comic Sans MS", Sans-serif;

A number of fonts can be listed. Separate the names by a comma. Enclose multi-word fonts in quotes. The browser will use the first font that it finds. List your fonts from most specific to most general. The generic font family names *serif, monospace, cursive, fantasy* and *sans-serif* can be used as the last option in the list. They act as defaults; if the browser can't find any other font specified, it will be guaranteed to have one of each of these font family categories.

Font-size: 30 pt;

Change the size of the font. The measurement is required. Do not have a space between the number and *pt*. Internet Explorer will default to *pt*, but other browsers will not. If you want your page to be readable in all browsers, then include the measurement.

Font-style: Italic;

Choices are italic, normal, oblique.

Font-weight: Bold;

Choices are bold, lighter, bolder, normal.

Text-align: Left;

Choices are left, right, center, justify.

Text-decoration: Underline;

Choices are underline, overline, none, line-through, blink, normal.

Text-transform: Lowercase;

Choices are lowercase, uppercase, normal, capitalize.

Margin-left: 20%;

Indents the object from the left margin. You can use a percentage or a number.

Margin-right: 20%;

Indents the object from the right margin. You can use a percentage or a number.

Text-indent: 20%;

Indents the first line of text from the margin. You can use a percentage or a number. The value may also be negative.

List-style-type: Lower-alpha;

Choices are decimal, lower-alpha, upper-alpha, lower-roman, upper-roman, disc, circle, square.

Width: 100 px;

Sets the width of the element. Any measurement can be used to define the width.

Default Styles

The above styles should be included within curly braces after the name of the HTML tag to be affected. To affect the entire document, include the properties with the style block for the body tag. The following will make the text colour red for the document, everything will be aligned to the centre and there will be a left margin that is 20% of the total width of the page.

```
body {
    color: red;
    text-align: center;
    margin-left: 20%;
}
```

It is also possible to define styles for just a paragraph, table or any other HTML tag. The following will force all paragraphs to have blue text and to be aligned to the right.

```
p {
    color: blue;
    text-align: right;
}
```

Since the <p> tag is nested within the <body> tag in HTML pages, it will inherit the left margin that was set in the body tag.

Multiple Definition

It is possible to have the same style apply to several tags. Use a comma to separate the names of tags that should use this style. The following style would apply to all <h1> and <h2> tags.

```
h1, h2 {
    text-align: center;
}
```

Nested Definition

It is possible to indicate that a style should be used only if it is nested inside other tags. Specify the order of nested tags that must appear in order to use this style. For example, to control a heading that appears inside a table element, use the following.

```
td h1 {
    font-size: 20pt;
}
```

Named Styles

It is also possible to define several styles for a specific tag. For instance, the <td> tag could have several styles like these.

```
td.money {
    color: green;
    text-align: left;
}

td.sky {
    color: lightblue;
    text-align: center;
}
```

Then the particular *td* would be specified with the class attribute within the *td* tag in the HTML code.

```
<table>
  <tr>
    <td>Normal
    <td class="sky">TD with sky style
    <td class="money">TD with money style
</table>
```

Generic Styles

Styles that can be applied to all tags can be created by naming the tag, but omitting the name of an HTML tag. For instance, to create a style to set the colour to orange that can be used with any HTML tag, just give it a name that starts with a period.

```
.warning {
  color: orange;
}
```

Then any tag could be specified with the class attribute within the tag in the HTML code.

```
<b class="warning">This is a bold warning.</b>
<i class="warning">This is an italicised warning.</i>
```

Pseudo Styles

In addition to the normal tags like *body*, *p* and *td*, there are some pseudo-tags that allow the hypertext links to be controlled.

A:Link

  Controls the appearance of an unvisited hypertext link.

A:Visited

  Controls the appearance of a visited hypertext link.

Style Examples

The following listing contains the code for a style sheet that includes styles similar to those listed above.

```
body {
  text-align: center;
}

p {
  font-style: italic;
  text-align: right;
}

td.under {
  text-decoration: underline;
  text-align: right;
}

td.center {
  font-weight: bold;
  text-align: center;
}

.warning {
  font-size: 150%;
}
```

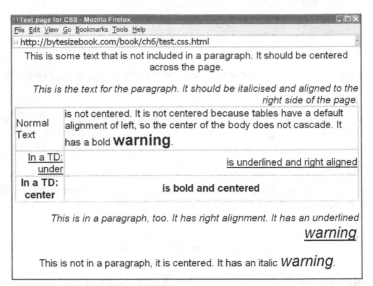

Figure 6.6 A page that uses a style sheet, as seen in a browser.

Next is an example of a page that uses the above style sheet. Notice how the specific *td* tag is specified by `<td class="under">` or `<td class="left">`.

```html
<html>
  <head>
    <title>Test page for CSS</title>
    <link REL="stylesheet" TYPE="text/css"
          HREF="test.css">
  </head>
  <body>
      This is some text that is not included in
      a paragraph. It should be centred across the page.
    <p>
      This is the text for the paragraph. It should
      be italicised and aligned to the right side of the
      page.
    <table border>
      <tr>
        <td>Normal Text</td>
        <td>is not centred. It is not centred because
            tables have a default alignment of left, so
            the centre of the body does not cascade. It
            has a bold <b class="warning">warning</b>.
        </td>
      </tr>
      <tr>
        <td class="under">In a TD: under</td>
    <td class="under">is underlined and right aligned</td>
      </tr>
      <tr>
```

```
      <td class="center">In a TD: centre</td>
      <td class="center">is bold and centred</td>
    </tr>
  </table>
  <p>
    This is in a paragraph, too. It has right alignment.
    It has an underlined <u class="warning">warning</u>.
  </p>
    This is not in a paragraph, it is centred.
    It has an italic <i class="warning">warning</i>.
  </body>
</html>
```

The above page will look like Figure 6.6, when viewed in a browser.

6.4   Form Elements

While being able to enter text in a form and to click a button is all that is needed for data entry, there are form element tags that allow more flexibility when entering data. These tags specify a layout to be used in the browser. There are tags for passwords, multiple lines of text, radio buttons, checkbox buttons and selection lists.

Although there are many ways for the user to enter data in a form, they all have one of three HTML syntaxes: those that look like the *input* tag, the *textarea* tag and the *select* tag.

The *input* tags already include the *text* tag and the *button* tag for submitting data. In addition, there is a variation for entering a password, displaying a radio button and displaying a checkbox button.

The *textarea* tag is used to enter multiple lines of text.

The *select* tag can display a drop down list or a multiple selection list. The drop down list only allows one option to be chosen and the available options can be viewed from a list that drops down from the element in the browser. The multiple selection list allows more than one option to be chosen and displays a scrollable window that displays the available options.

6.4.1   Input Elements

Up until this point, all HTML forms have used only three different form elements: text, hidden, and submit. All three of these use the same tag: `input`.

```
<input type="text" name="hobby"
                   value="${helper.data.hobby}">
<input type="hidden" name="hobby"
                   value="${helper.data.hobby}">
<input type="submit" name="confirmButton"
                   value="Confirm">
```

Additional elements have this same format. The only difference is the content of the *type* attribute.

The *password* type behaves just like a text box, but the value in the browser appears as a row of asterisks. There is not really any security in this. If the form uses the GET method, then the value will appear as plain text in the query string.

```
<input type="password" name="pswd"
                        value="${helper.data.pswd}">
```

The *radio* type has the appearance of a radio button. The user cannot change the value: it is hidden. The button can have two states: checked and unchecked. If it is in the checked state when the form is submitted, then the value will be sent to the server.

There is an additional attribute for radio elements named *checked*. If this word appears in the tag, then the button will be checked whenever the page is loaded.

```
<input type="radio" name="happiness"
                     value="1" checked>
```

The *checkbox* type has the appearance of a checkbox button. The user cannot change the value: it is hidden. It can have two states: checked and unchecked. If it is in the checked state when the form is submitted, then the value will be sent to the server.

There is an additional attribute for check box elements named *checked*. If this word appears in the tag, then the button will be checked whenever the page is loaded.

```
<input type="checkbox" name="extra"
                       value="sprinkles" checked>
```

Radio Group

Radio buttons are most useful when they are placed in groups. A group of radio buttons all have the same name, with different values. Only one of the radio buttons with that name can be in the checked state at any time. Whichever one is checked, that is the value that will be sent in the query string.

In the following listing, if *Ecstatic* is checked by the user, then the radio group will be included in the query string as happiness=2. Even though *Elated* is checked when the page is loaded, the value that the user selects will override the initial value.

```
Level of Happiness:<br>
<input type="radio" name="happiness"
       value="1" checked>
       Elated
<input type="radio" name="happiness"
       value="2">
       Ecstatic
<input type="radio" name="happiness"
       value="3">
       Joyous<br>
```

It is not necessary that the values for a radio group be numeric. All values are actually strings, even if they appear to be numeric. Numbers were used in this example only to demonstrate that numbers can be used as values.

Checkbox Group

A group of checkboxes all have the same name, with different values. More than one element in a checkbox group can be in the checked state at any time. Checkbox groups are especially useful for the programmer. In a servlet, a checkbox group can be processed using a loop.

All the checked values will be sent in the query string as separate *name = value* pairs. For instance, if *Chocolate Sprinkles* and *Hot Fudge* are checked, then they would be included in the query string as extra=sprinkles&extra=fudge.

```
Preferred Extras:<br>
<input type="checkbox" name="extra"
       value="sprinkles">
       Chocolate Sprinkles
<input type="checkbox" name="extra"
       value="fudge" checked>
       Hot Fudge
<input type="checkbox" name="extra"
       value="cream">
       Whipped Cream<br>
```

6.4.2   Textarea Element

Text boxes can only include one line of text. To enter multiple lines of text, use a *textarea* element.

```
<textarea name="comments"></textarea>
```

This will display as a box in which text can be typed. All the text in the box will be sent to the server when the form is submitted. If you want an initial value to display when the page is loaded, place it between the opening and closing *textarea* tags.

6.4.3   Select Elements

There are two types of select lists: single selection lists and multiple selection lists. The single selection list is also known as a drop down list. The multiple selection list is also known as a scrollable list.

Single Selection List

This appears in the browser as a drop down list of values. Whichever value the user selects, that is the value that will be sent to the browser. The first value in the list is the default value that will be sent to the browser, if the user does not make a selection.

The selection list has nested tags for each of the options in the list. To have one of them selected as the default, include an attribute named *selected* in the option.

```
Grade
<select name="grade">
  <option value="4.0">A
  <option value="3.67">A-
  <option value="3.33" selected>B+
  <option value="3.00">B
  <option value="2.67">B-
  <option value="2.33">C+
  <option value="2.00">C
</select>
```

It is not necessary that the values for a select list be numeric. All values are actually strings, even if they appear to be numeric. Numbers were used in this example only to demonstrate that numbers can be used as values.

Multiple Selection List

The only differences between the single selection list and the multiple selection list are two attributes: multiple and size. The attribute *multiple* indicates that more than one option may be selected by using the shift or control keys. The attribute *size* is used to set the number of options that are visible in the scrollable window. If the size is omitted then all the options will be visible in the window and the scroll bars will not function.

```
<select name="team" multiple size="2">
  <option value="heat">Heat
  <option value="marlins">Marlins
  <option value="dolphins">Dolphins
  <option value="panthers">Panthers
</select>
```

6.4.4   Bean Implementation

With the introduction of additional form elements, the bean must be modified to handle the new elements. Some of the new elements are handled the same way that text boxes are handled. Other elements require more work to store the multiple values in the bean and to display the values in a JSP.

Bean Properties

All the bean properties we have seen until now have been single-valued: the variable is a primitive type; the mutator has a primitive parameter; the accessor returns a primitive type (Listing 6.1).

```
protected String comments;
public void setComments(String comments) {
    this.comments = comments;
}

public String getComments() {
    return comments;
}
```
Listing 6.1 Template for a single-valued property.

With the introduction of checkbox groups and multiple selection lists, there must be a way to store the multiple values in the bean. This requires the notion of a multiple-valued bean property. If a property in a bean is multiple-valued, then declare the variable as an array and change the signatures of the mutator and accessor to agree (Listing 6.2).

```
protected String[] extra;
public void setExtra(String[] extra) {
    this.extra = extra;
}

public String[] getExtra() {
    return extra;
}
```
Listing 6.2 Template for a multiple-valued property.

Even though there are many different form elements, there are only two types of bean properties: single-valued and multiple-valued. In the bean, there is no way to determine if a single-valued property was set using a text box or a radio button; there is no way to determine if a multiple-valued property was set using a checkbox group or a multiple selection list. This makes it easier for the developer to implement a bean: there are only two possible choices for implementing a bean property.

Filling the Bean

For multiple-valued elements, there will be multiple *name = value* pairs in the query string. For instance, if a checkbox group named *team* has the teams *heat* and *marlins* checked, then the query string will appear as

```
?team=heat&team=marlins
```

For these elements, another method that is part of the request object will retrieve all of these values: getParameterValues. This method returns an array of strings that contains all of the values that are in the query string. If there are no values, then the method returns *null*.

In order to copy all the values from the query string, it would be necessary to call the property's accessor with the values from the query string.

```
data.setTeam(request.getParameterValues("team"));
```

The good news is that the fillBeanFromRequest method that has been used to copy the values from the query string to the bean will also work for multiple-valued properties. The fillBeanFromRequest method that is in the bean base class does not need to be modified to work for multiple-valued properties.

Until now, all properties have been strings. In the bean for this example, the happiness property has been defined as an integer and the grade property has been defined as a double.

```
protected int happiness;
protected double grade;
public void setHappiness(int happiness) {
    this.happiness = happiness;
}

public int getHappiness() {
    return happiness;
}
...
public void setGrade(double grade) {
    this.grade = grade;
}

public double getGrade() {
    return grade;
}
```

This was done to demonstrate that the fillBeanFromRequest method could also process these types; it will convert the value from the string in the form into the correct numeric type. If there is an error, then a value of zero is returned.

Please do not think that all radio groups must use integers or that all single select lists must use doubles. These types were chosen for demonstration purposes and a string could have been used for either of these properties.

Resetting Nullable Fields

As long as a form element that is a text box has a name, then data for the text box will be sent in the query string. If no data is entered by the user, then the name of the text box will be in the query string, but the value will be the empty string.

```
hobby=&confirmButton=Confirm
```

This is also true for hidden elements, password elements, text areas and single selection lists.

Radio groups, checkbox groups and multiple selection lists are different. If the user does not make a choice in these elements, then the name of the element will not be in the query string.

This causes a problem for the fillBeanFromRequest method. It calls the mutators for all the properties that are named in the query string. If the name of a property is not in the query string, then the mutator of that property will not be called.

Imagine that the user makes some choices in a checkbox group and hits the confirm button. The values that the user chose will be placed into the query string.

```
extras=fudge&extras=cream&confirmButton=Confirm
```

When the values from the query string are copied to the bean, the mutator for the property will be called, with an array containing *fudge* and *cream*. A bean with these values will be placed in the session.

Now imagine that the user clicks the edit button, returns to the edit page and unchecks all the values. When the user clicks the confirm button, the name of the checkbox group will not be in the query string, because all of the values were unchecked.

```
confirmButton=Confirm
```

In this case, the mutator for the checkbox group's property will not be called, since the fillBeanFromRequest method only calls the mutators for properties that are in the query string. The effect of this is that the old values from the session will not be erased. The only way to erase those values is to call the setter again with new values. Since the user did not specify any new values, then the old values will still be there.

The solution to this problem is to manually call the setters for those properties that might not be included in the query string. These types of elements are often called *nullable* elements. Create a method that will call the mutators for each of the nullable elements.

```
public void resetNullable() {
  data.setExtra(null);
  data.setTeam(null);
  data.setHappiness(0);
}
```

Use appropriate values to reset the properties. Call this method before new values are copied from the request into the bean.

```
resetNullable();
fillBeanFromRequest(data);
```

Accessing Multiple-Valued Properties

Since the accessors for multiple-valued elements return arrays, the JSP can access the values using a loop like the one that was used for displaying the database in Chapter Five. In this case, the array contains strings, so it is easy to display each of the values.

Notice that the *taglib* statement must appear in the confirm page once and before any references to its tags.

```
<%@ taglib uri="http://java.sun.com/jsp/jstl/core"
           prefix="core" %>
<ul>
<core:forEach var="extra"
              items="${helper.data.extra}">
  <li>${extra}
```

```
</core:forEach>
</ul>
...
<ul>
<core:forEach var="team"
               items="${helper.data.team}">
  <li>${team}
</core:forEach>
</ul>
```

In these two examples, the multiple values have been displayed using one of the advanced layout tags: unordered list. The opening and closing list tags are placed before and after the loop tag. In the loop, each element in the array is displayed with a list item tag.

6.5   Application: Complex Elements

An application will be developed that uses all of these new form elements. There will be a password field, a radio group, a checkbox group, a textarea for multiple lines of text, a single selection list (drop down list) and a multiple selection list (scrollable list).

6.5.1   Controller: Complex Elements

In order to see what the query string looks like for each request, all forms will use the GET method. The controller will only need to be able to process GET requests.

6.5.2   ControllerHelper: Complex Elements

The controller helper will be the same as the controller helper from the *Enhanced* example in Chapter Four, except for the name of the bean, the helper base class and the location of the JSPs. The helper base will be the one from Chapter Five.

6.5.3   Edit.jsp: Complex Elements

The edit page is the page that defines the data for the application. The edit page is where the user will enter all the data, so this is the page that will be defined first. All the other pages depend on this page; the bean will depend on the names of the form elements that are added to this page.

Listing 6.3 shows the edit page. It has a password field, a radio group, a checkbox group, a textarea, a single selection list and a multiple selection list. Each of these elements in the form is identical to the examples that were just developed above.

```
<!DOCTYPE html PUBLIC "-//W3C//DTD html 4.01//EN">
<html>
<head>
  <meta http-equiv="content-type"
        content="text/html;charset=utf-8">
```

```
  <title>Complex Form - Edit Page</title>
  <link rel="stylesheet" href="/book/complex.css"
        type="text/css">
</head>
<body>
  <form method="get" action="Controller">
    Secret Code
    <input type="password" name="secretCode"><br>
    Level of Happiness:<br>
    <input type="radio" name="happiness"
           value="1" checked>
           Elated
    <input type="radio" name="happiness"
           value="2">
           Ecstatic
    <input type="radio" name="happiness"
           value="3">
           Joyous<br>
    Preferred Extras:<br>
    <input type="checkbox" name="extra"
           value="sprinkles">
           Chocolate Sprinkles
    <input type="checkbox" name="extra"
           value="fudge" checked>
           Hot Fudge
    <input type="checkbox" name="extra"
           value="cream">
           Whipped Cream<br>
    Comments<textarea name="comments"></textarea>
    <br>
    Grade
    <select name="grade">
      <option value="4.0">A
      <option value="3.67">A-
      <option value="3.33" selected>B+
      <option value="3.00">B
      <option value="2.67">B-
      <option value="2.33">C+
      <option value="2.00">C
    </select>
    <br>
    Team
    <select name="team" multiple size="2">
      <option value="heat">Heat
      <option value="marlins">Marlins
      <option value="dolphins">Dolphins
      <option value="panthers">Panthers
    </select>
    <br>
    <input type="submit" name="confirmButton"
                         value="Confirm">
  </form>
</body></html>
```

Listing 6.3 An edit page that uses complex form elements.

Table 6.4 Correlation between the form elements and the bean properties.

Element		Property	
Name	Type	Accessor	Type
secretCode	password	getSecretCode	single-valued
happiness	radio	getHappiness	single-valued
extra	checkbox	getExtra	multiple-valued
comments	textarea	getComments	single-valued
grade	select	getGrade	single-valued
team	select	getTeam	multiple-valued

6.5.4 Java Bean: Complex Elements

The edit page is the most important file in the application; it defines the data. Once the edit page has been created, it is a straightforward process to create the bean.

The names of the bean properties will correspond to the names of the form elements in the edit page. The type of form element that is used in the edit page will determine whether the bean uses a single-valued property or a multiple-valued property.

The names and types of the form elements from the edit page are listed in Table 6.4 along with the corresponding name of the accessor for the property and the type of the property.

All of the single-valued properties will look like the property for the text area field, `comments`, from Listing 6.1.

All of the multiple-valued properties will look like the property for the checkbox group, `extra`, from Listing 6.2.

The only differences for the other elements will be the name of the property and, possibly, the type of the property.

6.5.5 Confirm.jsp, Process.jsp: Complex Elements

The data from the bean is displayed in the confirm page. A nested ordered list is used to display the data from the bean. A loop is used to display the data from the multiple-valued elements: extra and team (Listing 6.4).

```
...
<%@ taglib uri="http://java.sun.com/jsp/jstl/core"
           prefix="core" %>
<html>
  <head>
    <meta http-equiv="content-type"
          content="text/html;charset=utf-8">
    <title>Complex Form - Confirm Page</title>
  </head>
  <body>
    <p>
       This page displays the values from some
       complex form elements.
    </p>
```

```
<ul>
  <li>Secret Code: ${helper.data.secretCode}
  <li>Level of Happiness: ${helper.data.happiness}
  <li>Extras:
    <ul>
    <core:forEach var="extra"
                  items="${helper.data.extra}">
      <li>${extra}
    </core:forEach>
    </ul>
  <li>Comments: ${helper.data.comments}
  <li>Grade: ${helper.data.grade}
  <li>Teams:
    <ul>
    <core:forEach var="team"
                  items="${helper.data.team}">
      <li>${team}
    </core:forEach>
    </ul>
</ul>
...
```

Listing 6.4 A confirm page that loops through the values in complex form elements.

Except for having only one button, instead of two, the process page is identical to the confirm page.

Try It   http://bytesizebook.com/book/ch6/complexForm/Controller

See how the elements look and interact with them. Submit the form to inspect the query string.

Choose some values in the form (Figure 6.7).

Click the confirm button. The chosen values are displayed in the page and appear in the query string (Figure 6.8).

The entire query string will not be visible in the location window of the browser. If it could all be seen at once, it would look like the following string. The multiple-valued properties each have more than one item selected, so each one has multiple entries in the query string.

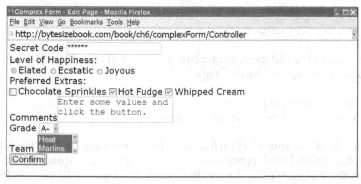

Figure 6.7 Make some choices in the form elements.

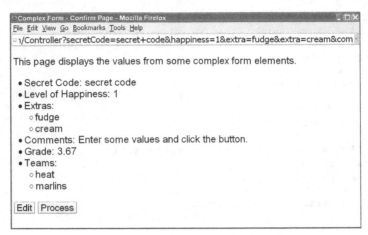

Figure 6.8 The confirm page with all the choices listed.

```
?secretCode=secret+code&happiness=1&extra=fudge&extra=cream
&comments=Enter+some+values+and+click+the+button.
&grade=3.67&team=heat&team=marlins&confirmButton=Confirm
```

6.6 Using Advanced Form Elements

Using these new tags makes it easier for the user to enter data, but makes life a little more complicated for the developer. There is a new technique for initialising buttons in the checked state and for initialising the selection lists with selected options that are in the query string. For elements that allow the user to select multiple choices, a new technique is needed to save the data to the database.

6.6.1 Initialising Form Elements

Initialising password fields is identical to initialising text elements.

```
<input type="password" name="secretCode"
       value="${helper.data.secretCode}">
```

Textareas are a little different, because they are paired tags. Place the initial value between the opening and closing tags.

```
<textarea name="comments"
       >${helper.data.comments}</textarea>
```

The radio, checkbox and selection lists are a bit more complicated. The initial state of a radio button or checkbox button is controlled by an attribute named checked. If this attribute is present in the tag, then the button will be in the checked state; if the attribute is missing, then the button will be in the unchecked state.

In the following listing, the radio button for *Elated* will be in the checked state every time the page is loaded; the *Ecstatic* button will not be checked.

```
<input type="radio" name="happiness"
       value="1" checked>
       Elated
<input type="radio" name="happiness"
       value="2">
       Ecstatic
```

Somehow, if the value associated with the checkbox or radio button is in the query string, then the button should have the word *checked* inserted into the tag.

One way to solve this problem is to place each tag in an if block and test if the corresponding value is in the query string. This gets very messy, very quickly. It would make the JSP very difficult to read, because there would be many if statements scattered amongst the HTML. There is a better solution that uses a map.

A solution to the problem of initialising form buttons, which avoids using any if statements to determine if *checked* should be inserted into the tag, is to add a map to the helper base that will associate the string *checked* with those values that are in the query string.

The idea is to create a map that associates a form element with the word *checked*. Each radio button or checkbox button in the form will have an entry in the map, if the button was checked by the user. If the user did not check the button, then that button will not have an entry in the map.

6.6.2 Map of Checked Values

The way this will be done is to create a map of maps. There will be a map for each radio group or checkbox group that has a button checked. Each of these maps will be placed in an all-encompassing map. This will allow the JSP to access the big map and be able to access the individual maps by the name of the radio group or checkbox group.

Each of the smaller maps will associate a string with a string, so the map should be instantiated as such.

```
Map<String, String>
```

The all-encompassing map will associate a string with one of the smaller maps. This map will have a key that is a string, but the value will be a smaller map.

```
Map<String, Map<String, String>>
```

The map will store the word *checked* for all those buttons that have been checked by the user, so it will be called *checked*.

```
Map<String, Map<String, String>> checked
        = new HashMap<String, Map<String, String>>();
```

One way to envision this is to think of a map of the world. Each country will be represented on the world map, but to obtain specific information about a country, a more detailed map for just that country would be needed.

A Small Map

For each radio and checkbox group that has a button checked, there must be a small map added to the big map. Each group will have its own small map inside the larger map.

Consider a radio group named *happiness*.

```
<input type="radio" name="happiness" value="1">Elated
<input type="radio" name="happiness" value="2">Ecstatic
<input type="radio" name="happiness" value="3">Joyous
```

A small map must be created for the radio group in the *checked* map. The name of the group will be used as the key to retrieve the small map from the *checked* map.

```
checked.put("happiness",
            new HashMap<String, String>());
```

Each checked button in the group will be added to this small map.

Adding a Key

If the user has chosen *Ecstatic* in the radio group, then the value in the query string for the radio group will be 2. That is the string that will be used as the key for the radio group's map; the value will be the word *checked*.

```
checked.get("happiness").put("2", "checked");
```

The call to checked.get("happiness") returns the map for the radio group. In this map, the word *checked* is associated with the key 2 by using the put method of the small map.

Figure 6.9 shows the big map with a small map for a radio group and a small map for a checkbox group.

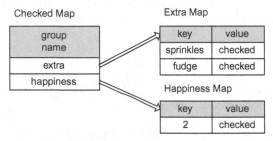

Figure 6.9 The big map with two small maps.

Retrieving Map Values

Later, to determine if the *Ecstatic* button should be checked, use the name of the group to retrieve the small map for the group, then retrieve the word stored in the map for the button, using the button's value as the key to the map.

```
checked.get("happiness").get("2")
```

Assuming that the user clicked this button, this will return the word *checked*.

Notice that the parameter to the first *get* is the name of the group for the button and the parameter to the second *get* is the value of the button.

```
<input type="radio" name="happiness" value="2">Ecstatic
```

What will be returned if the map is accessed with the other values in the radio group?

```
checked.get("happiness").get("1")
checked.get("happiness").get("3")
```

In both cases, the map will return *null*. Since neither button was clicked, then neither value was sent in the query string and neither value was placed into the map for the radio group.

Select lists use the word *selected* to select an option in the list. In addition to a map for the checked values, a similar map will be created for the selection lists. This map will associate the word *selected* with those values that have been chosen by the user.

Modifying the Helper Base

Both of these maps will be added to the helper base class.

```
protected Map<String, Map<String, String>> checked =
    new HashMap<String, Map<String, String>>();
protected Map<String, Map<String, String>> selected =
    new HashMap<String, Map<String, String>>();
```

Two accessors will be added to the helper base class so that the maps can be accessed from a JSP.

```
public Map getChecked() {
  return checked;
}
public Map getSelected() {
  return selected;
}
```

For each selected group or list, a new map must be created. If the map for a group or list does not exist when an item is added, then the map will be created for that group. This will be encapsulated in a method that accepts the name of the group or list and the value that the user has chosen. If there is no map for the group or list, then a new map will be created. Then, the appropriate word will be added to the map for the value.

```java
public void addChecked(String group, String item) {
  if (checked.get(group) == null) {
    checked.put(group,
              new HashMap<String, String>());
  }
  checked.get(group).put(item, "checked");
}
public void addSelected(String list, String item) {
  if (selected.get(list) == null) {
    selected.put(list,
              new HashMap<String, String>());
  }
  selected.get(list).put(item, "selected");
}
```

A method will be added for clearing all values from the maps.

```java
public void clearMaps() {
  checked.clear();
  selected.clear();
}
```

Figure 6.10 contains a diagram of the helper base class. The maps, accessors and helper methods have been added. An additional method has been added, which will be explained in the next section.

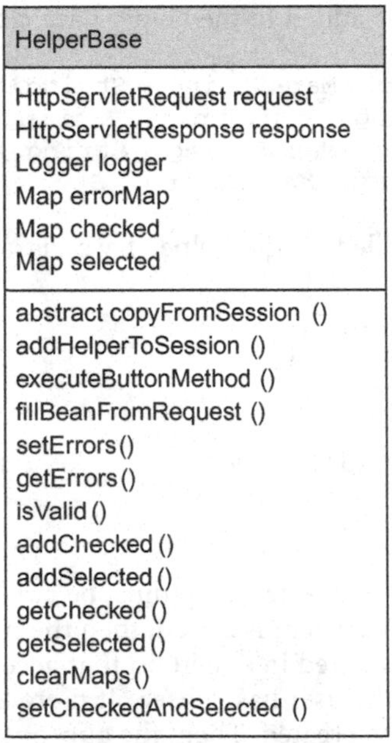

HelperBase
HttpServletRequest request
HttpServletResponse response
Logger logger
Map errorMap
Map checked
Map selected
abstract copyFromSession ()
addHelperToSession ()
executeButtonMethod ()
fillBeanFromRequest ()
setErrors ()
getErrors ()
isValid ()
addChecked ()
addSelected ()
getChecked ()
getSelected ()
clearMaps ()
setCheckedAndSelected ()

Figure 6.10 The helper base class with the checked and selected maps.

6.6.3 Automating the Process

The process of calling the addChecked and addSelected methods can be automated by annotating the properties in the bean that correspond to radio groups, checkbox groups and selection lists. A new annotation will be used to mark the accessors of those properties.

Since these properties are set by adding the *checked* or *selected* attribute to the element in the form, the annotation will be called SetByAttribute. The annotation will have an attribute that indicates whether this property is set by using the word *checked* or *selected*. To reduce errors, an enumeration has been created for the two possible values (Figure 6.11).

The annotation uses a value from the enumeration to configure the property. For those properties that correspond to radio and checkbox groups, use the AttributeType.CHECKED value; for those that correspond to selection lists, use the AttributeType.SELECTED value.

```
import shared.SetByAttribute;
import shared.AttributeType;
...
@SetByAttribute(type=AttributeType.CHECKED)
public int getHappiness() {
   return happiness;
}

@SetByAttribute(type=AttributeType.SELECTED)
public double getGrade() {
   return grade;
}
```

Like the *ButtonMethod* annotation, a method has been added to the helper base that loops through all the methods in the bean and looks for those that have been marked with the SetByAttribute annotation. For those accessors that have been marked, the appropriate addChecked or addSelected method will be called. If the accessor returns an array, then all of the values will be added to the map. The name of this method is setCheckedAndSelected; it has been added to the helper base class.

```
protected void setCheckedAndSelected(Object data) {
   ...
}
```

By calling setCheckedAndSelected, all the values in the bean for radio groups, checkbox groups and selection lists will be added to the corresponding

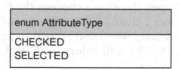

enum AttributeType
CHECKED
SELECTED

Figure 6.11 The enumeration of AttributeType.

checked or selected map. As long as the annotations have been added in the bean, this is the only method that needs to be called to add the values to the maps.

Setting the Maps

The maps should be filled every time that the bean has new data added to it. This corresponds to the time when fillBeanFromRequest is called.

```
fillBeanFromRequest(data);
setCheckedAndSelected(data);
```

JSP Access

The big payoff for this technique can be seen from a JSP. Since accessors were added to the helper base that return the all-encompassing maps for *checked* and *selected*, then EL can access the maps from a JSP.

```
${helper.checked}
${helper.selected}
```

EL is especially useful when accessing a map; the *get* method of a map can be accessed using the dot notation. Therefore, the map for the radio group can also be retrieved.

```
${helper.checked.happiness}
```

Finally, the word associated with the value *2* in the radio group can be retrieved. For those values in a map that are numbers or have embedded spaces, the dot notation cannot be used to retrieve them. However, EL also allows array notation to be used to access the get method of a map.

```
${helper.checked.happiness["2"]}
```

Consider the complete radio group that has the code added to it for retrieving the values from its map.

```
Level of Happiness:
<input type="radio" name="happiness" value="1"
       ${helper.checked.happiness["1"]}>Elated
<input type="radio" name="happiness" value="2"
       ${helper.checked.happiness["2"]}>Ecstatic
<input type="radio" name="happiness" value="3"
       ${helper.checked.happiness["3"]}>Joyous
```

Ask yourself what will happen if the user chooses the *Ecstatic* button.

In this case, ${helper.checked.happiness["2"]} will return the value *checked*. Both ${helper.checked.happiness["1"]} and ${data.checked.happiness["3"]} will return *null*, which EL will render as the empty string.

The radio group will be returned to the browser with the button for *Ecstatic* checked and the other buttons unchecked.

```
Level of Happiness:
<input type="radio" name="happiness" value="1"
            >Elated
<input type="radio" name="happiness" value="2"
            checked>Ecstatic
<input type="radio" name="happiness" value="3"
            >Joyous
```

A similar process will occur if the user checks one of the other buttons. The trick is that the value that was sent in the query string to the controller has been used as a key in the map for the radio group, while the other values in the radio group have not been added to the map.

Data Flow

To take a closer look at how the data moves from the JSP to the controller and back again, modify the checkbox group in the JSP so that all the boxes whose values are in the query string are checked when the page is loaded.

```
<input type="checkbox" name="extra" value="sprinkles"
        ${helper.checked.extra.sprinkles}>
        Chocolate Sprinkles
<input type="checkbox" name="extra" value="fudge"
        ${helper.checked.extra.fudge}>
        Hot Fudge
<input type="checkbox" name="extra" value="cream"
        ${helper.checked.extra.cream}>
        Whipped Cream
```

Assuming that the user selects *sprinkles* and *fudge*, this is the path that the data would follow.

1. There are three options in the checkbox group: *sprinkles*, *fudge*, and *cream*.
2. The user selects *sprinkles* and *fudge*.
3. The query string would contain extra=sprinkles&extra=fudge.
4. These values would be placed into an array by the servlet engine: {"sprinkles", "fudge"}
5. This array would be returned by the getExtra method in the bean.
6. The setCheckedAndSelected method would loop through these values and call addChecked for each, adding *sprinkles* and *fudge* to the hash map for the checkbox group.
7. The map for the checkbox group would be created before the first value is added to it.
8. The map for the checkbox group would have the pairs ("sprinkles", "checked") and ("fudge", "checked") in it.
9. In the JSP

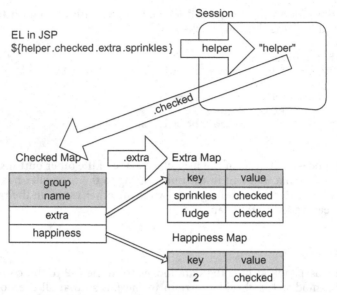

Figure 6.12 Accessing the small map for a checkbox group.

a. `${helper.checked.extra["sprinkles"]}` would return the value *checked*.

b. `${helper.checked.extra["fudge"]}` would return the value *checked*.

c. `${helper.checked.extra["cream"]}` would return `null` and would be displayed as the empty string.

Figure 6.12 demonstrates how the EL statement in a JSP accesses a small map for a checkbox group named *extra*.

6.7 Application: Initialised Complex Elements

The *Complex Form* example will be modified so that the form elements are initialised with data that is in the query string. This means that if the user enters data in the edit page, proceeds to the confirm page and returns to the edit page, then all of the user's choices will be initialised in the form.

1. The controller will handle GET and POST requests.
2. The JSP forms will be modified so that they use the POST method.
3. The maps for the checked and selected values will be added to the helper base.
4. The accessors and helper methods for the checked and selected maps will be added to the helper base.
5. The methods for automating the process of setting the values in the maps will be added to the helper base.
6. The bean will be annotated with the `SetByAttribute` annotation.
7. The edit page will have the EL added to it for retrieving the *checked* and *selected* attributes.

6.7.1   Java Bean: Initialised Complex Elements

Annotate all the accessors for radio groups, checkbox groups and select lists with the *SetByAttribute* annotation.

```
...
@SetByAttribute(type=AttributeType.CHECKED)
public int getHappiness() {
   return happiness;
}

@SetByAttribute(type=AttributeType.SELECTED)
public double getGrade() {
   return grade;
}

@SetByAttribute(type=AttributeType.CHECKED)
public String[] getExtra() {
   return extra;
}

@SetByAttribute(type=AttributeType.SELECTED)
   public String[] getTeam() {
   return team;
}
...
```

6.7.2   HelperBase: Initialised Complex Elements

The maps for *checked* and *selected* values will be added to the helper base class as member variables. The helper methods for setting values in the maps will be added. Accessors will be added for retrieving the maps from JSPs. The method for automating the process will be added.

```
protected Map<String, Map<String, String>> checked =
   new HashMap<String, Map<String, String>>();

protected Map<String, Map<String, String>> selected =
   new HashMap<String, Map<String, String>>();
...
public Map getChecked() {
  return checked;
}

public Map getSelected() {
  return selected;
}
...
protected void setCheckedAndSelected(Object data) {
   ...
}
```

Additional methods for using the maps have also been added to the helper base. See the Appendix for a complete listing of the Helper Base class for Chapter 6.

6.7.3   ControllerHelper: Initialised Complex Elements

Up until now, whenever data was copied from the session, only the bean was copied. Now, there is additional data to be copied from the session into the current helper: the maps for selected and checked values. The copy method needs to be updated so that the maps are copied from the data in the session into the current helper.

```
. . .
public void copyFromSession(Object sessionHelper) {
  if (sessionHelper.getClass() == this.getClass()) {
    ControllerHelper helper =
        (ControllerHelper) sessionHelper;
    data = helper.data;
    checked = helper.checked;
    selected = helper.selected;
  }
}
. . .
```

The radio groups, checkbox groups and multiple select lists might not have any choices chosen by the user. In order to delete all the old values from the session, call the mutator for each nullable property. A method named *resetNullable* will be added to the controller helper. In it, each of the mutators for the radio, checkbox and multiple selection list have been called with appropriate values.

```
. . .
public void resetNullable() {
  data.setExtra(null);
  data.setTeam(null);
  data.setHappiness(0);
}
. . .
```

Reset the nullable elements before new data is added to the bean. Add the values for the checked and selected maps after new data has been added to the bean. Perform these tasks in the method for the confirm button, since this is the only time when there is new data.

```
. . .
@ButtonMethod(buttonName="confirmButton")
public String confirmMethod() {
  resetNullable();
  fillBeanFromRequest(data);
  setCheckedAndSelected(data);
  String address;
  if (isValid(data)) {
    address = jspLocation("Confirm.jsp");
```

```
  } else {
    address = jspLocation("Edit.jsp");
  }
  return address;
}
...
```

It is not necessary to reset the maps for the selected and checked values, since these are reset every time that `setCheckedAndSelected` is called.

6.7.4   Edit.jsp: Initialised Complex Elements

Initialise the checkbox buttons with the values from the query string, by including the code that accesses the maps. Each reference will be similar.

```
<input type="checkbox" name="extra" value="sprinkles"
       ${helper.checked.extra.sprinkles}>
       Chocolate Sprinkles
```

The radio group is initialised in a similar way.

Initialise each option in the multiple selection list with the values from the query string by including the code that accesses the maps. Each reference will be similar.

```
<option value="heat"
        ${helper.selected.team.heat}>
        Heat
```

The single selection list is initialised in a similar way.

Try It   http://bytesizebook.com/book/ch6/complexInit/Controller

Enter some values into the form, then click the confirm button. From the confirm page, click the edit button and you will see the edit page initialised with all the values that were selected before.

6.7.5   Saving Multiple Choices

It is not difficult to save a bean that uses the advanced form elements. The single-valued properties behave just like text boxes. For multiple-valued properties, the accessors need two additional Hibernate annotations.

```
@CollectionOfElements
@IndexColumn
```

The `CollectionOfElements` attribute means that Hibernate will create an additional table for the multiple-valued property. This is completely transparent at the Java class level. Figure 6.13 is an example of data that is in the main table for the bean that has been developed in this chapter. It does not include the data for the multiple-valued properties; that data is stored in separate tables.

```
mysql> select * from complexdatapersistent;
+----+-----------+--------------+-----------+-------+
| id | secretCode | comments     | happiness | grade |
+----+-----------+--------------+-----------+-------+
|  1 | rutabega  | Nothing much |         1 | 3.33  |
|  2 | blahblah  | No comment.  |         2 |    4  |
+----+-----------+--------------+-----------+-------+
2 rows in set (0.00 sec)
```

Figure 6.13 The data for the one-to-many properties is not in the main table.

The data for each multiple-valued property is stored in a separate table. Each separate table is related to the main table for the bean. In order to build this relationship, each row in the separate table will contain the primary key of the related row in the main table. However, there can be multiple rows in the separate table for one row in the main table.

In order to identify each of the rows uniquely, there is a secondary key in the related table. The secondary key distinguishes amongst multiple values for the same row in the main table. This is an example of a table that has a composite primary key. It is made up of two columns: the primary key from the main table and the secondary key from the related table. The secondary key will be generated by the database and is referred to as an index column.

Figure 6.14 shows the values for the checkbox group, named *extra*. The first column in the table contains the primary key from the main table. The last column in the table contains the secondary key. The primary key and the secondary key together will uniquely identify each row in this table.

The `IndexColumn` attribute sets the name of the column for the secondary key in the separate related table. The `base` attribute is where to start indexing. The usual values are zero or one.

```
...
@CollectionOfElements
@IndexColumn(name="extra_pos", base=0)
@SetByAttribute(type=AttributeType.CHECKED)
public String[] getExtra() {
    return extra;
}
...
```

Only annotate properties that return an array with these annotations. If single-valued properties are annotated with them, there will be a runtime error.

```
mysql> select * from complexdatapersistent_extra;
+-------------------------+----------+-----------+
| ComplexDataPersistent_id | element  | extra_pos |
+-------------------------+----------+-----------+
|                       1 | sprinkles |         0 |
|                       1 | fudge     |         1 |
|                       1 | cream     |         2 |
|                       2 | fudge     |         0 |
+-------------------------+----------+-----------+
4 rows in set (0.00 sec)
```

Figure 6.14 The data for each one-to-many property is in a separate table.

6.8   Application: Complex Persistent

The *Complex Initialised* example will be extended by saving data to the database. Review the steps from Chapter Five for writing an application that saves data to a database.

The only additional step that is needed to write a multiple-valued property to the database is to annotate the accessor of the property.

In the controller helper, instead of using Java to configure hibernate, use a `hibernate.cfg.xml` (see Chapter Five). Place this file in the classes directory of the web app. Be sure to update the file with your server, port, username, password and database.

```
. . .
<property name="connection.url">
  jdbc:mysql://your-server:your-port/your-database
</property>
<property name="connection.username">
  your-user-name
</property>
<property name="connection.password">
  your-password
</property>
. . .
```

6.8.1   Java Bean: Complex Persistent

Each of the multiple-valued properties from the *Initialised Complex Elements* application needs to be annotated with two annotations. Only place these annotations before the properties that return arrays, *CollectionOfElements* and *IndexColumn*.

```
import org.hibernate.annotations.IndexColumn;
import javax.persistence.CollectionOfElements;
import shared.SetByAttribute;
. . .
@CollectionOfElements
@IndexColumn(name="extra_pos", base=0)
@SetByAttribute(type=AttributeType.CHECKED)
public String[] getExtra() {
    return extra;
}

@CollectionOfElements
@IndexColumn(name="team_pos", base=0)
@SetByAttribute(type=AttributeType.SELECTED)
public String[] getTeam() {
    return team;
}
. . .
```

6.8.2   Process.jsp: Complex Persistent

The only JSP that needs to be changed is the process JSP. It will display the list of data that is in the database. This is not a normal feature in an application; it is done in this application to demonstrate that the data has been updated in the database.

A table is used to organise the data in the database. An outer loop is used to access each row in the database; each field from the row is displayed in its own cell in the table. For a cell that contains a multiple-valued property, there is an inner loop that displays all of the property's values. The *taglib* statement for the JSTL must be included in the JSP before the first reference to a *core* tag.

```
<%@ taglib uri="http://java.sun.com/jsp/jstl/core"
           prefix="core" %>
...
<table>
  <core:forEach var="record" items="${database}">
    <tr>
      <td>${record.secretCode}
      <td>${record.happiness}
      <td>
        <ul>
          <core:forEach var="extra"
                        items="${record.extra}">
            <li>${extra}
          </core:forEach>
        </ul>
      <td>${record.comments}
      <td>${record.grade}
      <td>
        <ul>
          <core:forEach var="team"
                        items="${record.team}">
            <li>${team}
          </core:forEach>
        </ul>
    </tr>
  </core:forEach>
</table>
...
```

 Try It   http://bytesizebook.com/book/ch6/complexPersistent/Controller

Enter some data in the form, confirm the data and view all the rows from the database.

6.9   Summary

The basic structure of a web application was developed in the first four chapters. This chapter introduced features that added more style to a web application, not more substance.

There are more advanced ways to arrange content in a web page than using paragraph tags and new line tags. These advanced layout tags give the developer more control over how the content is arranged in the page. List tags allow indexes and table of contents to be generated with ease. A table tag allows content to be arranged like a newspaper page.

There are also additional tags that add style to the page. These tags are of a generic sort; they allow the developer to arrange content according to what the content represents and not the actual style of the content. It is up to the browser to decide how to display these elements.

Some tags allow the developer to set the style directly. These tags are an aberration from the generic style of most HTML tags. They were added to HTML when it was assumed that all display monitors could display basic styles like italic, bold and underline.

Web designers wanted more ways to set the style of a page. Developing more tags like italic was one possibility, but it was not a good possibility. Instead, it was recommended that style be separated from the HTML as much as possible. The way to do this was with cascading style sheets. This allowed the developer to define the style for a web site in one file and let all the HTML files use the same style sheet. This is now the preferred way to add style to a web site.

There are also additional tags for specifying input in an HTML form. While text boxes and submit buttons are all that are needed for user input, there are additional input elements that use radio buttons, checkbox groups, drop down lists, scrollable lists, password fields and multi-line text boxes. These elements make it easier for a user to enter data in a form.

While these new tags make it easier for the user, they add some complexity to the web application for the developer. It is more difficult to initialise some of these elements with data in the query string and it is more difficult to save some of them to a database.

6.10   Chapter Review

Terms

1. Inline tag
2. Block tag
3. Ordered list
4. Unordered list
5. Definition list
6. Table
   a. Table row
   b. Table data
   c. Table heading
7. Embedded image
8. Cascading Style Sheet (CSS)
   a. Scales
   b. Default styles

   c. Multiple definitions
   d. Nested styles
   e. Named styles
   f. Generic styles
   g. Pseudo styles
   h. Class
   i. Font family
   j. Generic font family
 9. External style sheet
10. Radio group
11. Checkbox group
12. Selection lists
13. Single-valued properties
14. Multiple-valued properties
15. Nullable fields
16. Map of checked values
17. Map of selected values

New Java

1. Annotations
   a. `@CollectionOfElements`
   b. `@IndexColumn(name = "...", base = 0)`
   c. `@SetByAttribute(type = AttributeType....)`
2. Enumerations
   a. `AttributeType { CHECKED, SELECTED }`

Tags

1. JSP
   a. `${helper.checked}`
   b. `${helper.selected}`
   c. `${helper.checked.extra}`
   d. `${helper.selected.team}`
   e. `${helper.checked.extra.fudge}`
   f. `${helper.selected.team.heat}`
   g. `${helper.checked.extra["whipped cream"]}`
   h. `${helper.selected.team["2"]}`
2. u
3. b
4. i
5. h1 ... h6

6. ol
   a. li
7. ul
   a. li
8. dl
   a. dt
   b. dd
9. table
   a. tr
   b. td
      i. *rowspan* attribute
      ii. *colspan* attribute
   c. th
10. img
    a. *src* attribute
11. link
    a. *href* attribute
    b. *rel* attribute
    c. *type* attribute
12. Form elements
    a. input
       i. password
       ii. radio
          A. *checked* attribute
       iii. checkbox
          A. *checked* attribute
    b. textarea
    c. select
       i. *multiple* attribute
       ii. *size* attribute
       iii. Option
          A. *selected* attribute

Style

1. background-color
2. background-image
3. color
4. font-family
5. font-size
6. font-weight
7. font-style

8. text-decoration
9. text-transform
10. text-align
11. text-indent
12. margin-left
13. margin-right
14. width
15. list-style-type

Questions

1. What is the difference between an inline tag and a block tag?
2. How many predefined headings are there?
3. How is the `<ol>` tag different from the `<ul>` tag?
4. How is the `<th>` tag different from the `<td>` tag?
5. What does the rowspan attribute control?
6. What does the colspan attribute control?
7. List the fixed scales in a style sheet.
8. List the relative scales in a style sheet.
9. What is a font family?
10. What is a generic font family?
11. How can bold tags inside paragraphs be given a different appearance from bold tags inside tables?
12. How can two paragraphs have different styles defined for them?
13. What is a generic style?
14. If *special* is a named style for paragraphs, how can a paragraph in an HTML page be given this named style?
15. List all the different types of input elements in a form (not just the new ones from this chapter).
16. Explain how a radio button can be placed into the checked state.
17. What would the query string look like if a password field named *secret* had the value *top secret code* typed into it?
18. What would the query string look like if a textarea named *comments* had the value *I love Java* typed into it?
19. What would the query string look like if a radio group named *team* had the value *marlins* checked?
20. What would the query string look like if a single selection list named *team* had the value *panthers* selected?
21. What would the query string look like if a checkbox group named *team* had the two values *heat* and *dolphins* checked?
22. What would the query string look like if a multiple selection list named *team* had the two values *hurricanes* and *dolphins* selected?
23. What is the difference between the mutator for a single-valued property and the mutator for a multiple-valued property in a bean?

24. Write the JSP code that will display all the values for a checkbox group named *team*.

25. Write the JSP code that will display all the values for a multiple selection list named *team*.

26. Explain how a hash map is used to simplify the initialisation of a checkbox group in a JSP.

27. What annotations are needed to save a checkbox group to a database?

28. What annotations are needed to save a multiple selection list to a database?

29. Explain how nested loops are used to display all the values in a collection of beans, if there are multiple-valued properties in the bean.

Tasks

1. Create an HTML page that has six paragraphs. Give each paragraph a different heading from the predefined headings. Include some content in each paragraph. Be sure that each heading is separate from each paragraph.

2. Create an HTML page that has three paragraphs. Make one paragraph bold, one italic and one underlined.

3. Create an HTML page that has a table with four rows and three columns. Include text or graphics in each cell in the table.

   a. Make one of the cells in the table span two rows.

   b. Make one of the cells in the table span two columns.

   c. Make one of the cells span two columns and two rows.

4. Create a style sheet that will set the colours, margins and font for a page. Give a list of preferred fonts, with a final choice that is one of the generic font families.

5. Create an HTML page that has an outline. There should be three levels in the outline. Create a style sheet for the page that will set the numbering for the outline as uppercase Roman letters, then uppercase English letters, then decimal numbers.

6. Create a style sheet that forces all predefined headings to be displayed in uppercase letters. Create an HTML page that uses this style sheet and demonstrates the styles.

7. Create a style sheet that sets the margin for all paragraphs to five widths of the letter 'x'. In this style sheet, also create a named style for paragraphs that creates a hanging indent. A hanging indent indents the entire paragraph, except for the first line. Create an HTML page that uses this style sheet and demonstrates the styles.

8. Create an HTML page that has three paragraphs. Make one paragraph bold, one italic, and one underlined. Do not use the bold, italic and underline tags. Create a style sheet for the page that defines three named styles for paragraphs.

9. Create a style sheet that will set the width of ordered lists to 3/4 the width of the page. Also set the width of horizontal rulers to 3/4 the width of the page. Create an HTML page that uses this style sheet and demonstrates the styles.

10. Create an application with a JSP that has a form with a textarea and a password.
    a. Create a bean to encapsulate the data.
    b. Create a controller.
    c. Validate that the password has at least six characters.
    d. Validate that the textarea has at least six words.
    e. If the data is invalid, display the form again with the textarea and password initialised with any values that the user had supplied.
    f. If the data is valid, display the data and allow the user to confirm it or edit it.
    g. If the user confirms the data, save it to a database and display a page with the user's data.

11. Create an application with a JSP that has a form with a radio group and a single selection list.
    a. Create a bean to encapsulate the data.
    b. Create a controller.
    c. Validate that at least one of the radio buttons has been checked.
    d. Validate that at least one of the options in the list has been selected.
    e. If the data is invalid, display the form again with the radio group and list initialised with any values that the user had supplied.
    f. If the data is valid, display the data and allow the user to confirm it or edit it.
    g. If the user confirms the data, save it to a database and display a page with the user's data.

12. Create an application with a JSP that has a form with a checkbox group and a multiple selection list.
    a. Create a bean to encapsulate the data.
    b. Create a controller.
    c. Validate that at least two of the checkboxes are checked.
    d. Validate that not all of the items in the selection list are selected.
    e. If the data is invalid, display the form again with the checkbox group and list initialised with any values that the user had supplied.
    f. If the data is valid, display the data and allow the user to confirm it or edit it.
    g. If the user confirms the data, save it to a database and display a page with the user's data.
    h. Note: There is an annotation for Hibernate that tests the size of an array

```
@Size(min=x,max=y)
```

7 Accounts, Cookies and Carts

An application will be developed that requires a user to log into the site. Once the user has logged in, the user's previous data will be retrieved from the database. Once a bean has been retrieved from the database, any changes to that bean will replace the data that is already in the database, instead of adding a new row. Hibernate determines if a bean has already been written to the database by looking at the primary key. If the primary key has not been set, then Hibernate will add the bean to the database; if the primary key is not null, then Hibernate will update the corresponding row in the database.

Finding a row in the database using the primary key is a simple matter. However, the primary key that we have been using has been generated by the database and its value is unknown to the user. In order to find a row in the database, there must be a way for the user to uniquely specify the desired row. In the simple case, there will be a field that uniquely identifies each row in the database, like social security number, phone number, email address or account number. In other cases, several fields might need to be combined to identify a row. We shall only consider the simple case where one field can identify a row. Once a bean has been retrieved from the database, it will be placed in the session and used to store all the information that the user enters. When this bean is written to the database, the values will be used to update the row that is already in the database.

Web applications are stateless: the developer must add code so that the application will remember what the user has done recently. Because of this, it is difficult to identify users until they log into a database. For this reason, cookies were developed. Cookies allow information to be stored on a user's computer. When the user visits a site, the stored information is sent to the site. The application can use this information to identify the user.

Cookies can be created for specific URLs and specific times. More than one cookie can be set by an application and more than one cookie can be received by an application. An application can delete a cookie by setting its time to zero. A user can delete a cookie through the browser's menus.

Most e-commerce sites allow the user to enter data into a shopping cart. This allows the user to browse the site, adding items to the cart for later purchase. A shopping cart is easy to implement using Java 1.5 generics. A complete application will be developed that uses a shopping cart.

7.1   Retrieving Rows from the Database

For all the applications that have been developed in this book, a primary key has been assigned by the database to each row that is added to a table. This primary key is used internally by the database and has no relationship with the data that is being stored. By allowing the database to assign the primary key, we are relieved of the responsibility of ensuring that each row in the database has a unique primary key value. However, there is a drawback; the user does not know the value of this primary key, so cannot use it to retrieve the row from the database.

In order to retrieve a row from the database, it is necessary to be able to identify a row based upon the values that are stored in the row. In many applications, there will be a field in the data that can be used to identify the row uniquely: social security number, phone number, username, email address or account number. In other applications, it may be more difficult. It may be necessary to look at several fields in order to identify a row. For instance, a person's address could be used to identify a row, but this would require looking at several fields: street, apartment, city, postal code.

When retrieving a row from the database, it is common to validate the fields that are used to identify a row, before validating any new data that the user will enter. The `isValid` method developed in Chapter Five is an all-or-nothing approach. A new method will be introduced that can validate one field at a time.

Once a row has been retrieved and placed into the session, it is only necessary to use the bean that has been added to the session. As long as all changes are made to that bean, then when the bean is written to the database, it will update the information that is in the database.

7.1.1   Finding a Row

Hibernate has the ability to retrieve a row from the database using one or more fields. There are several methods that can be used: SQL, Hibernate SQL, Criteria. The Criteria technique will be used in this book; it uses Java and requires no knowledge of SQL. The Hibernate Criteria class is a robust class. Only a simple example will be used here. Refer to the references for more information.

The Hibernate helper class has a method that will retrieve all rows that match a given field. The class that contains the property, the name of the property and the value to match are passed to the method. The method then creates search criteria that Hibernate will use to find all rows that match the criteria.

```
public java.util.List getListData(
    Class classBean, String strKey, Object value)
{
  java.util.List result = new java.util.ArrayList();

  Session session = sessionFactory.openSession();
  Transaction tx = session.beginTransaction();

  Criteria criteria =
      session.createCriteria(classBean);
  if (strKey != null) {
```

```
      criteria.add(Restrictions.like(strKey, value));
   }
   result = criteria.list();

   tx.commit();
   session.close();
   return result;
}
```

Another method in Hibernate helper will return the first row that matches the given criteria.

```
public Object getFirstMatch(
      Class classBean, String strKey, Object value) {
   java.util.List records =
         getListData(classBean, strKey, value);
   if (records != null && records.size() > 0) {
      return records.get(0);
   }
   return null;
}
```

The method getFirstMatch will be used to retrieve the bean for a persistent row and set it as the bean in the session. If a bean is returned from this method, it will be set as the bean in the session.

```
...
Object dataPersistent = HibernateHelper
      .getFirstMatch(data, "accountNumber",
                     data.getAccountNumber());
if (dataPersistent != null) {
   data = (RequestDataAccount)dataPersistent;
}
...
```

7.1.2   Validating a Single Property

The account number will be used to find a row in the database. It should be validated before it is used to access the database. At the least, it should be tested that it is not null or empty. New methods have been added to the helper base class that allow for one field in a bean to be tested, instead of testing all the fields in the bean at once.

To validate one field, the validation messages must be set first. In order to do this, call the setErrors method. Previously, this method was called by the isValid method, but now it will be more efficient if it is called directly. It only needs to be called once, since it will create the validation errors for all the properties in the bean.

After calling setErrors, the isValidProperty method can be called for as many properties as need to be validated. Only call setErrors once, no matter how many times isValidProperty is called.

```
...
setErrors(data);
if (isValidProperty("accountNumber")) {
...
```

7.2 Application: Account Login

An application will be developed that is based upon the *Persistent Data* example from Chapter Five.

1. The bean will be modified so that it has an account number.
2. The account number will be validated as being two letters followed by three digits.
3. Each user will be required to log into the site by specifying an account number.
4. If the user has saved data before, then the data from the database will be used to initialise the data in the edit page.
5. The bean that is retrieved from the database will be placed in the session and will be accessible from all of the JSPs.
6. When the data is written to the database, the new data will overwrite the previous data in the database.

The simplicity of this application is that once the user has logged into the site, the code is exactly the same is it was in Chapter Five. By adding a front end of a login page, the user is able to retrieve and edit the data in the database.

7.2.1 Java Bean: Account Login

The only change to the bean is the addition of the account number property. It is important to realise that this field is not the primary key for the bean; the primary key is still needed. The primary key is used internally by the database; the account number is used by the user to identify each row in the database.

```
...
@Pattern(regex="[a-zA-Z]{2}\\d{3}",
         message="must be in the format AA999.")
public String getAccountNumber() {
    return accountNumber;
}
public void setAccountNumber(String accountNumber) {
    this.accountNumber = accountNumber;
}
...
```

7.2.2 Login.jsp: Account Login

There is a new JSP added to this application. It contains the account number element and a button for logging into the site.

```
<!DOCTYPE HTML PUBLIC "-//W3C//DTD HTML 4.01//EN">
<html>
  <head>
    <meta http-equiv="content-type"
    content="text/html;charset=utf-8">
    <title>Login Page</title>
  </head>
  <body>
    <p>Please enter your account number
        to access your data.
    <form method="POST" action="Controller">
      <p>
        Account Number ${helper.errors.accountNumber}
        <input type="text" name="accountNumber"
               value="${helper.data.accountNumber}">
        <input type="submit" name="loginButton"
               value="Login">
      </p>
    </form>
  </body>
</html>
```

7.2.3   ControllerHelper: Account Login

When the user selects the login button from the login page, the controller will
validate that the account number has the correct format and will search the database for a row that has that account number. If it finds one, then the bean that is
returned from Hibernate will replace the one that is in the session.

For the rest of the session, all changes that are entered by the user will be stored
in this bean. When the bean is written to the database, Hibernate will realise that
it is a bean that came from the database and will update the values for that row in
the database, instead of adding a new row.

The method for the login page is similar to the method for the confirm page, except
it is only validating that the account number has the right format. The other properties
in the bean will still be validated when the user selects the confirm button.

```
@ButtonMethod(buttonName="loginButton")
public String loginMethod() {
  String address;
  fillBeanFromRequest(data);
  setErrors(data);
  if (isValidProperty("accountNumber")) {
    Object dataPersistent = HibernateHelper
        .getFirstMatch(data, "accountNumber",
                       data.getAccountNumber());
    if (dataPersistent != null) {
        data = (RequestDataAccount)dataPersistent;
    }
    address = "Edit.jsp";
  } else {
    address = "Login.jsp";
  }
  return jspLocation(address);
}
```

Try It   http://bytesizebook.com/book/ch7/accountLogin/Controller

Log into the site. Use an account that is two letters followed by three digits. Enter some data into the database.

Move the cursor into the location bar of the browser and hit the enter key. This will start the application from the beginning. Log into the site with the same account number. The data that was entered into the site will still be there.

Close the browser and reopen it. This will close the session. Log into the application again with the same account number. The data is still there. Change the data and save it to the database. Log into the site again. The new data will be retrieved.

7.3   Removing Rows from the Database

Building on the last application, it is an easy matter to remove rows from the database. The method `removeDB`, in the Hibernate helper class, allows a row to be removed from the database.

```
public void removeDB(Object obj) {
    . . .
}
```

Once the bean has been saved to the database, it can be removed by calling this method.

7.4   Application: Account Removal

This application only has a few changes from the last one, so inheritance can be used to implement the controller helper. The process page has a new button for removing the account that was just added. There is a new method in the controller helper to process the new button.

7.4.1   Process.jsp: Account Removal

The process page has a new button for removing the current bean from the database. This could have been done from any page in the application, once the user has logged in.

```
. . .
<form method="POST" action="Controller">
  <p>
    Edit the current record.
    <input type="submit" name="editButton"
                          value="Edit">
    Remove the current record.
    <input type="submit" name="removeButton"
                          value="Remove">
  </p>
</form>
. . .
```

7.4.2   ControllerHelper: Account Removal

Since this application is identical to the previous application, except for the addition of a new button for removing rows, the controller helper can be extended from the *Account Login* controller helper. The bean from that application can also be reused.

The method to process the removal button calls the removeDB method with the bean that was just saved to the database. If the removeDB method is called with a row that was never saved, then Hibernate will ignore the request. After removing the row, it is necessary to erase all the data from the bean. The simplest way to do this is to create a new bean.

```
package ch7.accountRemove;

import javax.servlet.ServletException;
import javax.servlet.http.HttpServletRequest;
import javax.servlet.http.HttpServletResponse;
import shared.ButtonMethod;
import shared.HibernateHelper;

public class ControllerHelper
    extends ch7.accountLogin.ControllerHelper {

  public ControllerHelper(HttpServletRequest request,
                          HttpServletResponse response)
  {
    super(request, response);
  }

  public String jspLocation(String page) {
    return "/WEB-INF/classes/ch7/accountRemove/" + page;
  }

  @ButtonMethod(buttonName="removeButton")
  public String removeMethod() {
    HibernateHelper.removeDB(data);
    data = new ch7.accountLogin.RequestDataAccount();
    return jspLocation("Login.jsp");
  }

  protected void doGet()
  throws ServletException, java.io.IOException {
    super.doGet();
  }

  protected void doPost()
  throws ServletException, java.io.IOException {
    super.doPost();
  }
}
```

Try It   http://bytesizebook.com/book/ch7/accountRemove/Controller

To see that a record has been removed from the database, follow these steps.

1. Log into the site with an account number that is already in the database.
2. Proceed to the process page.
3. Click the remove button to delete the current bean from the database.
4. Click in the location window of the browser and hit the enter key. This will delete the data from the session and display the login page.
5. Enter a different account number, enter some data and view the database.
6. The database will appear on the process page, but there will be no row for the account number that was just deleted.

7.5 Cookies

A server has the ability to ask a browser to store information. The next time the browser requests data from that server, the browser will send the stored data back to the server. A piece of information that is being stored is known as a *cookie*.

Many sites use cookies to identify users. Sites will ask if you would like your information remembered on the current computer, so that the next time you access the same site from that computer, you will not need to enter your data again. It is important to understand that the information is only being stored on the current computer; if you log into the site from a different computer, you will need to enter your data again.

Many sites offer to remember a user on the current computer. Such sites typically have a checkbox to indicate that the user's information should be stored on the local computer (Figure 7.1).

If this is checked, then the user's data will be stored as a cookie on the current computer. Whenever you see such a request, the site is asking to store information on your computer in a cookie.

Don't have a
Yahoo! ID?
Signing up is easy.

Sign up for Yahoo!

Already have a Yahoo! ID?
Sign in.

Yahoo! ID: |

Password:

☐ Remember my ID on this computer

Sign In

Forget your ID or password? | Help

Figure 7.1 Yahoo! offers to remember data on the current computer.

Table 7.1 Information stored in a cookie.

Property	Purpose
name	The *name* is used as the index into the browser's store of cookies.
value	The *value* is the data associated with the cookie.
expiration	The *expiration* is the date and time when the browser should remove the cookie from its store.
domain	The *domain* is the Internet domain that can receive the cookie from the browser.
path	The *path* is the prefix for all URLs in the domain that can receive the cookie.
secure	*Secure* indicates if the cookie should only be sent over secure connections.

7.5.1 Definition

Cookies are stored in a cookie jar. In computer terms, a cookie is a row in a database and the cookie jar is the database. The primary key to the database is the URL of the site that the user is requesting.

On every request that is made by the user, the browser searches through the database, looking for any cookies that were created for the current URL. All the cookies that are found are sent to the server as part of the request headers.

Table 7.1 lists the information that is stored in a cookie.

The cookie is stored in the browser under the name with the given value. Every time a request is made, the browser looks through all the cookies and sends all cookies to the request that match the domain and path of the request. Periodically, the browser will inspect the expiration date of all its cookies and delete those that have expired.

7.5.2 Cookie Class

The java package `javax.servlet.http.cookie` encapsulates this information and is defined in the `Cookie` class. There are accessors and mutators for all of the above properties.

Cookie

The constructor takes the name and value as parameters.

```
Cookie team = new Cookie("team","marlins");
```

setName/getName

It is not necessary to call `setName` since the name is included in the constructor.

setValue/getValue

It is not necessary to call `setValue` since the value is included in the constructor.

setMaxAge/getMaxAge

The default age is −1 seconds, which means that the cookie will be deleted when the browser closes. Set the age to 0 seconds to have the browser delete

---

the cookie immediately. Use a positive number of seconds to indicate how long the browser will keep the cookie. The number of seconds will be translated into a date by the `Cookie` class.

setDomain/getDomain

The default domain is the server that set the cookie. This can be changed to the subdomain of the computer. If the domain starts with a dot, then the cookie can be sent back to all servers on the subdomain. The domain must always be to an actual domain or subdomain and it must be the domain or subdomain of the server that set the cookie.

setPath/getPath

The default path is the path to the directory of the servlet that set the cookie.

setSecure/getSecure

The default security level is that the cookie can be sent over any type of connection.

7.6   Application: Cookie Test

A controller application will now be developed to explain and test the different actions for creating, deleting and finding cookies. The application will not receive any data from the user, so there is no need for a bean. This simplifies the `doGet` method in the controller helper, since there is no need to update the session.

```
. . .
protected void doGet()
throws ServletException, IOException
{
  String address = executeButtonMethod();

  request.getRequestDispatcher(address)
     .forward(request, response);
}
. . .
```

The controller is the same as the controller for the *Enhanced* application from Chapter Four.

7.6.1   JSPs: Cookie Test

There is only one JSP for this application. The primary function of the page is to list the cookies that were sent to it from the browser. The page loops through the cookies that were sent to it.

A map of the cookies can be retrieved from a JSP using the EL statement of `${cookie}`. A loop can be placed into the JSP to access the elements in the map.

Each element in the map has public accessors to retrieve the key and the value. The key is the name of the cookie and the value is the cookie.

If there is a loop control variable named `element`, then each cookie can be retrieved from the map with `${element.value}`. Since the value in the map is a cookie, its name and value can be retrieved from the cookie's public accessors. The EL statements to access the name and value from the cookie in the map are `${element.value.name}` and `${element.value.value}`. The name and value of the cookie are displayed in a table.

```
. . .
<table border>
  <tr><th>Name<th>Value
  <core:forEach var="element" items="${cookie}">
    <tr><td>${element.value.name}<td>${element.value.value}
  </core:forEach>
</table>
. . .
```

This application will also create a cookie that can only be read by one URL. Two servlet mappings will be created so that this servlet can be called by two different URLs. In this way, the servlet will have access to different cookies based upon the URL that is used to access it. Edit the *web.xml* file to add two mappings for this application.

```
<servlet-mapping>
  <servlet-name>CookieController</servlet-name>
  <url-pattern>
    /ch7/cookie/Controller
  </url-pattern>
</servlet-mapping>
<servlet-mapping>
  <servlet-name>CookieController</servlet-name>
  <url-pattern>
    /ch7/cookie/specific/Controller
  </url-pattern>
</servlet-mapping>
```

There are two forms in the JSP. Each form has a different URL in the *action* attribute. However, each URL is mapped to the same servlet in the *web.xml* file. The buttons in the second form create and access a cookie that can only be accessed from the URL used in that form. The buttons in the first form create cookies that can be accessed by both URLs.

```
. . .
<form action="/book/ch7/cookie/Controller">
  <input type="submit" name="showCookieButton"
         value="Show Cookies">
  <input type="submit" name="setCookieButton"
         value="Set Cookies">
  <input type="submit" name="deleteCookieButton"
         value="Delete Cookie">
```

```
<input type="submit" name="findCookieButton"
        value="Find Cookie">
</form>
<form action="/book/ch7/cookie/specific/Controller">
  <input type="submit" name="showCookieButton"
        value="Show Specific Cookies">
  <input type="submit" name="setSpecificCookieButton"
        value="Set Specific Cookie">
</form>
. . .
```

Figure 7.2 shows how the page will appear in a browser.

7.6.2 Showing Cookies

All the work for showing cookies is done in the JSP. The default button in the
controller helper only needs to return the address of the JSP.

```
. . .
buttonName="showCookieButton", isDefault=true)
  public String showMethod() {
    return jspLocation("ShowCookies.jsp");
  }
. . .
```

7.6.3 Setting Cookies

Setting a cookie is a two-step process: create the cookie and then attach it to the
response with the addCookie method.

    The action for the *Set Cookie* button will construct two cookie objects, change
some default values and attach the cookies to the response. One of the cookies will
have the default age, so it will be deleted when the browser is closed. The other

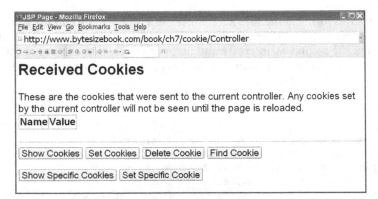

Figure 7.2 The JSP for testing cookies.

cookie will have its age set to 15 seconds. After setting the cookie, the browser will delete it after 15 seconds.

```
...
@ButtonMethod(buttonName="setCookieButton")
public String setMethod() {
   Cookie dolphins
      = new Cookie("dolphins",
                     "The Dolphins are here to stay");
   dolphins.setPath("/");
   response.addCookie(dolphins);

   Cookie marlins
      = new Cookie("marlins",
                     "The Marlins will be gone soon");
   marlins.setMaxAge(15);
   marlins.setPath("/");
   response.addCookie(marlins);

   return jspLocation("ShowCookies.jsp");
}
...
```

Be sure to change any default values before attaching the cookie to the response. The addCookie method generates a string that contains all the information about the cookie. This string is created during the call to addCookie and is added to the response headers at that time. Subsequent changes to the cookie will not alter the string that is already in the response headers.

 Try It   http://bytesizebook.com/book/ch7/cookie/Controller

An additional cookie might be displayed, named *JSESSIONID*, which was not created by the application. This is the cookie that is used to maintain the session for the servlet engine.

Since web applications are stateless, information must be stored on the browser in order to identify the current session. There are several places where the identifying data could be stored: in a hidden field, in the URL or in a cookie. The simplest solution is to use a cookie. The servlet engine can also be configured so that it will use the URL to store the identifying information.

Click the *Set Cookies* button, followed by the *Show Cookies* button. Cookies are only set in the response. In order to see the state of the cookies after the previous response, it is necessary to make a new request.

7.6.4   Deleting Cookies

The path and domain of a cookie must be known in order to delete the cookie. The cookies that are retrieved from the browser only have a name and value: the domain and path information are null. There is no way to know the path and domain of the original cookie by reading the cookie from the browser. If the domain was set to something other than the default when the cookie was created, then that domain will need to be set again, in order to delete that cookie.

The action for the *Delete Cookie* button will delete one of the cookies that was created when the *Set Cookies* button was clicked. It will delete the cookie that expires in 15 seconds. So, if too much time has elapsed, there won't be a cookie to delete. By setting the age to zero and adding the cookie to the response, the browser will delete the cookie that it has in its store.

```
. . .
@ButtonMethod(buttonName="deleteCookieButton")
public String deleteMethod() {
    Cookie marlins = new Cookie("marlins", "bye-bye");
    marlins.setMaxAge(0);
    marlins.setPath("/");
    response.addCookie(marlins);
    return jspLocation("ShowCookies.jsp");
}
. . .
```

 Try It   http://bytesizebook.com/book/ch7/cookie/DeleteCookies

Run the application and click the *Set Cookies* button. Click the *Show Cookies* button to see the current state of the cookies. Remember that cookies are sent in the response, so an additional request is needed to see what happened to the cookies after the last response.

To delete a cookie, click the *Delete Cookies* button. This will delete one of the cookies. To see that it has been deleted, click the *Show Cookies* button once again.

7.6.5   Finding Cookies

There can be more than one cookie that is sent to the servlet, even if the servlet only sets one cookie. This can happen when other servlets on the same subdomain set a cookie that can be accessed from the entire subdomain.

It is necessary to do a linear search through the array of cookies in order to find the desired one in a controller. If there are no cookies, then the array will be null, so it is important to test for this before accessing the array.

The action for the *Find Cookie* button will look for one of the cookies that was created when the *Set Cookies* button was clicked. It will look for the cookie that expires in 15 seconds. So, if too much time has elapsed, there won't be a cookie to find.

Whether or not the cookie is found, a value is set and made available to the JSP. The value is added to the request object. Since the cookie is sent from the browser on each request, it does not make any sense to save this value in the session object.

```
. . .
@ButtonMethod(buttonName="findCookieButton")
public String findMethod() {
    Cookie[] cookieArray = request.getCookies();
    Cookie marlins = null;
    if (cookieArray != null) {
        for (Cookie cookie : cookieArray) {
            if (cookie.getName().equals("marlins")) {
                marlins = cookie;
            }
        }
    }
```

```
String result = "The Marlins have left town";
if (marlins != null) {
    result = marlins.getValue();
}
request.setAttribute("marlins",result);

return jspLocation("ShowCookies.jsp");
}
...
```

In a JSP it is possible to locate a cookie without doing a linear search, if you know the name of the cookie.

```
${cookie.marlins.value}
```

Try It   http://bytesizebook.com/book/ch7/cookie/FindCookie

To see a search in action, follow the buttons in this order.

1. Set Cookies
2. Find Cookie
3. Delete Cookie
4. Find Cookie

Each time that *Find Cookie* is called, a linear search is performed on the cookies that are received by the application.

7.6.6   Cookie Utilities

A class has been added to the `shared` package that has two static methods for retrieving cookies. Each method performs a linear search through the cookies that are sent from the browser. Each looks for a cookie with a given name: one returns the cookie, the other returns the value in the cookie. The name of the class is `CookieUtil`.

```
public class CookieUtil {

  static
  public Cookie findCookie(HttpServletRequest request,
                           String name)
  {
    ...
  }

  static
  public String findCookieValue(HttpServletRequest request,
                                String name)
  {
    ...
  }

}
```

The complete listing of the *CookieUtil* class can be found in the Appendix.

7.6.7 Path Specific Cookies

The cookies that were created above changed the path to /, meaning that all servlets on the server will receive the cookie. If the path is not set, then it will default to the path of the directory of the servlet that set the cookie.

The action for the *Set Specific Cookie* button will create a cookie without setting its path. This means that only the current URL will receive the cookie. The button is located in the second form in the JSP. This form accesses the controller through a different URL. Only the buttons for setting and showing the specific button will have access to this cookie.

All of the cookies from the previous examples can be viewed from this URL, since the path was set so that those cookies are sent to all URLs on the server.

```
...
@ButtonMethod(buttonName="setSpecificCookieButton")
public String setSpecificMethod() {
  Cookie specific
    = new Cookie("specific",
                 "Not all pages can see this cookie");
  specific.setMaxAge(15);
  response.addCookie(specific);
  return jspLocation("ShowCookies.jsp");
}
...
```

 Try It   http://bytesizebook.com/book/ch7/cookie/specific/SetCookie

To experiment with the cookie that is only seen from one URL, click the buttons in the following order.

1. Set Specific Cookie
2. Show Specific Cookie
3. Show Cookie – the specific cookie will not be seen, since the URL does not match the one that set the cookie.
4. Show Specific Cookie – the specific cookie will be seen. The cookie will expire after 15 seconds.

7.7   Application: Account Cookie

The *Account Login* application can be extended to implement cookies. Whenever a bean is written to the database, its account number will be stored as a cookie. The next time a GET request is made, the account number can be retrieved from the cookie and used to retrieve the user's data. By using a cookie, the user will not have to see the login page. A new button will be added to the edit and process pages, in case a different user wants to log in.

7.7.1   Edit.jsp: Account Cookie

A new button is added to the edit page, to allow a different user to log in.

```
. . .
<input type="submit"  name="confirmButton"
                      value="Confirm">
<input type="submit"  name="newUserButton"
                      value="New User">
. . .
```

7.7.2   Process.jsp: Account Cookie

A new button is added to the process page, to allow a new user to log in.

```
. . .
<input type="submit"  name="editButton"
                      value="Edit">
<input type="submit"  name="newUserButton"
                      value="New User">
. . .
```

7.7.3   ControllerHelper: Account Cookie

When using a cookie, two questions need to be answered:

1. When will it be created?
2. When will it be read?

In this application the cookie will be written whenever the data is saved to the database. This makes the most sense, since the idea of having a cookie is so that data that has already been stored in the database can be retrieved automatically. Notice that only the account number is being saved in the cookie.

```
@ButtonMethod(buttonName="processButton")
public String processMethod() {
  if (!isValid(data)) {
    return jspLocation("Expired.jsp");
  }
  response.addCookie(
      new Cookie("account", data.getAccountNumber()));
  HibernateHelper.updateDB(data);
  List list = HibernateHelper
      .getListData(RequestDataAccount.class);
  request.setAttribute("database", list);
  return jspLocation("Process.jsp");
}
```

The cookie will be retrieved whenever there is a GET request to the application. A GET request signifies that a new user is trying to access the application. At that time, the cookies will be searched for an account number. If there is an account number, then the database will be searched. If a bean is returned from the database, it will replace the bean that is stored in the session and the next page will be the edit page, instead of the login page.

```
@ButtonMethod(isDefault=true)
public String getMethod() {
  String address = "Login.jsp";
  Cookie accountCookie =
      CookieUtil.findCookie(request, "account");
  if (accountCookie != null) {
    Object dataPersistent = HibernateHelper
      .getFirstMatch(data,
                  "accountNumber",
                  accountCookie.getValue());
    if (dataPersistent != null) {
      data = (RequestDataAccount)dataPersistent;
    }
    address = "Edit.jsp";
  }
  return jspLocation(address);
}
```

When the *New User* button is clicked from the edit or process pages, it signifies that the cookie does not have the correct account number for the current user. As a result, the data that is stored in the bean should be cleared, by creating a new bean.

```
@ButtonMethod(buttonName="newUserButton")
public String newUserMethod() {
  data = new RequestDataAccount();
  return jspLocation("Login.jsp");
}
```

 Try It   http://bytesizebook.com/book/ch7/accountCookie/Controller

Enter an account number and save some data to the database. When the process page is displayed, the cookie is sent to the browser.

Click in the URL location in the browser and hit the enter key. This will create a new request that will not read data from the session. The cookie will be sent from the browser. The value of the cookie will be used to retrieve data from the database. The login page will be skipped and the edit page will be displayed with the data from the database.

Click the *New User* button and a new request will be made that does not read the cookie.

7.8   Shopping Cart

A shopping cart is designed to access a database of items and to keep track of which items the user wants. A simple shopping cart application will be developed in this section. The application will be for a bookstore. The first page will display all the books that are available (Figure 7.3).

The user can click on any of the buttons to view the details for that item: name, description, cost and item Id (Figure 7.4).

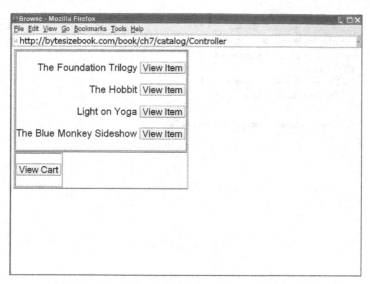

Figure 7.3 All items are listed when the user visits the site.

After the user has selected some items, the *View Cart* button can be clicked to see a summary of the items that have been selected (Figure 7.5).

After reviewing the items, the user can process the cart, which calculates the total cost and the number of items (Figure 7.6).

The most important aspect of a shopping cart is the item that will be placed in the cart. The item is the data that will be entered by the user. The data will be specific to the application.

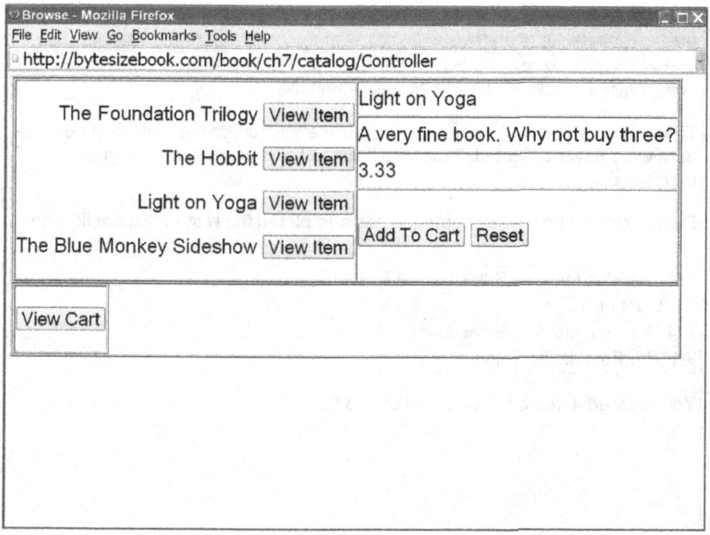

Figure 7.4 Details of a selected item are displayed.

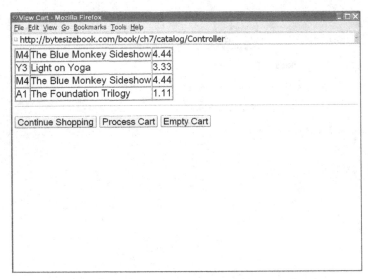

Figure 7.5 The cart contains all the items that were selected.

There will be a database of items that are available from the store. It is the developer's responsibility to keep this database up to date.

Keeping the item information in a separate table makes it easier to keep the information on the web site up to date. The only information that is hard coded into the JSP is the item Id, which should never change. The rest of the information about an item is generated from the database whenever a page is reloaded.

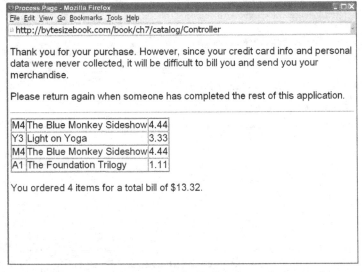

Figure 7.6 The total cost is calculated when the cart is processed.

The shopping cart itself is very simple. It only needs a collection of objects and methods for adding and deleting items from the collection. Shopping carts are all very similar. Generics from Java 1.5 can be used to develop the shopping cart class.

7.8.1 Catalogue Item

The first thing that is needed for a shopping cart is a database that defines all the items that can go into the cart. An item in the database should have the following.

1. a name
2. a description
3. a price
4. an item Id

These would be implemented as standard properties in the bean. Only two of them will need annotations, as described below.

Catalogue Item Class

A separate table for the items will be created in the database, so the bean should be marked as an entity. Even though the item Id could be used as the primary key in the database, this application will still let the database manage an internal column that will be used as the primary key. The item class will extend the *PersistentBase* class, which contains an identifier for a primary key.

```
@Entity
public class CatalogItem
extends shared.PersistentBase {
```

Catalogue Item Constructors

Besides the default constructor, there will be a constructor that will set the values of all the properties. This will make it easy to create a complete item that can be added to the database of items. The default constructor will choose some default values for the properties. The default item Id will be null. An item with an Id of null should never be added to the database.

```
public CatalogItem() {
  this (null, "", "", 0.00);
}
public CatalogItem(String itemId, String name,
                   String description, double price)
{
  setItemId(itemId);
  setName(name);
  setDescription(description);
  setPrice(price);
}
```

Catalogue Item Text Fields

When a column for a string property is added to a database table, the maximum length of the string must be set. The default length of a string column is database specific, but might be 255 characters. If a field represents a phone number of an identification number, then 255 characters would be too many. If a field represents a catalogue description, then 255 characters might not be enough. Figure 7.7 show the default implementation of three text fields from the `CatalogItem` class in the MySQL database server.

Hibernate has annotations that will give the database server a hint for setting the width of a column in a table.

The Hibernate annotation `@Length` validates the minimum and maximum length of a string. This annotation also tells the database server what the width of the column in the database should be. For example, by adding validation that tests that the length of a text field in the database does not exceed 50, Hibernate will give the column a width of 50 in the table.

```
@Length(min=1,max=50)
public String getName() {
   return name;
}
```

The description of a catalogue item could be very long. The default length of a string column in a table is database specific, but might only be 255 characters. When large amounts of text need to be entered, the field should be declared as a *large object*. The annotation that defines a property as a large object is `@Lob`. As the name implies, a large object property can contain a lot of information.

```
@Lob
public String getDescription() {
   return description;
}
```

The `@NotNull` annotation is very useful for a database. By marking a field with it, then the field must always have a value before data is entered into the database. This is particularly helpful when the session is being used to store user data.

If the user does not interact with the server for an extended period, then the session will be closed and the user data will be lost. If the user subsequently attempts to save that data, a check should be made by the database that the user data is still valid. The simplest way to accomplish this is to mark at least one

```
mysql> describe catalogitemdefault;
+-------------+--------------+------+-----+---------+----------------+
| Field       | Type         | Null | Key | Default | Extra          |
+-------------+--------------+------+-----+---------+----------------+
| id          | bigint(20)   | NO   | PRI | NULL    | auto_increment |
| itemId      | varchar(255) | YES  |     | NULL    |                |
| price       | double       | NO   |     |         |                |
| name        | varchar(255) | YES  |     | NULL    |                |
| description | varchar(255) | YES  |     | NULL    |                |
+-------------+--------------+------+-----+---------+----------------+
5 rows in set (0.03 sec)
```

Figure 7.7 Strings have a default width of 255 characters.

```
mysql> describe catalogitem;
+-------------+-------------+------+-----+---------+----------------+
| Field       | Type        | Null | Key | Default | Extra          |
+-------------+-------------+------+-----+---------+----------------+
| id          | bigint(20)  | NO   | PRI | NULL    | auto_increment |
| itemId      | varchar(10) | NO   |     |         |                |
| price       | double      | NO   |     |         |                |
| name        | varchar(50) | YES  |     | NULL    |                |
| description | text        | YES  |     | NULL    |                |
+-------------+-------------+------+-----+---------+----------------+
5 rows in set (0.00 sec)
```

Figure 7.8 Text fields whose length has been specified.

field as not null. If there is an attempt to write a null field to that column in the database, an exception will be thrown. This is considered a last chance test. Hopefully, the controller will test that the data is valid before attempting to write to the database.

```
@NotNull
@Length(min=1,max=10)
public String getItemId() {
  return itemId;
}
```

Figure 7.8 shows the `CatalogItem` class that has used annotations to set the length of two of the text fields and has marked the third as a large object. The `itemId` field has also been marked as not null, since every item in the database should have an item identification code.

7.8.2   Create Catalogue Database

The next step is to define some items and create a database for them. This will only be done once by the site administrator. This database will not be modified by the cart: it is just a list of items that are available. Additional controllers could be defined to add items to the current database of items.

The controller will need access to Hibernate, but will not need any JSPs. The user interface is very simple in this administrator application, so the controller will send the response directly to the browser without using a JSP.

Controller with No JSPs

This controller is only supposed to be run by the site administrator to create the catalogue database. It does not need a sophisticated user interface; just a simple message, indicating that the database was created successfully, is enough. In such a situation, it is possible for the controller to write text directly to the browser.

As part of the response object, there is a method that returns a *PrintWriter* that has direct access to the browser. Whatever is written to the writer will be sent to the browser. It is possible to create an entire HTML page to send, but it is easier to just send a simple text message.

```
response.getWriter().print("Catalogue Created");
```

Catalogue Controller

The complete controller to create the catalogue must initialise Hibernate in the *init* method. It is assumed that the properties for initialising Hibernate are in a configuration file.

The *doGet* method is very simple; it only needs to call *updateDb* to write the catalogue items to the database and to use the writer from the response object to send a simple message to the browser. The *updateDb* method in the hibernate helper has been overloaded to accept a list of items.

```java
package ch7.catalog;
import java.io.IOException;
import java.util.ArrayList;
import java.util.List;
import java.util.Properties;
import javax.servlet.ServletException;
import javax.servlet.http.HttpServlet;
import javax.servlet.http.HttpServletRequest;
import javax.servlet.http.HttpServletResponse;
import org.hibernate.cfg.Environment;
import shared.HibernateHelper;
public class CreateCatalog extends HttpServlet {

  public void init() {
    HibernateHelper.createTable(CatalogItem.class);
    HibernateHelper.initSessionFactory(CatalogItem.class);
  }

  static List<CatalogItem> itemList =
    new ArrayList<CatalogItem>();

  static {
    itemList.add(new CatalogItem(
      "A1", "The Foundation Trilogy",
      "A very fine book. Why not buy one?", 1.11));
    itemList.add(new CatalogItem(
      "T2", "The Hobbit",
      "A very fine book. Why not buy two?", 2.22));
    itemList.add(new CatalogItem(
      "Y3", "Light on Yoga",
      "A very fine book. Why not buy three?", 3.33));
    itemList.add(new CatalogItem(
      "M4", "Blue Monkey Sideshow",
      "A very fine book. Why not buy four?", 4.44));
  };

  protected void doGet(HttpServletRequest request,
                       HttpServletResponse response)
  throws ServletException, IOException {
    if (HibernateHelper.testDB(response)) {
      HibernateHelper.updateDB(itemList);
      response.getWriter().print("Catalogue Created");

    }
  }
}
```

7.8.3   Shopping Cart Bean

Now that the catalogue of items exists, the shopping cart can be defined. The shopping cart should be able to store all the items that a user has selected. The details of the item are not important for the shopping cart; the cart only needs to be able to add an item, retrieve all items and clear all items. Additional properties will be added to the cart for storing the total cost and number of items that are in the cart.

Other features could be added to the cart, like the ability to delete an individual item or to maintain a count for each item in the cart. The implementation of these additional features will be left as exercises.

Since the details of the item that is being placed into the cart are unimportant to the cart, generics from Java 1.5 will be used to define the cart. By using generics, the objects returned from the cart will not need to be cast to the correct type and syntax checking can be performed on objects returned from the cart.

```
public class ShoppingCart<Item> {
    ...
}
```

When the cart is created, the type of item that will be placed into the cart is included in the definition. For example, in the shopping cart application in this chapter, a shopping cart for the *CatalogItem* will be created.

```
private ShoppingCart<CatalogItem> cart =
    new ShoppingCart<CatalogItem>();
```

This will allow the shopping cart to return a specific type from a method, instead of returning an *Object*.

Cart Data Structure

The cart will have a list of items from the database. Since the cart was declared with a generic type named *Item*, this generic type can be used to define the type of object that is placed into the list.

```
private List<Item> items;
```

The cart will be recreated whenever all the items should be removed from it. When creating the cart, the type of element that is in the cart is included in the call to the constructor. An *ArrayList* will be used to store the items. The method resetItems will be used to clear all the items from the cart.

```
public void resetItems() {
    items = new ArrayList<Item>();
...
```

When the shopping cart is created, it will also create the list that stores the items, by calling the *resetItems* method.

```
public ShoppingCart() {
    resetItems();
...
```

Accessing Items

There are only two additional features that are essential for a shopping cart: adding items and retrieving items.

When retrieving the items, the entire list of items will be returned. Individual access to the items can be handled in the controller helper, where the details of the items will be known. The getItems method will return a generic list of items, so that the objects retrieved from it will not need to be cast to the correct type.

```java
public List<Item> getItems() {
    return items;
}
public void addItem(Item item) {
    items.add(item);
}
```

Total and Count

Additional properties will be added to the shopping cart for storing the total cost of the items and the count of all the items. There will be normal accessors and mutators for the total and count. These properties are not essential to a cart, they could always be generated when needed; however, they demonstrate that additional features could be added to the cart to make it more robust.

```java
private double total;
private int count;

public void setTotal(double total) {
    this.total = total;
}

public double getTotal() {
    return total;
}

public void setCount(int count) {
    this.count = count;
}

public int getCount() {
    return count;
}
```

Additionally, there will be an accessor that returns the total as currency, a method for adding to the total and a method for incrementing the count. To format the total as currency, create a number format for the currency that is defined for the current region.

```java
private static NumberFormat currency =
    NumberFormat.getCurrencyInstance();

public void addTotal(double amount) {
    total += amount;
}
```

```java
public String getTotalAsCurrency() {
    return currency.format(total);
}

public void incrCount() {
    count++;
}
```

Complete Shopping Cart

The complete cart is simple and generic. It could be used for any application with any item. Any application that needs a shopping cart would only need to define the item class and use it to construct the shopping cart, as will be done in the shopping cart application in this chapter.

```java
package ch7.catalog;
import java.util.List;
import java.util.ArrayList;
import java.text.NumberFormat;
public class ShoppingCart<Item> {

    private static NumberFormat currency =
        NumberFormat.getCurrencyInstance();
    private List<Item> items;
    private double total;
    private int count;

    public ShoppingCart() {
        resetItems();
    }

    public void resetItems() {
        items = new ArrayList<Item>();
        total = 0.0;
        count = 0;
    }

    public void setItems(List<Item> items) {
        this.items = items;
    }

    public List<Item> getItems() {
        return items;
    }

    public void addItem(Item item) {
        items.add(item);
    }

    public void setTotal(double total) {
        this.total = total;
    }
```

```java
public double getTotal() {
   return total;
}

public void setCount(int count) {
   this.count = count;
}

public int getCount() {
   return count;
}

public void addTotal(double amount) {
   total += amount;
}

public String getTotalAsCurrency() {
   return currency.format(total);
}

public void incrCount() {
   count++;
}
```
}

7.9   Application: Shopping Cart

Now that the items, the item database and the shopping cart bean have been
defined, it is possible to define the shopping cart application. The controller for
this application is identical to previous controllers that save data to a database; all
the work is done in the controller helper.

This is a simple cart. If more than one item is added to the cart, then two identical beans will be added to the cart. Figure 7.9 shows how the cart would appear if

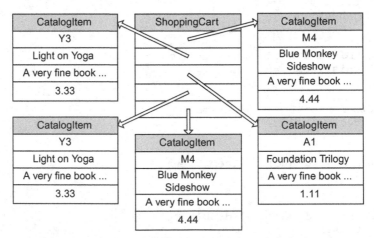

Figure 7.9 Multiple beans with the same values might be in the cart.

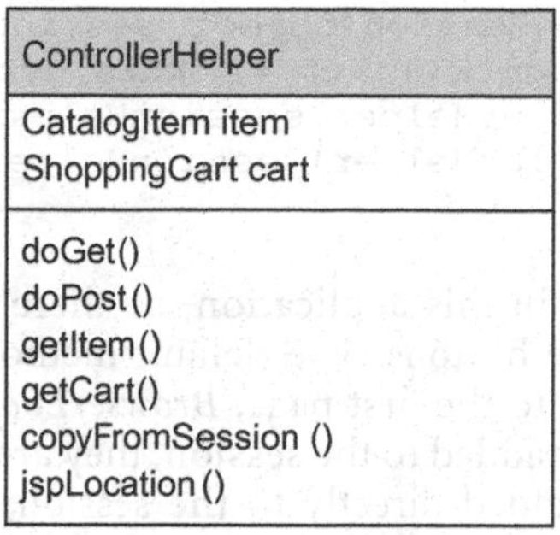

ControllerHelper
CatalogItem item
ShoppingCart cart
doGet()
doPost()
getItem()
getCart()
copyFromSession ()
jspLocation ()

Figure 7.10 The controller helper for the shopping cart has two beans.

two of the same items were added to the cart. It is left as an exercise to modify the cart so that there is only one bean for each item that is ordered.

7.9.1   ControllerHelper: Shopping Cart

If the user is viewing a catalogue item, then the item Id should be sent to the controller when a button is clicked. When the application receives the item Id, the item information will be read from the database. The bean that is returned from Hibernate will be set as the bean in the controller helper. When the bean is returned in the next response, the details of the item can be viewed in the JSP.

In addition to the current item bean, the shopping cart bean is also kept in the helper. This is the first application that has two beans: the current catalogue item and the shopping cart (Figure 7.10).

The controller helper will have member variables for both of these beans.

```
private CatalogItem item = new CatalogItem();
private ShoppingCart<CatalogItem> cart =
    new ShoppingCart<CatalogItem>();
```

Both of these beans should be accessible from the JSPs, so accessors for each will be added to the controller helper.

```
public Object getItem() {
  return item;
}

public Object getCart() {
  return cart;
}
```

The *copyFromSession* method should copy both beans from the session data. It is necessary to copy all the member variables that hold user data or the data will be lost.

```
public void copyFromSession(Object sessionHelper) {
  if (sessionHelper.getClass() == this.getClass()) {
    item = ((ControllerHelper)sessionHelper).item;
    cart = ((ControllerHelper)sessionHelper).cart;
  }
```

There are many buttons in this application, so there will be many methods to perform the tasks for the buttons. The default method should make the list of catalogue items available to the first page, *BrowserLoop.jsp*. As before, the items from the database are not added to the session, they are only added to the request attributes. If they were added directly to the session, then the web application would crash whenever it was reloaded.

```
@ButtonMethod(isDefault=true)
public String methodDefault() {
  java.util.List list = HibernateHelper
      .getListData(CatalogItem.class);
  request.setAttribute("allItems", list);
  return jspLocation("BrowseLoop.jsp");
}
```

The remaining buttons perform specific actions based on the button that the user clicked. Two of these methods encapsulate calls to methods in the shopping cart. When the user selects *Add Cart* or *Empty Cart*, the controller helper only has to call the corresponding method from the cart. After doing the specific tasks, the methods call the default method.

Using the session always complicates matters, especially when an item that is in the session has also been placed into a separate collection (Figure 7.11). In this case, after an item has been added to the cart, the item will still be in the session. Upon the next request, the item in the session could be populated with new data. If this happens, then the data in the collection will be changed, too.

This problem can be avoided by creating a new bean after the current item is added to the cart. This will create a new, empty bean that will be accessed from the session. The item that was just added will no longer be accessible from the session.

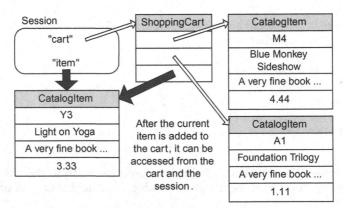

Figure 7.11 The item is in the session and in the shopping cart.

```
@ButtonMethod(buttonName="addCart")
public String methodAddCart() {
  cart.addItem(item);
  item = new CatalogItem();
  return methodDefault();
}

@ButtonMethod(buttonName="emptyCart")
public String methodEmptyCart() {
  cart.resetItems();
  return methodDefault();
}
```

The button for viewing an item is more complicated. When the user chooses an item to view, the item Id is sent to the controller. The helper needs to look in the database of items and check that a valid Id was sent. If it is a valid Id, then the bean from the database is set as the bean in the helper. This is similar to the technique used in the *Account Login* application, when testing if the account was already in the database.

```
@ButtonMethod(buttonName="viewItem")
public String methodViewItem() {
  fillBeanFromRequest(item);
  if (item.getItemId() != null) {
    Object dbObj = HibernateHelper.
      getFirstMatch(item, "itemId",
                        item.getItemId());
    if (dbObj != null) {
      item = (CatalogItem)dbObj;
    }
  }
  return methodDefault();
}
```

The *View Cart* method only has to redirect the application to the JSP that displays the contents of the cart. All the details of displaying the cart are encapsulated in the Cart page.

```
@ButtonMethod(buttonName="viewCart")
public String methodViewCart() {
  return jspLocation("Cart.jsp");
}
```

The final button is the one to process the cart. The corresponding method will loop through all the items, counting them and adding the price to the total in the cart. The method redirects to the final JSP in the application, *Process.jsp*.

```
@ButtonMethod(buttonName="processCart")
public String methodProcessCart() {
  for(CatalogItem item : cart.getItems()) {
    cart.addTotal(item.getPrice());
    cart.incrCount();
  }
  return jspLocation("ProcessCart.jsp");
}
```

The JSPs will be located in the same directory as the Controller.

```
public String jspLocation(String page) {
  return "/WEB-INF/classes/ch7/catalog/" + page;
}
```

7.9.2   BrowseLoop.jsp: Shopping Cart

The main page of the application is the page that displays all the catalogue items
that are in the catalogue item database. These are the items that can be placed in
the shopping cart. If the user selects an item from the catalogue, its details will be
displayed in the page.

When the page is first loaded, no item has been selected from the catalogue.
In this case, the bean that has been sent to the JSP contains default information,
including a null item Id. A bean with a null item Id should not be displayed in
the page. There needs to be a way to hide the details of the bean when the item
Id is null.

There are several ways to resolve the problem of conditionally showing an item
from the catalogue. The simplest solution is to use a valid, default item Id when
the page is first loaded, so that an item will always be displayed. A second solution
is to conditionally generate the HTML for the item information in the controller
and send it to the JSP. A third solution is to put an **if** statement into the JSP. The
third solution will be used in this page, using another custom tag from JSTL.

Another problem in this page is to identify which item the user selected. A
common technique for doing this is to have a separate button for each item in the
catalogue, but then how is each button made unique?

A complicated solution would be to name each button with the item Id, but this
would require many button methods in the controller. A simpler solution is to
place each button in a separate form and to place a hidden field in each form,
containing the item Id. Each button will have the same name, so there will only
be one button method for all the items. The item Id can be retrieved from the
hidden field.

Display Catalogue

The catalogue of items was added to the request attributes in the controller helper.
This is the same way that the database was sent to the JSP in previous examples.

```
@ButtonMethod(isDefault=true)
public String methodDefault() {
  java.util.List list = HibernateHelper
     .getListData(CatalogItem.class);
  request.setAttribute("allItems", list);
  return jspLocation("BrowseLoop.jsp");
}
```

The catalogue database can be retrieved using EL as ${allItems}. The
individual items can be accessed just like any other collection: using a *forEach*
tag.

```
<core:forEach var="oneItem" items="${allItems}">
    access ${oneItem} here
</core:forEach>
```

Each item will have its own form, button and hidden field. The hidden field will contain the item Id and can be used by the controller to access the database of catalogue items. When the user clicks a button, the data for that item will appear in the page.

...

```
<core:forEach var="oneItem" items="${allItems}">
  <form method='post' action="Controller">
    <p>
    ${oneItem.name}
    <input type='hidden' name='itemId'
                          value='${oneItem.itemId}'>
    <input type='submit' name='viewItem'
                          value='View Item'>
  </form>
</core:forEach>
```

...

This is an example where a hidden field is needed; this technique could not be implemented using the session. There must be some information in the form that identifies the item Id.

Each button has the same name, which will correspond to one method in the controller helper. The controller helper will retrieve the value from the hidden field and use it to read the item information from the catalogue database.

Conditional Tag

The JSP will always receive a bean, but sometimes it will only have default data and not data from the database. In this case, the page should not display the bean. This means that a decision needs to be made in the JSP. As before, there are two ways to do this: use a custom HTML tag that performs an **if** statement or use Java code in the JSP.

It is better to use a custom HTML tag to solve the problem. It is better if the code in a JSP contains as much HTML as possible, so that an HTML designer could maintain the page more easily. Using a custom HTML tag also eliminates the possibility of unfriendly stack traces.

There is a tag from JSTL that defines an if statement.

```
<core:if test="boolean condition">
    conditional processing
</core:if>
```

With this tag, it is possible to conditionally include details about an item. The condition will be that the item Id is not null. If it isn't, then the additional HTML code between the tags will be displayed.

```
<core:if test="${helper.item.itemId != null}">
    HTML for item details
</core:if>
```

BrowseLoop

The BrowseLoop JSP will use nested tables to layout the data. One nested table will contain the list of catalogue items with their forms, hidden fields and buttons. If the user has selected an item, then the details will appear in another cell of this table. The other nested table contains the button for viewing the cart.

The first nested table contains the loop that generates the form for each button and contains the conditional code for displaying the item details. The Boolean condition for the core:if statement tests if the item Id is not null. If the item Id is null, then the bean is a default bean and the user did not choose an item yet.

```
...
<table border>
  <tr>
  <td rowspan="4" align="right">
  <core:forEach var="oneItem" items="${allItems}">
    <form method='post' action="Controller">
      <p>
      ${oneItem.name}
      <input type='hidden' name='itemId'
                           value='${oneItem.itemId}'>
      <input type='submit' name='viewItem'
                           value='View Item'>
    </form>
  </core:forEach>
  <core:if test="${helper.item.itemId != null}">
    <td>
      ${helper.item.name}
    <tr>
    <td>
      ${helper.item.description}
    <tr>
    <td>
      ${helper.item.price}
    <tr>
    <td>
    <form action="Controller" method="post">
      <p>
      <input type="hidden" name="itemId"
             value="${helper.item.itemId}">
      <input type="submit" name="addCart"
             value="Add To Cart">
      <input type="reset">
    </form>
    </tr>
  </core:if>
</table>
...
```

7.9.3 Cart.jsp: Shopping Cart

The cart page is simple: it only needs to display the items that are in the cart. The cart has been added to the session, so it can be retrieved in the JSP. Once again, a loop will be used to display all the items from a collection. A table will be used to organise the items from the catalogue into a grid.

```html
<!DOCTYPE HTML PUBLIC "-//W3C//DTD HTML 4.01//EN">
<%@ taglib uri="http://java.sun.com/jsp/jstl/core"
           prefix="core" %>
<html>
  <head>
    <meta http-equiv="content-type"
          content="text/html;charset=utf-8">
    <title>View Cart</title>
  </head>
  <body>
    <table border>
      <core:forEach var="oneItem"
                    items="${helper.cart.items}">
      <tr>
        <td>${oneItem.itemId}
        <td>${oneItem.name}
        <td>${oneItem.price}
      </core:forEach>
    </table>
    <hr>
    <form method="post" action="Controller">
      <p>
      <input type="submit" name="shop"
                           value="Continue Shopping">
      <input type="submit" name="processCart"
                           value="Process Cart">
      <input type="submit" name="emptyCart"
                           value="Empty Cart">
    </form>
  </body>
</html>
```

The process cart page is similar. It displays the cart.

Try It   http://bytesizebook.com/book/ch7/catalog/Controller

View some items, add them to the shopping cart, process the cart.

7.9.4 Shopping Cart: Enhancement

The shopping cart is only part of a complete web application. After obtaining the cart of items from the user, a typical web site would than obtain the user's billing information. This could be accomplished from the process page, by adding a button that would send the user to an edit page, in which the user would enter the billing information. The edit page would be like the edit pages from the other examples in this book. There would then be a confirm page and a process page. The user's data would be entered into a database of user data.

Such an application would be using two tables from the database: one for the catalogue items and one for the user's data. There would also be three beans in the application: catalogue item, shopping cart, user information. Each of these beans would need an accessor in the controller helper and would need to be copied from the session data.

```java
protected RequestDataAddress data =
    new RequestDataAddress();
private CatalogItem item = new CatalogItem();
private ShoppingCart<CatalogItem> cart =
    new ShoppingCart<CatalogItem>();
...
public Object getData() {
  return data;
}

public Object getItem() {
  return item;
}

public Object getCart() {
  return cart;
}
...
public void copyFromSession(Object sessionHelper) {
  if (sessionHelper.getClass() == this.getClass()) {
    data = ((ControllerHelper)sessionHelper).data;
    item = ((ControllerHelper)sessionHelper).item;
    cart = ((ControllerHelper)sessionHelper).cart;
  }
}
```

The details of implementing such an application are left to the reader. The only difference between this application and previous applications is that two tables are being used in the database. When Hibernate is configured, all the tables that are marked as entities must be included in the call to initSessionFactory.

```java
HibernateHelper
    .initSessionFactory(RequestDataAddress.class,
                        CatalogItem.class);
```

The catalogue item table should not be created by this application. It is created with a separate controller. For this reason, the call to createTable will only have one table, while the call to initSessionFactory will have both tables.

```java
static public void initHibernate(boolean create) {

  if (create) {
    HibernateHelper
```

```
        .createTable(RequestDataAddress.class);
    }

    HibernateHelper
        .initSessionFactory(RequestDataAddress.class,
                            CatalogItem.class);
}
```

7.10   Summary

It is better to let Hibernate manage the primary key, since it is used to indicate data persistence. There is often a separate key in the user's data that can also be used to identify a row. Other times, several fields will need to be combined to uniquely identify each row.

Finding a value in the database can be accomplished by using the Criteria class in Hibernate. Once an object has been retrieved from the database, Hibernate will remember that it came from the database and will update the row, instead of adding a new one.

An application was developed that forced the user to log into the site. By doing this, the user's data can be retrieved from the database and stored in the session. When the bean in the session is written to the database, it will replace the old data in the database.

Cookies can be used to remember information about a user, so that personal information can be displayed every time the user visits a site. Cookies are stored in the browser and are sent back to the site that created it, whenever that site is visited. The user has control over cookies and can delete them at any time.

Cookies have a name and a value. Cookies can be created that will exist for a specific time and be sent to a specific server or page. Cookies can be configured so that they are only sent over a secure connection. Cookies are sent to the browser as part of the response headers.

Cookies can be used to save a user Id, so that the next time a site is accessed, the user does not have to log in. The browser will send the Id to the controller and the controller will use it to access the database.

Many sites have shopping cart applications that allow users to select and add items. Shopping carts are fairly simple in that they only need to be able to store the items, clear the items and add an item. The item that is stored in the shopping cart is not important when implementing a shopping cart. A shopping cart can be developed using Java 1.5 generics.

An application that uses a shopping cart was developed. A database of items was created. The same bean that was used to create the database was also used in the application. It is a natural choice, since the user will be selecting items from the catalogue to be added to the shopping cart.

The database will set the maximum length for a text field when a column is added to the table for the field. It is better to set the maximum value than to use the default length. Hibernate has annotations that will indicate the preferred length of the column in the table.

A new tag that implements an if statement was introduced from the JSTL. By using this tag, conditional content can be added to a JSP. This is a better approach than using Java, since Java can generate stack traces and Java can be difficult to change for an HTML developer.

7.11   Chapter Review

Terms

1. Criteria Class
2. Cookie
   a. Name
   b. Value
   c. Expiration
   d. Domain
   e. Path
   f. Secure
3. Cookie Operations
   a. Sending
   b. Accessing
   c. Deleting
   d. Finding
4. Path Specific Cookies
5. Catalogue Item and Catalogue
6. Shopping Cart Bean
   a. add
   b. reset
   c. set total
   d. set count

New Java

1. Cookie Class
   a. Constructors
   b. getName, setName
   c. getValue, setValue
   d. getMaxAge, setMaxAge
   e. getDomain, setDomain
   f. getPath, setPath
   g. getSecure, setSecure
   h. Default Values
2. isValidProperty

Tags

1. core:if

Questions

1. Why was a new bean created after a row was removed from the database?
2. Explain the steps that are followed to retrieve a bean from the database and copy it into the current controller helper.
3. Explain the steps that are followed to read a cookie from the browser and then test if there is a corresponding row in the database.
4. Why does the new user method create a new bean?
5. What are the default values for all the properties in a cookie?
6. In a cookie, what does a maximum age of zero mean? What does a maximum age of – 1 mean?
7. What does it mean when the value of the domain property in a cookie starts with a period?
8. What does it mean when the value of the path property in a cookie is "/accounting"?

Tasks

1. Create the following cookie and add it to the response.
    a. Name it *fruit* and give it a value of *orange*.
    b. Have it expire when the browser closes.
    c. Have it returned only to the domain and path that created it.
    d. It may be sent over a non-secure connection.
2. Create the following cookie and add it to the response.
    a. Name it *vegetable* and give it a value of *broccoli*.
    b. Have it expire in one year.
    c. Have it returned to all subdomains of fiu.edu and to all paths.
    d. It may be sent over a secure connection only.
3. For the create catalog servlet, add a web interface, so that items can be added to and deleted from the database.
4. Write the code that belongs in a JSP that will loop through all the cookies that it received.
5. Write the code that belongs in a controller that will delete a cookie named *pen* that can be read by all paths that begin with /bic on the *www.pensforsale.com* domain. Don't just create the cookie, be sure that the cookie is sent to the browser.
6. Write the code that belongs in a servlet that will find a cookie named *auto*.
7. Modify the getListData method so that two different properties and values can be sent to it. Add an additional criterion to the search.
8. Modify the getListData method so that a variable number of properties and values can be sent to it. Add an additional criterion to the search for each new property. Hint: The initSessionFactory method has a parameter that can accept a variable number of arguments.

9. For the shopping cart application, only allow one instance of an item in the cart and keep a total of the number of copies that are wanted. On the confirm page, add a text box for changing the current item count and a button to recalculate the total, for each item.

10. For the shopping cart application, after the cart has been processed, allow the user to proceed to additional pages, named edit, confirm and process, in which the user's billing information is added. Save the billing address and the purchased items in a new table in the database.

Appendix

The relationship between the CLASSPATH and packages is explained. When complex applications are developed that require the use of many additional packages, it is necessary to understand how Java finds packages at runtime.

With any complex software package, there can be difficulties using it. There can be conflicts between separate packages that lead to memory leaks. Some of these problems can be avoided by moving the packages to another location. Some need to be modified. Two packages need to have methods called to avoid memory leaks and errors. The details of memory leaks are explained in this Appendix.

Hibernate can be used without any knowledge of SQL. For those that still want to see what Hibernate is doing on the database server, simple commands for the MySQL database server have been explained. Using these commands it will be possible to log onto the server and list the contents of the tables that have been created by Hibernate.

The remainder of the Appendix lists the contents of the auxiliary classes that were used in the book. The helper classes use many standard Java techniques to implement some of the features in the book. A detailed explanation of these techniques belongs in a book on Java. Hopefully, the contents of these files are easy to understand. The Javadoc statements have been removed from these files, but can be accessed at http://bytesizebook.com/book/doc.

A.1   Classpath and Packages

When using Java, it is important to understand the concepts of the classpath and packages. The two concepts are intertwined; one will not make any sense until the other is understood. When Java looks for packages, it searches the classpath.

A.1.1   Usual Suspects

There is a great scene at the end of the movie *Casablanca*. Humphrey Bogart has just killed the German Commander in front of the Chief of Police. The Chief then calls his office and informs them that the Commander has been murdered and that they should round up the usual suspects.

For Java, the CLASSPATH variable is a list of the usual suspects. When Java wants to find a class file, it searches through all of the directories that are listed in the CLASSPATH. In order to have Java look in new places, just add more paths to the CLASSPATH variable.

For example, suppose the CLASSPATH contains

1. `/myData`
2. `/myFiles`
3. `/myStuff`

Java will check the following paths to find a class file named `myFile.class`.

1. `/myData/myFile.class`
2. `/myFiles/myFile.class`
3. `/myStuff/myFile.class`

There are also system paths that are searched that are not listed in the CLASSPATH.

A.1.2   What Is a Package?

The simplest definition of a package is a folder that contains Java class files. However, packages do more than that. They also indicate where a Java class can be found. Essentially, packages allow for an extension to the CLASSPATH list, without adding new paths to it.

If the class file `myFile.class` was in a package named `jbond007`, then Java will check the following paths to find the class file.

1. `/myData/jbond007/myFile.class`
2. `/myFiles/jbond007/myFile.class`
3. `/myStuff/jbond007/myFile.class`

If the class file `myFile.class` was in a package named `agents.jbond007`, then Java will check the following paths to find the class file.

1. `/myData/agents/jbond007/myFile.class`
2. `/myFiles/agents/jbond007/myFile.class`
3. `/myStuff/agents/jbond007/myFile.class`

Every section of the package name corresponds to a subdirectory in the file system. The first part of the package name corresponds to a directory on the file system that must be a subdirectory of a path in the CLASSPATH variable.

A.2   JAR File Problems

Java loads *.class* files when they are first accessed. At different times, Java uses different class loaders to create the class that is defined in the *.class* file. When a class is created, its information is stored in a separate part of memory that is never garbage-collected by the JVM. The memory can be released when the class loader is removed; however, if there is still a reference from a different class loader to any object that was created by the class loader being removed, then none of the class definitions that were loaded by the class loader will be released. This is known as a memory leak.

Each web application has its own class loader. This is what makes it possible to restart a web application without restarting the entire JVM. There are class loaders for running the JVM and there is a class loader for the web application. When the web application is restarted, the class loader is reinitialised. As long as there are no active references to the objects created by the web application's class loader, all of the permanent memory that was allocated by the class loader will be released. If there is still an active reference, then none of the class information will be released and there will be a memory leak.

Other memory leaks can be caused by the programmer. Many packages have methods that should be called in order to release all the reources that are being used by the package. This is analogous to closing a file: there is a method to close the file, but the programmer must call it. If the file is not closed, then some data might not be written to the file. In the same way, the methods that exist for releasing resources must be called by the programmer, or the application will have a memory leak.

There are two types of memory leaks: catastrophic and one-timers. Catastrophic errors can cause the servlet engine to crash. The one-timers will usually not cause the servlet engine to crash; they will only force the engine to hold onto more resources than it needs.

If a web application with a catastrophic leak is reloaded enough times, then it will crash the servlet engine. Each time it is reloaded, it maintains a reference to the previous class loader. All the class data from the old class loader cannot be released and then a new class loader is created. If it is reloaded ten times, then there will be ten copies of the class data. If it is reloaded enough times, all of the memory in the servlet engine will be used and the engine will crash.

The one-timers only hold onto extra memory during the first reload; they do not leak more memory on subsequent reloads. The one-timers are usually caused by a static reference to an object. When the static reference is loaded by one class loader and the object is loaded by a different class loader, then there is a memory leak. Often, these leaks can be removed by using a weak reference to the object.

As of the publication of this book, Tomcat 6 is available as well as Hibernate 3.2.4. These packages have removed all of the catastrophic memory leaks. However, it is still up to the programmer to call all the necessary methods to release resources; otherwise, there will be catastrophic memory leaks.

A.2.1 Hibernate

Hibernate can cause a catastrophic memory leak, if the programmer does not release Hibernate's resources. There is a method in the Hibernate package that must be called before the web application closes: `closeFactory()`. If this is not called, then every time the web application is reloaded, the previous class loader and all of its memory will not be released.

The call to this method has been encapsulated in the `closeHibernate` method of the `HibernateHelper` class.

A.2.2 MySQL Driver

The MySql driver is used in this book, but this section applies to any SQL driver that is used. Once a driver has been registered with Java, then it must be deregistered before the web application is stopped; otherwise, there will be a catastrophic memory leak.

One technique is to deregister all of the drivers. An enumeration of all of the drivers can be obtained from the `DriverManager` class. Loop through each driver and deregister it.

```
try {
  Enumeration<Driver> enumer = DriverManager.getDrivers();
  while (enumer.hasMoreElements()) {
    DriverManager.deregisterDriver(enumer.nextElement());
  }
} catch (java.sql.SQLException se) {
  se.printStackTrace();
}
```

A.2.3 Hibernate Annotations

This section is not about a memory leak, but it is a warning to developers who have used earlier versions of Hibernate. In earlier versions, a multiple-valued bean property was annotated with `@OneToMany` to indicate that it will have a separate table created for it in the database. This table was created by Hibernate, without having to be defined. In Hibernate 3.2, this annotation is only to be used for entities that have been defined by the programmer, an implicit table cannot be created by using this annotation. The `@CollectionOfElements` annotation should be used, instead, to indicate that Hibernate should create an implicit, related table in the database.

A.3 MySQL

Although Hibernate eliminates the necessity of knowing SQL, sometimes curiosity gets the better of us and we want to see what Hibernate is doing. An example will be presented that demonstrates how to issue a few SQL commands in the MySQL database server to see the structure of the tables that Hibernate has created. A command will also be supplied that shows all the records in a table. These commands are very simple SQL commands. Only the bare minimum of statements will be introduced.

Additional commands will be supplied that are specific to the MySQL database. These additional commands are needed in order to log onto the server. The MySQL server is a free relational database. The source code can be obtained at http://mysql.org.

Two essential pieces of information are needed to log onto any server: user-name and password.

To access the MySQL database, issue the following command. This command will connect to the MySQL server that is installed on the local machine. Enter your password after MySQL prompts you for it.

```
mysql -u username -p <Enter Key>
password
```

View all databases in the server with the following command. Don't forget the ; at the end.

```
show databases;
```

Select a database named *db_name* with the following command. This is the only command that does not need a ; at the end.

```
use db_name
```

Once a database has been chosen, the names of all the tables can be displayed.

```
show tables;
```

There won't be any tables until you create a servlet that saves data to a database. Once you have a table, you can view the structure of a table named *name-of-table* with the following command.

```
describe name-of-table;
```

Use the select statement to see all the records in the table.

```
select * from name-of-table;
```

Exit MySQL with the following command.

```
exit;
```

These are the only commands that are needed to see what Hibernate has done.

A.4 Auxiliary Classes

Many classes that were used in the book were not explained in complete detail. The parts that were relevant to the theme of the book were covered, but the remaining parts of these classes were not covered. Most of the uncovered details deal with annotations, enumerations, error handling and reflection. A complete explanation of the code from these files belongs in a Java programming text.

A.4.1   Annotations

In addition to the annotations that are used by Hibernate, two other annotations were used in the book. ButtonMethod was used to annotate a method that does the processing associated with a button on a form. SetByAttribute was used on bean property accessors to indicate if the property is initialised by including an extra attribute in the definition of the form element in the JSP.

ButtonMethod

Listing A.1 is the ButtonMethod annotation. Place this annotation before a method that does the processing associated with a button in a form. The method that is annotated should have no parameters and should return a string.

```
package shared;

import java.lang.annotation.*;

@Retention(RetentionPolicy.RUNTIME)
@Target({ElementType.METHOD})
public @interface ButtonMethod {
    String buttonName() default "";
    boolean isDefault() default false;
}
```

Listing A.1 The ButtonMethod annotation.

SetByAttribute

Listing A.2 is the SetByAttribute annotation. Place the annotation before the accessor of a bean property that is associated with a form element that is a button group or a select list. These types of form elements are initialised by including an extra attribute in the element. The type of the additional attribute is defined in the AttributeType parameter of the annotation.

```
package shared;

import java.lang.annotation.*;

@Retention(RetentionPolicy.RUNTIME)
@Target({ElementType.METHOD})
public @interface SetByAttribute {
    AttributeType type();
}
```

Listing A.2 The SetByAttribute annotation.

A.4.2   Cookie Utility

The cookies that are retrieved in a servlet cannot be accessed randomly; it is necessary to do a linear search each time a cookie is needed. To facilitate this task, a utility class of static methods was created that will perform such linear searches. A cookie can be retrieved by name; either the cookie or the cookie's value can be returned (Listing A.3).

```java
package shared;
import javax.servlet.http.Cookie;
import javax.servlet.http.HttpServletRequest;

public class CookieUtil {

  static
  public Cookie findCookie(HttpServletRequest request,
                           String name)
  {
    if (request.getCookies() == null ) return null;
    for(Cookie cookie : request.getCookies()) {
      if (cookie.getName().equals(name)) return cookie;
    }
    return null;
  }

  static
  public String findCookieValue(HttpServletRequest request,
                                String name)
  {
    Cookie cookie = findCookie(request, name);
    if (cookie != null) {
      return cookie.getValue();
    }
    return null;
  }

}
```

Listing A.3 The CookieUtil class.

A.4.3   Enumerations

Enumerations are new in Java 1.5. They are an excellent way to create self-documenting code. The SessionData enumeration is used to indicate if the data that is already in the session should be read or ignored. The AttributeType enumeration is used by the SetByAttribute annotation to indicate the type of the attribute that is used to initialise a form element.

Session Data

Listing A.4 is the SessionData enumeration, which is defined in the HelperBaseCh4 class. It is used as a parameter to the addHelperToSession method. While this parameter could have been implemented with a boolean variable, it is clearer to understand what SessionData.READ means than to remember what true means in this context.

```
protected enum SessionData { READ, IGNORE };
```
Listing A.4 The SessionData enumeration from HelperBaseCh4.

Attribute Type

Listing A.5 is the AttributeType enumeration. This is used in the SetByAttribute annotation. Certain form elements are initialised by adding an attribute to the form element. This form element attribute is named either checked or selected. This enumeration encapsulates these values.

```
package shared;
```

```
public enum AttributeType { CHECKED, SELECTED }
```
Listing A.5 The AttributeType enumeration.

A.4.4 Helper Base

The helper base classes have been used since Chapter Four. The subsequent helper base classes from each chapter extend the helper base from the previous chapter. Most of the details of the classes were covered in the book, but not every version of an overloaded method was covered. Reflection was also used in several places to simplify the work of the controller helper; the details of using reflection should be covered in a Java programming text.

Helper Base Chapter Four

This base class has member variables for the request, response and logger. These are initialised when the base class is constructed. There are also default implementations of the doGet and doPost methods that only display an error. The session is used to store data, the population of a bean is automated and reflection is used to execute a method that is associated with a button. Listing A.6 is the helper base class from Chapter Four.

```
package shared;

import java.io.IOException;
import java.io.PrintWriter;
import java.lang.reflect.InvocationTargetException;
import java.lang.reflect.Method;
import javax.servlet.ServletException;
import javax.servlet.http.HttpServletRequest;
import javax.servlet.http.HttpServletResponse;
import org.apache.log4j.Level;
import org.apache.log4j.Logger;

public abstract class HelperBaseCh4 {

protected enum SessionData { READ, IGNORE };
```

```java
private Method methodDefault = null;

protected HttpServletRequest request;
protected HttpServletResponse response;
protected Logger logger;

public HelperBaseCh4(HttpServletRequest request,
    HttpServletResponse response) {
this.request = request;
this.response = response;
logger = Logger.getLogger("bytesizebook.webdev");
logger.setLevel(Level.DEBUG);
}

protected void doGet()
throws ServletException, IOException {
  response.getWriter()
     .print("The doGet method must be overridden" +
             " in the class that extends HelperBase.");
}

protected void doPost()
throws ServletException, IOException {
  response.getWriter()
    .print("The doPost method must be overridden" +
            " in the class that extends HelperBase.");
}

protected abstract void copyFromSession(Object helper);

public void addHelperToSession(String name,
                               SessionData state) {
  if (SessionData.READ == state) {
    Object sessionObj =
       request.getSession().getAttribute(name);
    if (sessionObj != null) {
      copyFromSession(sessionObj);
    }
  }
  request.getSession().setAttribute(name, this);
}

public void addHelperToSession(String name,
                               boolean checkSession) {
  if (checkSession) {
    Object sessionObj =
       request.getSession().getAttribute(name);
    if (sessionObj != null) {
      copyFromSession(sessionObj);
    }
  }
  request.getSession().setAttribute(name, this);
}
```

```java
protected String executeButtonMethod()
throws ServletException, IOException {
  String result = "";
  methodDefault = null;
  Class clazz = this.getClass();
  Class enclosingClass = clazz.getEnclosingClass();
  while (enclosingClass != null) {
    clazz = this.getClass();
    enclosingClass = clazz.getEnclosingClass();
  }

  try {
    result = executeButtonMethod(clazz, true);
  } catch (Exception ex) {
    writeError(request, response,
            "Button Method Error", ex);
    return "";
  }

  return result;
}

protected
String executeButtonMethod(Class clazz,
                           boolean searchForDefault)
throws IllegalAccessException, InvocationTargetException
{
  String result = "";
  Method [] methods =  clazz.getDeclaredMethods();
  for(Method method : methods) {
    ButtonMethod annotation =
       method.getAnnotation(ButtonMethod.class);
    if (annotation != null) {
      if (searchForDefault && annotation.isDefault())
      {
        methodDefault = method;
      }
      if (request.getParameter(annotation.buttonName())
           != null)
      {
        result = invokeButtonMethod(method);
        break;
      }
    }
  }
  if (result.equals("")) {
    Class superClass = clazz.getSuperclass();
    if (superClass != null) {
      result =
        executeButtonMethod(superClass,
                          methodDefault == null);
    }
    if (result.equals("")) {
      if (methodDefault != null) {
        result = invokeButtonMethod(methodDefault);
      } else {
```

```
            logger.error(
                    "(executeButtonMethod) No default method " +
                    "was specified, but one was needed.");
            result = "No default method was specified,.";
        }
      }
    }
    return result;
}

protected String invokeButtonMethod(Method buttonMethod)
throws IllegalAccessException, InvocationTargetException
{
  String resultInvoke = "Could not invoke method";
  try{
    resultInvoke =
        (String) buttonMethod.invoke(this,
                                    (Object[]) null);
  } catch (IllegalAccessException iae) {
    logger.error("(invoke) Button method is not public.",
                iae);
    throw iae;
  } catch (InvocationTargetException ite) {
    logger.error("(invoke) Button method exception",
                ite);
    throw ite;
  }
  return resultInvoke;
}

public void fillBeanFromRequest(Object data) {
  try {
    org.apache.commons.beanutils.BeanUtils.
        populate(data, request.getParameterMap());
  } catch (IllegalAccessException iae) {
    logger.error("Populate - Illegal Access.", iae);
  } catch (InvocationTargetException ite) {
    logger.error("Populate - Invocation Target.", ite);
  }
}

public void populateThrow(Object data)
throws IOException, ServletException {
  try {
    org.apache.commons.beanutils.BeanUtils.
        populate(data, request.getParameterMap());
  } catch (IllegalAccessException iae) {
    logger.error("Populate - Illegal Access.", iae);
    writeError(request, response,
                "Populate - Illegal Access.", iae);
  } catch (InvocationTargetException ite) {
    logger.error("Populate - Invocation Target.", ite);
    writeError(request, response,
                "Populate - Invocation Target.", ite);
  }
}
```

```
static public void writeError(
    javax.servlet.http.HttpServletRequest request,
    javax.servlet.http.HttpServletResponse response,
    String title,
    Exception ex)
    throws IOException, ServletException
{
  java.io.PrintWriter out = response.getWriter();
  response.setContentType("text/html");
  out.println("<html>");
  out.println("  <head>");
  out.println("    <title>" + title + "</title>");
  out.println("  </head>");
  out.println("  <body>");
  out.println("<h2>" + title + "</h2>");
  if (ex.getMessage() != null)
    out.println("    <h3>" + ex.getMessage()+ "</h3>");
  if (ex.getCause() != null)
    out.println("    <h4>" + ex.getCause()+ "</h4>");
  StackTraceElement[] trace = ex.getStackTrace();
  if (trace != null && trace.length > 0)
    out.print("<pre>");
  ex.printStackTrace(out);
  out.println("</pre>");
  out.println("  </body>");
  out.println("</html>");
  out.close();
  }
}
```

Listing A.6 The helper base class from Chapter Four.

Helper Base Chapter Five

The Chapter Five helper base class adds the enhanced interface for accessing the Hibernate validation messages (Listing A.7).

```
package shared;

import java.io.IOException;
import javax.servlet.ServletException;
import javax.servlet.http.HttpServletRequest;
import javax.servlet.http.HttpServletResponse;
import org.hibernate.validator.ClassValidator;
import org.hibernate.validator.InvalidValue;

public abstract class HelperBaseCh5 extends HelperBaseCh4 {

    public HelperBaseCh5(HttpServletRequest request,
            HttpServletResponse response) {
        super(request, response);
    }

    java.util.Map<String, String> errorMap =
            new java.util.HashMap<String, String>();
```

```java
    public void setErrors(Object data) {
        InvalidValue[] validationMessages;
        ClassValidator requestValidator =
                new ClassValidator(data.getClass());
        validationMessages =
                requestValidator.getInvalidValues(data);


        errorMap.clear();
        if (validationMessages.length != 0) {
            for(InvalidValue msg : validationMessages) {
                errorMap.put(msg.getPropertyName(),
                                msg.getMessage());
            }
        }
    }


    public boolean isValid(Object data) {
        setErrors(data);
        return errorMap.isEmpty();
    }


    public java.util.Map getErrors() {
        return errorMap;
    }


    public boolean isValidProperty(String name) {
        String msg = errorMap.get(name);
        return msg == null || msg.equals("");
    }


}
```

Listing A.7 The helper base class from Chapter Five.

Helper Base Chapter Six

The Chapter Six helper base class adds the maps for initialising complex form elements (Listing A.8).

```java
package shared;

import java.lang.reflect.InvocationTargetException;
import java.lang.reflect.Method;
import java.util.HashMap;
import java.util.Map;
import javax.servlet.http.HttpServletRequest;
import javax.servlet.http.HttpServletResponse;

public abstract class HelperBaseCh6 extends HelperBaseCh5 {

  protected Map<String, Map<String, String>> checked =
      new HashMap<String, Map<String, String>>();
```

```
  protected Map<String, Map<String, String>> selected =
     new HashMap<String, Map<String, String>>();


  public HelperBaseCh6(HttpServletRequest request,
     HttpServletResponse response) {
    super(request, response);
  }

  protected void setCheckedAndSelected(Object data) {
    setCheckedAndSelected(data, data.getClass());
  }

  protected void setCheckedAndSelected(Object data,
     Class clazz) {
    Method [] allMethods = clazz.getDeclaredMethods();
    Method methodDefault = null;
    for (Method method : allMethods) {
      SetByAttribute propAnnotation = method
         .getAnnotation(SetByAttribute.class);
      if (propAnnotation!=null) {
        String property = method.getName();
        java.util.regex.Pattern pattern
           = java.util.regex.Pattern.compile("get(.+)");
        java.util.regex.Matcher matcher
           = pattern.matcher(property);
        int index = property.indexOf("get");
        if (!matcher.matches()) {
          logger.error(property + " must be an accessor.");
        } else {
          property = matcher.group(1);
          property = property.substring(0,1).toLowerCase()
                      + property.substring(1);
          clearProperty(property,
                      propAnnotation.type());
          if (method.getReturnType().isArray()) {
            Object[] result =
               (Object[]) invokeGetter(data, method);
            if (result != null) {
              for(Object obj: result) {
                addChoice(property, obj.toString(),
                      (AttributeType)propAnnotation.type());
              }
            }
          } else {
            Object result = invokeGetter(data, method);
            if (result != null) {
              addChoice(property, result.toString(),
                   (AttributeType)propAnnotation.type());
            }
          }
        }
      }
    }
    Class parentClass = clazz.getSuperclass();
```

```java
    if (parentClass != null) {
      setCheckedAndSelected(data, parentClass);
    }
  }

  protected Object invokeGetter(Object obj, Method method)
  {
    Object result = null;
    try{
      result =  method.invoke(obj, (Object[]) null);
    } catch (IllegalAccessException iae) {
      logger.error("(invoke) Accessor needs public access",
                   iae);
    } catch (InvocationTargetException ite) {
      logger.error("(invoke) Accessor threw an exception",
                   ite);
    }
    return result;
  }

  public Map getChecked() {
    return checked;
  }

  public Map getSelected() {
    return selected;
  }

  public void addChecked(String group, String item) {
    if (checked.get(group) == null) {
      checked.put(group,
                  new HashMap<String, String>());
    }
    checked.get(group).put(item, "checked");
  }

  public void addSelected(String list, String item) {
    if (selected.get(list) == null) {
      selected.put(list,
                   new HashMap<String, String>());
    }
    selected.get(list).put(item, "selected");
  }

  public void addChoice(String list,
      String item,
      AttributeType type) {
    if (type == null ) return;
    if (AttributeType.CHECKED == type) {
      addChecked(list, item);
    }
    if (AttributeType.SELECTED == type) {
      addSelected(list, item);
    }
  }
```

```
public void clearProperty(String property,
    AttributeType type) {
  Map<String, String> propMap;
  if (AttributeType.CHECKED == type) {
    propMap = checked.get(property);
    if (propMap != null) {
      propMap.clear();
    }
  } else if (AttributeType.SELECTED == type) {
    propMap = selected.get(property);
    if (propMap != null) {
      propMap.clear();
    }
  }
}

public void clearMaps() {
  checked.clear();
  selected.clear();
}

}
```

Listing A.8 The helper base class from Chapter Six.

A.4.5 Hibernate Helper

The Hibernate helper class encapsulates access to the Hibernate methods. Hibernate uses transactions and session to access the database. The details of using these are placed in the Hibernate helper methods.

Saving Data

The saveOrUpdate method is used to add new objects in, or update existing objects to the database. Hibernate uses sessions and transactions to interact with the database. The details of sessions and transactions are outside the scope of this text.

```
public void updateDB(Object obj) {
  Session session = null;
  try {
    session = sessionFactory.openSession();
    Transaction tx = session.beginTransaction();

    session.saveOrUpdate(obj);

    tx.commit();
  } finally {
    if (session != null) session.close();
  }
}
```

```
static
public void updateDB(java.util.List list) {

  Session session = sessionFactory.openSession();
  Transaction tx = session.beginTransaction();

  for(Object obj : list) {
    session.saveOrUpdate(obj);
  }

  tx.commit();
  session.close();
}
```

Retrieving Data

Retrieving data is accomplished by using a `Criteria` object. This method returns all the records from the database. If a key and value are sent to the method, then only the records that match the value for that key will be returned. This method could be extended to include additional criteria, so that a more complicated search could be performed.

```
public java.util.List getListData(
    Class classBean, String strKey, Object value)
{
  java.util.List result = new java.util.ArrayList();

  Session session = sessionFactory.openSession();
  Transaction tx = session.beginTransaction();

  Criteria criteria =
      session.createCriteria(classBean);
  if (strKey != null) {
    criteria.add(Restrictions.like(strKey, value));
  }
  result = criteria.list();

  tx.commit();
  session.close();
  return result;
}
```

Removing Data

Once a record has been found, Hibernate will remember that it was retrieved from the database. By sending the same object to the remove method, it will be deleted from the database.

```
public void removeDB(Object obj) {
  Session session = null;
  try {
    session = sessionFactory.openSession();
    Transaction tx = session.beginTransaction();
```

```
    session.delete(obj);

    tx.commit();
  } finally {
    if (session != null) session.close();
  }
}
```

Hibernate Helper Class

Listing A.9 is the complete Hibernate helper class.

```
package shared;

import java.io.IOException;
import java.io.PrintWriter;
import java.util.ArrayList;
import java.util.List;
import java.util.Properties;
import javax.servlet.ServletException;
import javax.servlet.http.HttpServletRequest;
import javax.servlet.http.HttpServletResponse;
import org.apache.log4j.Logger;
import org.hibernate.Criteria;
import org.hibernate.HibernateException;
import org.hibernate.Query;
import org.hibernate.Session;
import org.hibernate.SessionFactory;
import org.hibernate.Transaction;
import org.hibernate.cfg.AnnotationConfiguration;
import org.hibernate.cfg.Configuration;
import org.hibernate.cfg.Environment;
import org.hibernate.criterion.Restrictions;

public class HibernateHelper {

  static protected Logger log =
      Logger.getLogger("bytesizebook.webdev");

  static protected List<Class> listClasses = new
ArrayList<Class>();
  static protected SessionFactory sessionFactory;
  static protected Exception lastError;

  static
  public void initSessionFactory(Properties props,
      Class... mappings) {
    if (addMappings(listClasses, mappings)) {
      closeFactory(sessionFactory);
      sessionFactory = createFactory(props, listClasses);
    }
  }
```

```
  static
  public void initSessionFactory(Class... mappings) {
    initSessionFactory(null, mappings);
  }

  static
  public void createTable(Properties props,
      Class... mappings) {
    List<Class> tempList = new ArrayList<Class>();
    SessionFactory tempFactory = null;

    addMappings(tempList, mappings);
    if (props == null ) props = new Properties();
    props.setProperty(Environment.HBM2DDL_AUTO, "create");
    tempFactory = createFactory(props, tempList);
    closeFactory(tempFactory);
  }

  static
  public void createTable(Class... mappings) {
    createTable(null, mappings);
  }

  static
  protected boolean addMappings(List<Class> list, Class...
mappings) {
    boolean bNewClass = false;
    for (Class mapping : mappings) {
      if (!list.contains(mapping)) {
        list.add(mapping);
        bNewClass = true;
      }
    }
    return bNewClass;
  }

  static
  protected SessionFactory createFactory(
                            Properties props,
                            List<Class> list) {
    SessionFactory factory = null;
    AnnotationConfiguration cfg =
        new AnnotationConfiguration();
    try {
      if (props != null) cfg.addProperties(props);
      configureFromFile(cfg);
      for (Class mapping : list) {
        cfg.addAnnotatedClass(mapping);
      }
      factory = buildFactory(cfg);
      testConnection(factory);
    } catch (Exception ex) {
      log.error("SessionFactory creation failed.", ex);
      lastError = ex;
      closeFactory(factory);
```

```java
      factory = null;
    }
    return factory;
}

static
protected void configureFromFile(Configuration cfg)
throws Exception {
  try {
    cfg.configure();
  } catch (HibernateException ex) {
    if (ex.getMessage().equals(
        "/hibernate.cfg.xml not found")) {
      log.warn(ex.getMessage());
    } else {
      log.error("Error in hibernate " +
          "configuration file.", ex);
      throw ex;
    }
  }
}

static
protected SessionFactory buildFactory(Configuration cfg)
throws Exception
{
  SessionFactory factory = null;
  try {
    factory = cfg.buildSessionFactory();
  } catch (Exception ex) {
    closeFactory(factory);
    factory = null;
    throw ex;
  }
  return factory;
}

static
protected void testConnection(SessionFactory factory)
throws Exception {
  Session session = null;
  try {
    session = factory.openSession();
    Transaction tran = session.beginTransaction();

    someDatabaseProcess();

    tran.commit();
    session.close();
  } catch (Exception ex) {
    log.error("Database transaction failed.", ex);
    if (session != null) session.close();
    throw ex;
  }
}
```

```
static
protected void someDatabaseProcess() {}

static
public void closeFactory(SessionFactory factory) {
  if (factory != null) {
    factory.close();
  }
}

static
public void closeFactory() {
  closeFactory(sessionFactory);
}

static
public Exception getLastError() {
  return lastError;
}

static
public void updateDB(Object obj) {
  Session session = null;
  try {
    session = sessionFactory.openSession();
    Transaction tx = session.beginTransaction();

    session.saveOrUpdate(obj);

    tx.commit();
  } finally {
    if (session != null) session.close();
  }
}

static
public void updateDB(java.util.List list) {

  Session session = sessionFactory.openSession();
  Transaction tx = session.beginTransaction();

  for(Object obj : list) {
    session.saveOrUpdate(obj);
  }

  tx.commit();
  session.close();
}

static
public void saveDB(Object obj) {
  Session session = null;
  try {
    session = sessionFactory.openSession();
    Transaction tx = session.beginTransaction();
```

```
      session.save(obj);

      tx.commit();
    } finally {
      if (session != null) session.close();
    }
  }

  static
  public void removeDB(Object obj) {
    Session session = null;
    try {
      session = sessionFactory.openSession();
      Transaction tx = session.beginTransaction();

      session.delete(obj);

      tx.commit();
    } finally {
      if (session != null) session.close();
    }
  }

  static
  public java.util.List getListData(
      Class classBean, String strKey, Object value)
  {
    java.util.List result = new java.util.ArrayList();

    Session session = sessionFactory.openSession();
    Transaction tx = session.beginTransaction();

    Criteria criteria =
        session.createCriteria(classBean);
    if (strKey != null) {
      criteria.add(Restrictions.like(strKey, value));
    }
    result = criteria.list();

    tx.commit();
    session.close();
    return result;
  }

  static
  public java.util.List getListData(
      Class classBean) {
    return getListData(classBean, null, null);
  }

  static
  public Object getFirstMatch(
      Class classBean, String strKey, Object value) {
    java.util.List records =
        getListData(classBean, strKey, value);
```

```java
    if (records != null && records.size() > 0) {
      return records.get(0);
    }
    return null;
  }

  static
  public Object getFirstMatch(
      Object data, String strKey, Object value) {
    return getFirstMatch(data.getClass(),
      strKey, value);
  }

  static
  public Object getKeyData(Class beanClass, long itemId) {
    Object data = null;
    Session session = sessionFactory.openSession();

    data = session.get(beanClass, itemId);

    session.close();

    return data;
  }

  static
  public boolean isSessionOpen() {
    return sessionFactory != null;
  }

  static
  public boolean testDB(HttpServletResponse response)
  throws IOException, ServletException {
    if (!isSessionOpen()) {
      writeError(response);
    }
    return isSessionOpen();
  }

  static
  public void writeError(HttpServletResponse response,
                         String title,
                         Exception ex)
  throws java.io.IOException, ServletException
  {
    java.io.PrintWriter out = response.getWriter();
    response.setContentType("text/html");
    out.println("<html>");
    out.println("  <head>");
    out.println("    <title>" + title + "</title>");
    out.println("  </head>");
    out.println("  <body>");
    out.println("<h2>" + title + "</h2>");
    if (ex != null) {
      if (ex.getMessage() != null) {
```

```
      out.println(
         "        <h3>" + ex.getMessage() + "</h3>");
    }
    if (ex.getCause() != null) {
      out.println(
         "        <h4>" + ex.getCause() + "</h4>");
    }
    StackTraceElement[] trace = ex.getStackTrace();
    if (trace != null && trace.length > 0) {
      out.print("<pre>");
      ex.printStackTrace(out);
      out.println("</pre>");
    }
  } else {
    out.println("Hibernate must be initialized");
  }
  out.println("   </body>");
  out.println("</html>");
  out.close();
}

static
public void writeError(HttpServletResponse response)
throws java.io.IOException, ServletException {
  writeError(response,
      "Hibernate Initialization Error",
      lastError);
}
}
```

Listing A.9 The Hibernate helper class.

A.4.6   InitLog4j Servlet

A servlet is used to configure Log4j. Listing A.10 is the complete InitLog4j servlet.

```
package shared;

import java.io.IOException;
import javax.servlet.http.HttpServlet;
import org.apache.log4j.FileAppender;
import org.apache.log4j.Level;
import org.apache.log4j.Logger;
import org.apache.log4j.PatternLayout;
import org.apache.log4j.RollingFileAppender;

public class InitLog4j extends HttpServlet {

  private static final String logPath =
     "/WEB-INF/logs/error.log";

  public void init() {
    FileAppender appender = getAppender(logPath);
    if (appender == null ) return;
    initLogger(null, appender, Level.ERROR);
```

```
      initLogger("org.apache.commmons.beanutils",
                  appender, Level.DEBUG);
   }

  private FileAppender getAppender(String fileName) {
    RollingFileAppender appender = null;
    try {
      appender = new RollingFileAppender(
          new PatternLayout("%-5p %c %t%n%29d - %m%n"),
          getServletContext().getRealPath(fileName),
          true);
      appender.setMaxBackupIndex(5);
      appender.setMaxFileSize("1MB");
    } catch (IOException ex) {
      System.out.println(
          "Could not create appender for "
          + fileName + ":"
          + ex.getMessage());
    }
    return appender;
  }

  private void initLogger(String name,
                          FileAppender appender,
                          Level level)
  {
    Logger logger;
    if (name == null) {
      logger = Logger.getRootLogger();
    } else {
      logger = Logger.getLogger(name);
    }
    logger.setLevel(level);
    logger.addAppender(appender);
    logger.info("Starting " + logger.getName());
  }
}
```

Listing A.10 The `InitLog4j` servlet.

A.4.7   PersistentBase Class

It is a repetitive task to make a bean into a persistent bean. To facilitate this task, a base class was created that contains the definition of a primary key (Listing A.11). By extending this class, a primary key will be added to the bean.

```
package shared;

import javax.persistence.GeneratedValue;
import javax.persistence.Id;
import javax.persistence.MappedSuperclass;

@MappedSuperclass
public class PersistentBase {
```

```
    protected Long id;

    @Id
    @GeneratedValue
    public Long getId() { return id; }

    protected void setId(Long id) { this.id = id; }


    public PersistentBase() {
    }

}
```

Listing A.11 The PersistentBase class.

It is recommended that such a primary key is used, even if there is a natural primary key in the data. This is because the primary key plays a fundamental role in how Hibernate maintains state.

A.4.8 Webapp Listener

In order to be sure that Hibernate is closed before the web application is stopped, a reference to a context listener was added to the *web.xml* file. Listing A.12 contains the source code for this listener.

```
package shared;

import java.sql.Driver;
import java.sql.DriverManager;
import java.sql.SQLException;
import java.util.Enumeration;
import javax.servlet.ServletContextEvent;
import javax.servlet.ServletContextListener;

public class WebappListener implements ServletContextListener
{
  public void contextInitialized(ServletContextEvent sce)
  {}

  public void contextDestroyed(ServletContextEvent sce)
  {
    try {
      Enumeration<Driver> enumer = DriverManager.getDrivers();
      while (enumer.hasMoreElements()) {
        DriverManager.deregisterDriver(enumer.nextElement());
      }
    } catch (java.sql.SQLException se) {
      se.printStackTrace();
    }
    shared.HibernateHelper.closeFactory();
  }
}
```

Listing A.12 The WebappListener class that is used to close Hibernate.

Glossary

CSS – Cascading Style Sheets
EL – Expression Language
HTML – Hypertext Markup Language
HTTP – Hypertext Transfer Protocol
IDE – Integrated Development Environment
JAR – Java Archive
JSP – Java Server Page
JSTL – Java Standard Template Library
JVM – Java Virtual Machine
MIME – Multipurpose Internet Mail Extensions
MVC – Model, View, Controller
SQL – Structured Query Language
URL – Uniform Resource Locator
W3C – WWW Consortium
WAR – Web Archive

References

Additional Resources

Books

Bauer C, King G, (2005) Hibernate in Action, Manning, Greenwich.
Chopra V, Galbraith B, Li S, Wiggers C, Bakore A, Bhattacharjee D, et al., (2002) Professional Apache Tomcat, Wrox, Birmingham.
Hall M, (2002) More Servlets and Java Server Pages, Sun, Palo Alto.
Hall M, Brown L, (2004) Core Servlets and Java Server Pages, Second Edition, Sun, Santa Clara.
Ragget D, Lam J, Alexander I, Kmiec M, (1998) Raggett on HTML 4, Second Edition, Addison-Wesley, Harlow.
Stein L, (1997) How to Set Up and Maintain a Web Site, Second Edition, Addison-Wesley, Reading.

Web Sites

Hibernate, http://www.hibernate.org/247.html
Hibernate Annotations, http://www.hibernate.org/hib_docs/annotations/api/index.html?org/hibernate/annotations/package-summary.html
Hibernate Validator, http://www.hibernate.org/hib_docs/annotations/reference/en/html/validator.html
Jakarta Commons, http://jakarta.apache.org/commons/
Java, http://sun.comJava
Log4j, http://logging.apache.org/log4j/docs/
Memory Leaks and Class Loaders, Frank Kieviet Blog,
http://blogs.sun.com/fkieviet/entry/classloader_leaks_the_dreaded_java
NetBeans, http://netbeans.org
Regular Expressions, http://java.sun.com/j2se/1.4.2/docs/api/java/util/regex/Pattern.html
Tomcat, http://tomcat.apache.org/

Index